Edmund Bogg

A Thousand Miles of Wandering along the Roman Wall,

The Old border Region, Lakeland, and Ribblesdale

Edmund Bogg

A Thousand Miles of Wandering along the Roman Wall,
The Old border Region, Lakeland, and Ribblesdale

ISBN/EAN: 9783744772822

Printed in Europe, USA, Canada, Australia, Japan

Cover: Foto ©Andreas Hilbeck / pixelio.de

More available books at **www.hansebooks.com**

A THOUSAND MILES

OF

WANDERING ALONG THE ROMAN WALL,

THE

OLD BORDER REGION,

LAKELAND, AND RIBBLESDALE.

BY EDMUND BOGG,

Member of the Yorkshire Archæological Society;

AUTHOR OF

"FROM EDENVALE TO THE PLAINS OF YORK," "A THOUSAND MILES IN WHARFEDALE,"
ETC.

ONE HUNDRED AND EIGHTY ILLUSTRATIONS.

Publishers:
LEEDS· EDMUND BOGG, 3, WOODHOUSE LANE.
JAMES MILES, GUILDFORD STREET.

1898.

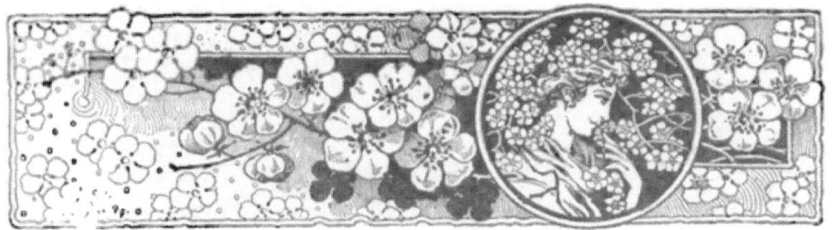

ᐁᕝ PREFACE. ᕗᐊ

THE success of the first edition of this work, in two parts, bound in one volume, comprising 1,200 copies, now exhausted, and demands for more, encouraged the author to issue the book in a more cheap and popular form, namely, in two volumes, each complete, if needs be, without the other.   Volume I. dealing principally with Durham, Northumberland, and the Border Country proper; Volume II. describing the district around Carlisle, The Roman Wall, South Tyne, and the Irthing and Eden Valleys, with chapters descriptive of the old-world border country around Upper Teesdale and Stain-Moor.   Then the pilgrimage is extended to the Lake Country, and from thence down Ribblesdale to the sea.   Our object is to excite that love for nature (inherent in the human heart), especially the varied and changeful scenery of our native land, which can hold its own with the fairest scenes beyond.   Few countries can match ours in the delightful undulation of hill, vale, and plain, decked with green woods, meadows, and corn field.   Old sleepy villages, sombre and grey, with church spire rising over the sunlit roofs, or, peradventure, an old castle or peel tower seen standing so shadowy and silent on the wild, desolate moorland, though shorn of former dignity, still seeming to defy the wreck of time, mute, yet eloquent, opening out pages of thrilling history, startling exploits, adventure, and romance, in days when "might was right."   And how delightful to the soul of a pilgrim is the scenery along the banks of a river anon hurrying, now tranquil, curving and flowing 'neath overshadowing trees; and perhaps in no other part of the world, in so small a compass as our English Lakes cover, can such exquisite phases of nature be found.   And, lastly, Ribblesdale, where the Ribble bursts from the wild mountainous country of Craven, with its wondrous caverns and curious pot holes, its latter course meandering and graceful.   Thus we obtain, in this valley, in a distance of 30 or 40 miles, all the charm of contrast which make the Northern counties so delightful and invigorating.   I owe my thanks to Mr. G. T. Lowe and Mr. L. Moore for their contributions—"The Roman Wall," "Climbs in Lakeland," and "High Ribblesdale."

Truly yours,

EDMUND BOGG.

✂ INTRODUCTION. ✂

VOLUME II.

AGAIN we have left behind the busy manufacturing centres, on this occasion our destination being the Border and Lake country, around which clings, as ivy to ruin, inspiring themes from old romance. As the train speeds onward, bewitching glimpses of lovely scenery spread in rapid succession before our eyes. How exquisite are the silver twinings of the Lune, receding away into the distant landscape; now through meadows, and over many a stream to the west—the blue waters of Morecambe glitter in a ripple of sheen; now the line passes for several miles up the vale of the Kent, woods, village, mansion, and distant church tower adds further interest to the beholder. The wild sweep of the Lake Hills rise and add their beauty to the scene. Kendal is passed, and for several miles we glide through a succession of hill country, the mountains towering in grandeur against the sky, and clouds cleaving and playing around as if things of life. The beauty of contour, and the ever-changing light and shade inspiring and elevating the mind of a city-pent man. What pleasurable anticipations spring to the mind as imagination conjures happy days of our future wanderings. Yonder to the west is the vale of the Lowther, where the Abbey of Shap rests in peaceful seclusion ; still further is the richly timbered park and regal demesne, formerly the seat of the Lowthers (now Lonsdale). Clifton, with its primitive church and grim peel-tower, reminds us of the skirmish of 1745, the last attempt made by the ill-fated Stuarts to regain their inheritance. Now the train speeds over the beautiful valley of the Lowther and Eamont, and a few hundred yards east, the ruins of Brougham rise in sombre dignity from a thickly timbered landscape, beyond which towers, in wall-like prominence, the great Penine Range, the highest point terminating in Cross Fell. Just a few glimpses at Penrith, with its grim and ragged fortress of red sandstone, situated in the forest of Inglewood, which the old chronicle of Lanercost describes as " A goodly and great forest full of red deer, fallow, wild swine, and all manner of wild beasts," a district which has often resounded with the tramp and clash of hostile armies, and which afforded a secure hiding-place for refugees and outlaws in the struggle and turmoil of past ages. Penrith is a place of great antiquity, as the many prehistoric remains in this district testify. It is also one of the entrances to the Lake country. All the way from Penrith to Carlisle we obtain delightful peeps and vistas of the dulcet Petrel meandering through rich pasture lands and past sleepy old villages to join the Eden. The landscape adorned with clumps of dark fir, and the grey walls of peel and manor. As the train draws up at Carlisle we pass through the city to the Walls, and scan the circling landscape of the old Borderland, resonant with echoes of vanished heroes and deeds of wild and lawless daring, the clang of armour, glittering of sword, lance, and spear, the hoarse cries of reivers, driving before them sheep and cattle, anon the frenzied and mad haste of troopers in pursuit—

> " Through the dark wood in mingled tone,
> Were border pipes and bugles blown."
> * * * * *
> " Glistening through the hawthorn green,
> Shine helm and shield and spear."

Away west can be discerned the glittering Solway, and on the further shore Dornock and Annan. Near by this place a raid, under the command of Sir Marmaduke Langdale and Lord Crosby, ended so disastrous to the invaders, for the few that escaped the fray with their lives were driven into the Solway and drowned ; and the victorious Scots are said to have washed their swords in a well near Annan, since that battle day known as the " Sword's Well." It was yonder on Solway Moss that James the Fifth of Scotland, and his army of fifteen thousand, was defeated by the English. This disaster broke the heart of the unfortunate James, for he died a few days after the battle. Still more to the north is Gretna, famed for the celebration of runaway-marriages, in Norman times in the possession of the Carlyles, lords of Annandale—in after centuries passing into the hands of the Johnstones. The ashes of many a scion of this noble family lie mouldering in Gretna kirkyard. Beyond the banks of the little river Sark, Solway Moss, a dreary expanse of waste stretches to the sparkling Esk, on whose bank dwelt for centuries in the old debatable land the redoubtable Græmes, celebrated as the most renowned thieves on the Border. Further up the Esk is Cannobie Lea, across which the Græmes chased " Young Lochinvar."

> " There was rideing and chaseing on Cannobie Lea,
> But the lost bride of Netherby ne'er did they see."

And further still the distant Cheviots fill up the background of the picture, while to the east the remains of the Roman Wall stretch from the Tyne to the Solway, which will be described in a later chapter, and from Carlisle we renew our wandering for the second volume.

CONTENTS

Contents.

ADIEU.

ERRATA.

Page   2—"Lugunallum" should read "Luguvallium" in the first line.

  ,,   36—"Stanard de Peel" should be "Stanward le Peel."

Pages 33 & 34—"Cholleford" should read "Chollerford."

Page 59—Fifteen lines down, "Wren," should read "Wreay."

  ,,   70—Last line in verse should read, "To (sit) in the roses and hear the birds sing."

  ,, 185—"Langsbrath" should be "Langstrath."

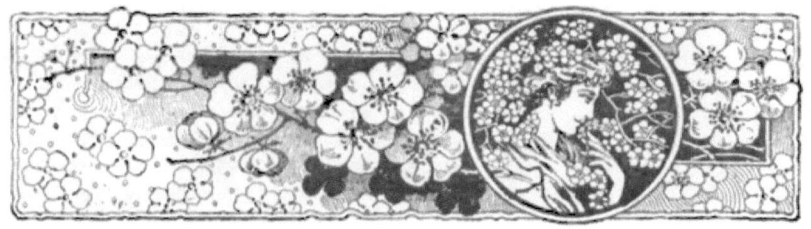

CHAPTER I.

☙ CARLISLE. ☙

STILL grim and defiant, the hoary towers of Carlisle keep frown on the traveller, as he crosses the river and enters the old city of strange memories and old-world associations. Historians tell us that far away back in the dim twilight of time, and generations before the Roman standard waved triumphant over this island, had the city of Carlisle been founded. The Celtic prefix, Caer (a place of strength), with the terminal Liul (the name of a British prince)—Caer-liul; hence Liul's city is obtained. And a glance at the map will prove the wisdom of this prince of prehistoric ages in selecting this site for the founding of his capital. Beautifully situated on the Eden, near the confluence of several other streams and rivers, teeming with fish, and a land of rich pasturage, it requires no stretch of imagination to picture to the mind the woad-stained Celt paddling his coracle along the different streams, or the ascending of the war-vessels up the Eden after some tribal foray along the Solway shore. Of British occupation scarcely a vestige remains, except what the earth now and again yields from its long slumber. Yet as a sure proof of the antiquity of man in this district, there is that immense circle of unhewn stone, and a smaller circle near by, which stand in solemn mystery guarding the moor, as it were, above the Eden, a few miles below the old city—a silent, yet strange testimony of a religion and people the knowledge of whom has become lost by the lapse of ages.

B

During the occupation of this place by the Romans it was known as Lugunallum, and on their departure, in the fifth century, to prop up their tottering empire, this district became the battle-ground of contending nations—Pict, Caledonian, Angle and Celt. The two former had, for three centuries, been held at bay by the strength of the Roman arm; but they now swept, wave after wave, across the barrier, shrieking forth, on the dreary night wind, their wild, unearthly battle-cry, immediately the Roman legions retired.

This was the state of things when that immortal hero, the famed King Arthur, appeared on the scene. Of royal British lineage, the blood of Vortigern flowed in his veins. He was the son of Uter Pendragon, the ruin of whose castle is still to be seen in the upper reaches of the Eden. Tradition has often connected this hero with the old city, but Sir Walter Scott has most delightfully associated the Flower of Kings with Carlisle in his "Bridal of Triermaen." What a mystery and charm floats over these old British days. Several of the twelve great battles fought by King Arthur took place in the northern part of the kingdom; and is not the round table, formed by Merlin the Wizard, still to be seen near Penrith? It was here that the magnificent tournament took place, when Gyneth, a natural daughter of King Arthur, was promised in marriage to the most valiant knight in Christendom.

Queen Mary looking towards Scotland from the battlements of Carlisle Keep.

" Within trumpet sound of the table round
    Were fifty champions free,
    And they all arise to fight that prize;
    They all arise but three.

And these three knights of Arthur's court
    Are from the tourney missed;
And still these lovers' fame survives,
    For faith so constant shown.
There were two who loved their neighbours' wives,
    And one who loved his own."

But Gyneth, we are told, suffered so many of the combatants to bite the dust without dropping her wand, and so earnest grew the game—

" The spears drew blood, the swords struck flame,
    And horse and man to ground they came;
    Knights who shall rise no more;
    Gone was the pride, the war that greed.
    Gay shields were cleft, and crests defaced,
    And steel coats riven, and helms unbraced,
    And pennons stream'd with gore."

Merlin, to save the noble knights from total annihilation, interposed, causing the beautiful woman to fall into an enchanted sleep, from which she was not to awake until a knight as unrivalled as those who had fallen in tournament should claim her in marriage.

> " But for the love of Arthur's race
> Punishment is blent with grace "

To the castle rock, in the lovely valley of Saint John, she is spirited by Merlin, where she sleeps in solitude for five hundred years. At the end of that period, Sir Roland de Vaux, Baron of Trierman, whose tomb is still to be seen at Lanercost, rides forth to break the mystic spell, and having overcome the four temptations—fear, avarice, pleasure, and ambition—he succeeds in his enterprise.

" A weighty curtal-axe he bare ;
  The baleful blade so bright and square,
  And the tough shaft of heben wood
  Were oft in Scottish gore imbrued.
  Backward his stately form he drew,
  And at the rocks the weapon threw.
  Just where one crag's projected crest
  Hung proudly balanced o'er the rest,
  Hurl'd with main force, the weapon's shock
  Rent a huge fragment of the rock.
  If by mere strength, 'twere hard to tell,
  Or if by the blow dissolved some spell,
  But down the headlong ruin came,
  With cloud of dust and flash of flame.

   *   *   *   *

" When ceased that thunder, Triermain
  Survey'd the mound's rough front again ;
  And, lo ! the ruin had laid bare,
  Hewn in the stone, a winding stair,
  Whose moss'd and fractured steps might lend
  The means the summit to ascend,
  And by whose aid the brave De Vaux
  Began to scale these magic rocks,
  And soon a platform won,
  Where the wild witchery to close,
  Within three lance's length arose
     The Castle of St. John.

   *   *   *   *

" Totters tower, and trembles keep,
  Burst the castle walls asunder,
  Fierce and frequent were the shocks ;
    Melt the magic halls away ;
  But beneath their mystic rocks,
  In the arms of bold De Vaux,
    Safe the princess lay ;
  Safe and free from magic power,
  Blushing like the rose's flower,
    Opening to the day."

Roland de Vaux ascending the winding stair to the Castle of St. John.

And as we ponder over these early days of King Arthur and his knights, and of merrie Carlisle, what a goodly array of noble warriors rise before us. 'Tis the banquet hour, the Flower of Kings graces the festive board with his commanding presence ; and mirth, jest, and song resounds, and the King pledges his loyal knights in a golden cup of blood-red wine.   There, in regal beauty, sits Queen Guenever, daughter of Leod Ogran, King of Camelaird ; Sir Hector, foster-father to the King ; Sir Kay, the Seneschal, mean-spirited and scornful ; and Mordred, the traitor, is also there ; and Sir Bors de Gluis, who, for his purity, was vouchsafed a vision of the holy grail, and noble Sir Hector de Maris, and Sir Caradoc, husband of that beautiful and virtuous dame, the only lady in the Queen's train who could wear the mantle of matrimonial fidelity.   Queen Guenever tried to wear it, but one while it was too long, another while too short, and wrinkled on her shoulders in most unseemly sort.   Sir Tristram, the sorrowful, who loved not wisely, but too well, the wife of his uncle, King Mark. She it was who told Tristram, "My measure of hate for Mark is as my measure of love for thee."   Sir Lamerock, the brave, who held his own against four knights— Sir Gavain and his brethren—for three hours ere they could slay him.   And Sir Lancelot, the peerless warrior who conquered the mighty Tarquin on the banks of the Eamont, and liberated three-score knights and four.   "He was the kindest man that ever struck with sword, and he was the goodliest person that ever rode among a throng of knights ; he was the meekest man, and the gentlest, that ever did eat in hall among ladies ; and he was the sternest knight to his mortal foe that ever laid lance in rest."   And by the side of Sir Lancelot sits Sir Perceval, a knight without reproach or stain ; it was he who was with Sir Bors when the visible Saviour went into the consecrated water which was given them by the Bishop.

  "Oh, mercy," said Sir Perceval, " what may this mean ? "   Sir Hector replied, " It is the holy vessel wherein is a part of the holy blood of our Blessed Saviour ; but it may not be seen except by perfect man."   Sir Bevidere, the last of Arthur's knights, it was whom the dying King thrice requested to throw his famous sword Excaliber into the mere.   When cast in, it was caught by an arm clothed in white samite, and drawn into the water.

  'Tis morn : the great bell tolls the alarm of war.   Trumpets blare, the battle-steeds are caparisoned, armour flashes, spears glisten, pennons wave, and there rides forth the noblest of kings, followed by the goodliest array of warriors that ever trod the wide Borders, each of them true Borderers.   Their names are immortalised in undying verse, and their glorious deeds of chivalry are imperishable.   With their disappearance, the horde of invaders, which had been held at bay, swarmed like locusts over the land, and a long night of unbelief and ignorance reigned supreme.   The body of Arthur rests deep in a vault in that beautiful, though mouldering, ruin of Glastonbury, but we should imagine his spirit still loves to dwell amongst the places he knew in the flesh. The grievously wounded and dying King, we are told by the bard, was borne off the field of battle by Sir Bevidere the faithful, and placed in a barge, in which were seated three Queens, who conveyed him to the island valley of Avillion, "where falls not hail or rain, or any snow, nor even wind blows loudly." Hither he was carried, to be healed of his grievous wound, but neither the love of his sister, the abbess, nor any skill could heal the dying king. His death was long kept secret, and for generations his people thought he would come again and lead them to victory.

Towards the end of the 6th century, during a fearful immigration of warriors from the north, Carlisle was pillaged, totally destroyed, and left in ashes. In this state of desolation it remained for nearly a century, and was rebuilt and fortified by Egfrid, King of Northumbria, about 650, he surrounding it with a strong wall. He also built a church, which was added to the bishopric of Lindisfarne, then ruled over by Saint Cuthbert. To this outlying part of his diocese Cuthbert sometimes journeyed, and here was met by that holy man, St. Herbert of Derwentwater, and the brethren held loving communion. The Venerable Bede says : "But it came to pass that Saint Herbert was told how that St. Cuthbert was come to the city of Lugubalic (Carlisle), and as soon as Herbert heard this, as was his wont, he journeyed to meet him, and, amongst other things, Saint Cuthbert told him that his dissolution was nigh at hand, all of which had been divinely revealed to him."

It was by the Roman Wall, still to be seen at the north end of Carlisle Keep, that a vision is said to have appeared to Saint Cuthbert, which foretold that if King Alred should persist in giving battle to the enemy, grievous calamity should overtake him. He disobeyed the warning, and was slain.

For two hundred years the city flourished, and waxed rich. Until the 9th century, when it was darkened by the incoming shadows of other wild foes, the Danes, who at that period infested the Irish Sea and the adjoining coasts, steered their war galleys into the estuary of the Eden, and fell with sudden fury on the city, burnt it, and destroyed everything that King Egfrid and his successors had reared. And again for two hundred years the old city lay black and desolate, in mourning and ashes, until the time of the Norman Rufus, who upreared that strong fortress on the site of the Roman castle ; fragments of the latter remain to this day. When the keep of the Red King was complete, and the city girded with strong walls and towers of defence, it became recognised as the most important key on the western Border. Of the troublous times witnessed, and all the stern and stirring scenes of incidents of siege and war, and terrible deeds enacted here, space forbids mention. Few cities in Great Britain have been the theatre of such startling adventures.

It has frequently changed masters, and oft been the abode of Kings and Queens. Momentous gatherings, stirring deeds of chivalry, mediæval glory and princely festivity. Oft in the darkness of night has the city been disturbed by the slogan's terrible yell, and the startling shriek of the pibroch sounding like a death-knell on the night air, when the city has been invested by kilted chieftains, and fierce, unkempt intruders from the wilds of Galloway and the far north, led by men the most famed in history—a Wallace, a Bruce, Randolph, Douglas, or Scott.

Hither, on his last invasion of Scotland, came the hoary old warrior, Edward ; and here, for some time after the unfortunate battle of Langside, dwelt the

Mary, Queen of Scots.

unhappy Mary Stuart, the beginning of those long, dreary years of bitterness and sorrow which were to follow the footsteps of that unhappy lady. The apartments which Mary occupied were on the south-east part of the castle, commanding a fine view of the Eden country, and we can easily imagine the beautiful queen gazing from the battlements, to the dim outline of her own country, the border line of which she was destined never more to cross. .

" Her name is linked with thine, O Carlisle, still,   Noteless and notable, thy dungeons old.
Linked with thy ancient walls, thy castle old ;   Close cavern'd in from all the green sweet rays,
She was thy captive sad, this lady fair,   Have born upon their basements, dark and cold,
And thou had'st many captives in those days.   The wearying form of many a child of care."

Here, in 1745, during his march to the south, Bonnie Prince Charlie took up his quarters for some time, through which cause such awful punishment fell on many of the principal citizens. But of all the gallant deeds ever performed on this or any other Border, the liberation of Kinmont Willie, from the Keep of Carlisle Castle, is the most startling and romantic.

William Armstrong, of Kinmont, or, in the more endearing name of the Borders, Kinmont Willie, was a man of great personal strength and stature, and had four sons—Jock, Francie. Geordie, and Sandie—each of them equally as brave as his father. Their exploits and feuds were dreaded over the whole district, and he was the most lawless and terrible moss-trooper thief on the Borders. His capture, according to the rules and usage of truce, was illegal. He had been attending a Warden's meeting, held on the little Kershope river, and was returning home in the company of a few other Scotchmen ; but on the Englishmen becoming aware of his presence at the meeting, they had determined on capturing him, and accordingly a troop followed, and, after a long, stern chase up Liddlesdale, arrested and bound him, and brought him, heavily ironed, into Carlisle Castle. This, as we have said, was in direct violation of Border law. Scott of Buccleugh, with whom Armstrong was a great favourite, at once wrote to Lord Scrope, the Governor of Carlisle and Warden of the English Border, demanding his instant release, but he refused to release him. So bold Buccleugh swore to bring Kinmont Willie out of Carlisle, quick or dead, with his own hand. Choosing a dark and stormy night (the 13th April), he assembled two hundred of his bravest men at the tower of Morton, a fortalice on the 'debateable land,' on the water of Sark, about ten miles from Carlisle. Amongst these, the leader whom he most relied on, was Awd Wat Scott of Harden ; but along with him were Wat Scott of Branxholm, Wat Scott of Goldielands, Jock Elliot of the Copeshaw, Sandie Armstrong, son to Hobbie ; the Laird of Mangerton, Kinmont's four sons, Rob of the Langholm, and Will Bell of the Redcloak—every one a Scott, except Jock Elliot.

"They were well mounted and armed, and carried with them scaling-ladders, besides iron crowbars, sledge-hammers, hand-picks, and axes, etc. Favoured by the extreme darkness, they passed the river Esk, and through the Graham's country, forded the Eden, and came to the brook Caday, close by Carlisle, where Buccleugh made his men dismount, and silently led eighty of them, with the ladders and iron tools, to the foot of the wall. Everything favoured them ; the heavens were as black as pitch, and the rain descended in torrents. The ladders proving too short, they undermined a postern in the wall of the base, and soon made a breach large enough for a soldier to squeeze through. In this way several of them passed into the outer court, and disarmed and bound the watch, wrenched open the postern from the inside, and thus admitting their companions, were masters of the place. Twenty-four troopers now rushed to the Castle jail (Buccleugh meantime keeping the postern), forced the door of the chamber where Kinmont was confined, carried him off heavily-ironed, and sounding their trumpet, the signal agreed on, were answered by loud shouts and the trumpet of Buccleugh, whose troopers now filled the outer court.   All was terror and confusion, both in town and castle.   The alarm-bell rang out on the stormy night, and was answered by the clang of the Cathedral and Town-house bells ; the beacon blazed from the top of the great tower, and red tongues of flame flitted ominously on the blackness of the night, and the shadowy forms, hoarse shouts, and flashing armour rather increased the horror and their numbers.   Willie was carried down the scaling ladders on the shoulders of Red Rowan, 'the starkest man in Teviotdale.'

The Rescue of Kinmont Willie.

Lord Scrope, believing, as he afterwards wrote to Burghley, that five hundred Scots were in possession of the castle, kept himself within his chamber.   Kinmont Willie himself, as he was carried on his friends' shoulders beneath the Warden's window, roared out a lusty 'Good-night' to his lordship.   Buccleugh remounted his troopers, forded once more the Esk and the Eden, and, bearing his rescued favourite in the middle of his little band, regained the Scottish Border before sunrise.   Kinmont, in swimming his horse through the Eden, which was then flooded, was much cumbered by the irons round his ankles, and is said to have drily observed that, 'often as he had breasted it, he had never had such heavy spurs before.' His master, Buccleugh, eager to rid him of these shackles, halted at the first smith's house they came to within the Scottish Border; but the door was locked, the family in bed, and the knight of the hammer so sound a sleeper, that he was only awakened by the Lord Warden thrusting his long spear through the window, and nearly spitting both Vulcan and his lady.

The storming of the castle and rescue of the prisoner was a serious affair to Lord Scrope, and no doubt he would almost feel disgraced in the eyes of the nation. Queen Elizabeth demanded of King James that Buccleugh should be instantly arrested, and sent as a prisoner to receive due punishment for such an outrage. But the whole Scottish nation was on the side of the baron, and for some time resented the demands of the Queen; at length Elizabeth became so peremptory, that, to save his country from spoliation, Buccleugh was committed a prisoner to the Castle of St. Andrew, and soon after

sent on *parole*, or prisoner at large, to England. No one admired bold, brave, and doughty deeds more than Elizabeth, and when Buccleugh was brought before her she demanded of him, with lion-like glance, how he had dared to assault and storm her castle at Carlisle? In no way daunted, the renowned Border chieftain replied, 'Madame, what is there that a brave man may not dare?' This answer so impressed her that, turning to her courtiers, she exclaimed: 'This is a man, indeed! With ten thousand such men, our brother of Scotland might shake the firmest throne in Europe.'

The castle is built of red sandstone, and occupies a prominent position on a sharply rising ascent on the north-west side of the city, and consists of outer and inner wards. The entrance is over a deep vallum, under the tower, and through a double gateway defended by portcullis, etc. The gateway to the keep, which is situated within the inner ward, is also defended by double gates. The keep is a square building of vast strength. Here, in the steps leading to the parapet, is to be seen the deep Roman well referred to by the Venerable Bede, and shown as a wonder to St. Cuthbert on his visit.* Within the corridor leading to the prison is a rare antique table, brought from the guest chamber. In the dungeon of the keep are to be seen the various modes of punishment and instruments of torture, enough to make the heart quake and flesh creep; and the mere recital of barbarous deeds by our loquacious guide, who was a veteran soldier, and who told us that on one

---

* As shown in picture, eight steps from the bottom.

occasion 382 prisoners were incarcerated in this gloomy prison house at one time ; if so, the scene must have presented a veritable " Black Hole of Calcutta." Built in the walls of the dungeon is the celebrated weeping-stone.

Early in the present century, and during some alterations in the second storey of the keep, the skeleton of a lady was found, built in the walls. She was dressed in a Scotch silk tartan, and had costly rings on her fingers, and her feet rested on silk handkerchiefs. An awful tragedy, we should imagine, has been enacted here. Scott depicts such a scene in " Marmion," " who for their sins the wall was to enclose alive

The Castle Gateway

within a tomb." A story is told of how a soldier of the 93rd Regiment, when on patrol duty in this ward, in 1842, fancied he saw someone walking, when, after the challenge was given, and, receiving no answer, he charged the imaginary object, and rousing the guard, who, on arriving, found the sentry senseless, and his bayonet stuck fast in the wall. The sentry was removed to the hospital, where the poor man soon died. The view from the battlements is very extensive and interesting.

The Cathedral has been greatly mutilated in bygone centuries ; the cloisters and chapter-house have been demolished, and only a fragment of the nave remains. The edifice, as it now stands, is the plainest of our English cathedrals. The choir, however, is very rich in carved work, and the east

window is the glory of the whole building, said to be the most perfect and exquisite specimen of flowing tracery in existence. Many impressive ceremonies and startling incidents have been witnessed in this cathedral. Here, in 1297, Robert Bruce took the oath of fealty to the first Edward, and ten years later was solemnly excommunicated by the Papal representative, who, with bell, book, and candle, cursed in terrible wroth Robert Bruce, the usurper. A few months later Edward came, and offered up to God the litter on which he had been forced to make his journey ; and again mounting his horse, he rode through the gateway of the Priory filled with projects for the conquest of Scotland, which he was never to reach, dying at Burgh Sands with the object of his ambition and the prize for which he had struggled within sight. Here, in 1793, Walter Scott was married to Miss Carpenter.

Few cities, we should imagine, so ancient and historic as Carlisle have undergone so rapid a transformation. Yet, for those who seek, there are curious old houses, thick walls, and antique windows, grim with memory and tradition ; narrow wynds, alleys, and by-places ; mazy courts and tower-like houses, dating from the Tudor period ; and on Fair-days she is still Merrie Carlisle ; then she is a perfect Tower of Babel, and it would be easy to imagine that all the riff-raff that ever dwelt on the borders had congregated together for some great carnival on these occasions. The old gates, English, Scotch, and Irish, which were closed at sunset, have disappeared, and the city walls have been cast down. Factories with tall chimneys have risen above keep and bastel towers, and she is still progressing, and spreading out her arms further and further into the meadow country. Most of her streets are wide and clean, and now in the night-time, instead of beacon fires, the tramp of armies, the clanging of the minster bells, bugles sounding the alarm and call to arms, or the whoop of half-wild clans,—it is the flash and shriek of the " Flying Scotchman," speeding north through the darkness like a demon of night, which disturbs the silence, carrying thousands of missives breathing of peace and commerce. Could the old borderers look on such a sight, surely they would fly affrighted ; for, as of old, she is still the key or gate to the north, and the screech and blare of engine, roar of traffic, and the whizz and whirr of passing trains seem never ending. The pretty little village of Stanwix, with its neat church, is on the right bank of the Eden, and is the site of a Roman station. It was from this bank of the river that Turner painted his picture of Carlisle, the bridge, castle, and cathedral are prominent features in the picture.

CHAPTER II

THE ROMAN WALL.

THE ROMAN WALL., frequently called the Picts' Wall, in its perfect state, was one of the most remarkable examples of military engineering in Europe. Even now, after a lapse of nearly 1,800 years, its remains tell in no feeble manner of its former strength and magnificence. It has generally been regarded as a barrier against the Picts and Scots of Caledonia, whose frequent inroads proved a terrible scourge to the inhabitants of Southern Britain, at that time becoming less warlike and self-reliant under the civilizing influence of the Roman rule.

From the double nature of the fortified line, as represented by the vallum or earth wall, which consists mainly of three ramparts and a fosse, and the murus, or stone wall, with a broad, deep fosse running uniformly on the north side, many archæologians hold the view that protection against the south was also an essential feature of the rampart. A more recent suggestion is that the vallum is the older structure, and that the stone wall was erected at a later date, and that invasion from the north was the only reason for the existence of the fortifications. Around this phase of the question enthusiasts dispute with the calmness and moderation characteristic of specialists. Whichever view may be correct, the scope of the present chapter will only permit of a general account of the Wall and its accompanying works.

Stretching with undeviating persistency along the most impregnable line of natural defence, it formed a huge bow from Bowness, on Solway Firth, to Wallsend-on-Tyne (Segedunum), a distance of over 70 miles. Between the Wall and the vallum, and pursuing an easier course, was the great military way from Newcastle to Carlisle. From Sewingshields, along the Nine Nicks of Thirlwall, an undulating series of precipitous basaltic cliffs, running some distance north of the most direct line across the isthmus, induced the military engineers to carry the structure along their verge, thus adding enormously to the strength of the barrier.

That the stations themselves were in existence before the Wall itself is evident from the fact that, where the latter is built up to continue the north face of the station, the rounded corners of the fort do not fall in with the line of the Wall, as may be seen at Borcovicus, and in the case of Cilurnum the Wall actually meets the station some distance from the corner. In several instances the stations lie to the north or south of the Wall, entirely separated from it, as at Vindolana, the present Chesterholm.

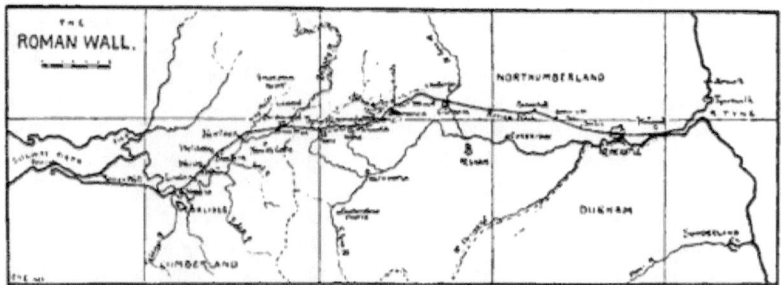

Neglected and deserted for nearly 1,300 years, its well-dressed stones have been utilized by generations of dwellers in its neighbourhood for the construction of castle, peel, and homestead, until the extremities of the Wall have practically disappeared, although the fosse may still show traces of its former course. In the central portion, however, the existing remains are such as to enable the wanderer along its line to reconstruct in imagination the ancient rampart in much of its original form. Careful observations, assisted by excavations, have given us a clear conception of this truly interesting monument of the Roman occupation of Britain.

The more easily accessible stations are frequently visited, but few care to undertake to follow its course from sea to sea. This latter excursion is one to be strongly recommended, not only for the benefits to be derived from the exercise, but from the intellectual advantages. To see these time-honoured remains *in situ*, to clothe the dry bones of history with fact, is to relive in the past, and to give birth to a desire to know more of the greatest nation of warriors the world has ever known.

In following the Wall it is advisable to trace its course from west to east, as the interest in the relic is augmented by the gradually increasing importance of the remains.

The Wall was built of carefully dressed stones, generally about eight by ten inches, resting on a double course of larger stones which projected a few inches on either side of the upper portion. The space between these facing stones was filled in with rough concrete composed of small stones and excellent lime, as existing fragments testify. It was probably about eighteen feet high, and below the parapet from six to nine feet thick. The narrowest portions are found where the Wall traverses the steep heights in the middle of its course. It seems the different gangs of workers under various overlookers followed no uniform plan, hence the breadth and minor details vary to some extent. The north face of the wall, however, is continuous.

At intervals of a Roman mile* small forts were placed, having two entrances, one to the north and the other to the south. Between each two mile-castles were small turrets or watch-towers, about a furlong apart. So close were these sentry-towers that an alarm raised at any point could be passed from one to the other with great rapidity, thus enabling assistance to be summoned at short notice. In addition to these mile-castles and turrets there were nearly twenty larger stations or camps, varying in extent from three to five acres, situated at convenient positions along the Wall, about four miles apart. They were quadrangular in form and rounded at the corners.

From the *Notitia*, compiled about the beginning of the fifth century, which is a kind of army list of the Roman Empire, a list of the prefects and tribunes of the cohorts located along the Roman Wall can be obtained. From this list, by comparison with inscriptions found on the spot, the names of many of the camps have been ascertained with absolute certainty. The number of these stations actually connected with the Wall was eighteen out of the twenty-three enumerated in the *Notitia*, the remaining five being supporting stations north or south of it.

It is convenient to consider the Wall in three distinct parts—I., the stone wall or murus with the fosse on the north ; II., the earth wall or vallum on the south side of the stone wall ; and III., the stations, mile-castles, turrets, roads, and habitations which would inevitably spring up in the vicinity of the great camps. For the most part the vallum and stone wall run within a few yards of each other right across the country ; but in the central portion, where the Wall is carried to the north to take advantage of the high ridges, the space is much greater, approaching in one instance to half-a-mile.

And now one naturally asks whom shall we credit with the authorship of the fortification ? Undoubtedly Agricola led the way when he built many of the stations

---

* About 1,618 English yards.

across the isthmus, afterwards traversed by the Wall. The main line of defence is attributed to Hadrian, although there are those who maintain the claims of Severus. As the matter at present stands the concensus of opinion is in favour of the former. Hadrian landed in Britain A.D. 119, and died A.D. 138, so that the Wall was probably constructed about the year A.D. 130.

In the course of two rambles along the Roman Wall, in one of which we traced the whole course from the Solway to Wallsend, we had ample opportunities of examining the principal points of interest. It is instructive to notice along the route how the place-names are significant of the existence of the Wall. It is unnecessary to enumerate examples, as a cursory examination of the map will instantly confirm the statement.

From Carlisle to Bowness the traces of the Wall are almost entirely absent, though the fosse gives feeble proofs of its former existence. To the east of Carlisle the first indications are to be observed in Drawdykes Castle and the peel at Linstock. The stones used in their construction are unmistakable, and make clear to the most careless observer the fate of the Wall. Such a convenient quarry could not be overlooked. Now, after 1,800 years, it is marvellous that so much of the original structure remains. From Wallby to Bleatarn the fosse is distinctly traceable on the left to the north. About a mile from Bleatarn the ditch passes through some gardens at Old Wall. Here a villager showed us a small stone nearly eleven inches long and nine broad, bearing an inscription to the century of Julius Tertullianus of the second legion. The stone was in the outer wall on the east side of a dilapidated hut near the end of the village.

After walking about half-a-mile in the fosse, we passed through Irthington and stopped at Cambeck Bridge for refreshments, and then went through the park by Castlesteads, which is probably the Petriana of the *Notitia*, to Walton. Westward of Amboglanna, *Burdoswald, no inscriptions have been found to enable us to identify the stations with the stations of the *Notitia*. Until one does turn up we must be content to take the order of the list from Amboglanna and trust to its accuracy.

On the hills beyond the Kingswater the fosse can be traced for a great distance. After crossing the stream we found a long heap of stones under a hedge, which indicated the site of the Wall. Before reaching Garthside Farm several detached portions of wall from three to four feet high, considerably grass-grown, appeared. The fosse was well marked and regular. Many of the portions were without facing stones, but showed rubble and lime. Below Craggle Hill, in the south-east corner of a field, we found an unfaced bit nearly six feet high. The lime was good, showing white and clear. In the next field, at the bottom, another piece seven feet high was

---

* Oswald's Burgh = Burdoswald or Birdoswald.

observed. On Hare Hill the fosse was magnificent. The view looking back embraced the Solway, Carlisle, Skiddaw, Blencathara, and the undulating country south of the Cheviots. A little to the south are Lanercost Priory and Naworth Castle.

At Banksburn the highest existing portion of the Wall is found in a garden by the side of the brook. It stands nine feet ten inches high, but has been deprived of its facing stones. It has, however, been refaced to keep it up.

Nearing Burdoswald the Wall appears on the south of the road in good preservation for a long distance, over seven feet thick and nearly six feet high. This station, the Roman Amboglanna, is the largest on the line, being five and a half acres in extent, exceeding the Chesters and Housesteads. It is situated behind a farmhouse

The Irthing, near Burdoswald.   GIBSON.

immediately above the steep right bank of the Irthing. The camp is typical of the rest. Looking out of the west gate the Wall on the right is six feet high, and on the left seven feet. The south-west corner is very high and solid, with the foundation stones very plain. The south entrance is broken down. The east wall is almost gone, but over the modern wall the best gate is still to be seen, with two side guard-chambers. The walls are nearly eight feet high, with the remains of ornamental capitals. The pivot holes for the gates are very good. There are two curved stones among the *débris* nearly two feet across, which probably formed portions of the arches.

A rough heap outside continues the Wall to a part of the foundation stones overhanging the Irthing, which, in the present state of the precipitous bank, causes one to wonder how the Wall was continued to the river, and the bridge which must have crossed it. Several more mounds and portions of courses behind the vicarage garden next appear. Near the railway station there are traces of the existence of a mile-castle. Next, *Thirlwall Castle, built of stones from the Wall, is reached. At the back of an outhouse close to the stream at Holmhead, and built into the wall wrong way up, is an inscribed stone—CIVITAS DUMNONI. Up the hill the fosse is in splendid condition, and by the quarries the Wall is three or four courses high. The prospect along this portion overlooking Spade Adam Waste is wild, and until Carrow is passed the route lies along the most perfect and picturesque part of the Wall.

From Magna, Caervoran, one can walk on the top of the Wall, which in some instances is over six feet high, in perfect courses. Much of the first part is among boulders and a thick growth of trees. Passing an excavation about twelve feet square we noticed the fosse was absent, and the configuration of the country shows no need of this precaution, which, however, appears at every point where the natural protection is inadequate. Over the Nine Nicks of Thirlwall the Wall rigorously pursues its course along their precipitous sides to Æsica, Great Chesters, a large station indicated by high grass-grown mounds. At this point the rampart may be left, and at the Red Lion, Haltwhistle, about two miles south, convenient accommodation is to be found. Resuming the journey, Cawfields mile-castle, beyond the Caw Burn, is next reached, and the Wall shows in courses and mounds over Whinshields to the pretty group of Northumbrian lakes. Before reaching Crag Lough over Whinshields (1,230 feet), the middle and highest part of the Wall is passed. Nearly to the top of the crag the Wall is in splendid condition, and the sharp angles formed by it as it follows the contour of the slopes are remarkably interesting. On the cliff we stopped for a long rest and thorough enjoyment of the varied scene. The pretty little lake at our feet was dotted with waterfowl, and in the crevices of the rocks dwelt jackdaws rock-doves, starlings, and other birds.

On the next hill, after leaving the lake, is Hotbank Farm, where a visitors' book is to be seen, given by the great antiquarian, Dr. Bruce, in 1856. He at the same time presented them with two of his works, which have since been borrowed.—Well, I need say no more! The farm is beautifully situated, and affords a delightful and convenient resting-place for visitors.

From Hotbank we walked on the top of the Wall, which is here five feet high and over six feet wide, for a considerable distance. A little before the long plantation which terminates in Housesteads a grand mile-castle is passed, with the northern wall over nine feet high; the southern doorway is broken down. Housesteads, the Borcovicus of the Romans, is a most interesting camp, and magnificently situated on the brow of a hill, which, on its southern slope, shows traces of a considerable number

---

* A.S. Thirl-ian = to penetrate. Said to be where the Caledonians first hurled down the Wall.

of exterior buildings, indicating the site of a town which had grown about the station. At some points the walls are over nine feet high. The western gateway is in excellent condition, with square columns standing, and two guard-rooms on each side about ten feet square. It has been reduced to half its width by closing the northern half of the outer, and the southern half of the inner, gate. When the garrisons were reduced this expedient was adopted at most of the camps. Bases of columns and other curious blocks of stone lie around the southern entrance. Rut-marks, as is often the case, caused by the chariot wheels, are plainly worn into the sill-stones of the

Crag Lough from the west.   GIBSON.

gateways. The width of these ruts, 4ft. 6in., is precisely the same as those to be seen in the streets of Pompeii. The narrow Pompeian streets surprised me not a little, and the high stepping-stones seemed to block vehicular traffic entirely. Probably their horses were inferior in size to our modern breed. It is noteworthy that this measurement exactly agrees with the gauge of the modern railway track.

The Wall on leaving the station is nearly eight feet wide, and at the bottom of the valley is broken by a gap with large stones on each side, and to the south there are traces of guard-rooms. This was, no doubt, a more convenient entrance to the camp and town on the hill above, or it may have given egress to the amphitheatre supposed to have existed on the site of a hollow immediately to the north of this lower portal. Up to the small plantation the Wall is good, then it disappears; but by heaps of rubble it may be followed to Sewingshields.

It is an interesting variation to walk along the foot of the basaltic cliffs from Sewingshields to Borcovicus. The additional security obtained by leading the Wall to the north, along the verge of the precipices, is obviously apparent. Those who can spare the time will be amply repaid for the extra exertion.

With the exception of the Chesters the most interesting, and certainly the wildest part of the Wall, is now left behind. Undulating hillocks succeed, steep towards the north, then a recently excavated mile-castle, with gateway and guard-rooms very plain. Several more castles were indicated by grassy mounds, and at Carrow we stopped to examine Proco-litia, on the south side of the present high-road. Carrow-burgh is a dreary-looking station, with grass-grown ramparts, and the ruins of the gateways plainly appearing. The antiquarian knowledge of a local farmer led him, in a season of

Thirlwall Castle.

EDMUND BOGG.

drought, to search here for water, and he was rewarded by the discovery of the ancient Roman well, which on examination yielded a remarkable quantity of coins, altars, carved stones, Roman pearls, etc.

A little further on, and about a mile from Walwick, there are some fine pieces of the Wall and ditch. In one instance the former is over eight feet high, and remarkably solid and strong. The top is covered with a thick growth of bushes. The change in the character of the scenery is now very noticeable. Cultivated fields and thick leafy woods replace the wild, rugged moorland. After passing Walwick, at the bottom of the hill Chesters is reached, at one time the residence of the late Mr.

John Clayton, who has done more than any other man to preserve and make known the relics of the finest monument of the Roman occupation of Britain. In the road going down the hill to the entrance the foundations of the Wall are very clear in the present high-road.

Permission being readily and courteously granted, we examined the numerous altars, inscribed stones, ear-rings, bones, pieces of pottery, etc., behind the house, and then proceeded to the park in front to inspect the remains of the Roman Cilurnum, which covered an area of five and a quarter acres, coming next to Amboglanna in size.

The ruins are nearly all exposed and free from earth accumulations, and present the most perfect examples of the camp buildings of the larger Roman stations. The Forum occupied the centre of the camp, and at the south end of the enclosure

The Seven Niches, Chesters.   GIBSON.

is a vaulted chamber in good preservation, which is supposed to have been the *aerarium,* or treasury of the station. Near the centre of the eastern wall was the *praetorium,* or general's quarters. The hypocaust, blackened by smoke, and formerly yielding quantities of soot, is in an almost perfect state. The slabs of stone which formed the floors of the rooms are in position. Close to the river a series of seven-arched niches, in good preservation, is noteworthy. What they were intended for is a matter of conjecture. At this point, facing the middle of the station, the North Tyne was crossed by a bridge of considerable size, as is evinced by the remains of the buttresses on the banks, and the piers in the river bed. On the left bank the river has receded, and a large mound of earth intervenes between the buttress and the stream. The stones are large and neatly fashioned, retaining their original positions. The lewis holes and grooves for the iron binders are clearly defined. One curious piece of stone, over a yard long, has the appearance of an axle-tree, with the holes round the centre. When the bridge was perfect it must have been a noble example of architectural skill.

Tired, yet thoroughly pleased with our day, we turned into the "George," a comfortable hostelry facing the lovely river.

Between Chollerford and Newcastle few obvious traces of the Wall are to be seen. Here and there the high-road passes directly over the foundation stones. This is especially noticeable before reaching the Errington Arms, and after heavy rain the stones are exceedingly plain.

At Heddon-on-the-Wall a long strip covered with a thorn hedge appears on the right of the road, and just over the hill there is another piece nearly four feet high, with the remains of a mile-castle. The winding Tyne is now seen far away to the south-east, and a canopy of smoke indicates the proximity of a large industrial centre.

At Dene House, two miles past Heddon, in the corner of a garden close to the road, is a heap of stones which have formed the columns of the gates of a mile-castle. Next, at Denton Burn, there are two irregular mounds between three and four feet high, surrounded by a wooden railing.

Of course, in addition to the remains enumerated in this brief outline, there are many less conspicuous which the keen antiquarian has disclosed, and to those who wish to have an exhaustive account of these I would suggest a study of Dr. Bruce's large work, and for actual use on the walk the Wallet Book. Even at Wallsend traces still linger.

A few general remarks must terminate this account. Each of the stations was occupied by a number of soldiers varying from 600 to 1,000, so that the whole garrison, consisting of legions of various nationalities, was probably about 12,000 In many places along the Wall specimens of rough inscriptions still linger, notably at the quarries on Fallowfield Fell, near Chollerford, at Coome Crag, and at the Written Crag, in the glen of the River Gelt, near Brampton.

As will be gathered from the foregoing remarks the central portion is in the most perfect preservation, and this it undoubtedly owes to its wild and isolated situation. Thanks to the exertions of the Earl of Carlisle, the late Mr. John Clayton, and others, the mutilation of the Wall has almost ceased, and it is to be sincerely hoped that what remains of this valuable relic will be preserved from the destructive propensities of the tripping vandal and the quarrying of the immediate inhabitants, ignorant of its antiquarian importance. Finally, a new era may be said to have opened for the Roman Wall, and now, late in the nineteenth century, careful and indefatigable attention is being devoted to its study and preservation, notably by the Society of Antiquaries of Newcastle-on-Tyne, whose journals contain notes on the most recent excavations, and the consequent theories advanced.

G. T. L.

CHAPTER III.

HEXHAM.

RATHER more than twelve centuries ago, a remarkable gathering of monks and artificers might have been witnessed in a wild, romantic spot at the slope of hills which rise in picturesque undulation, a mile or so below where the North and South Tyne unite into one broadly flowing river, at the time we speak of winding through a charming forest vale, uncontaminated by manufactories. At the head of that company was Bishop Wilfred, who had just returned from a pilgrimage to Rome, where he had passed through a severe training, both ecclesiastical and monastic, his mind filled with ambitious projects and holy zeal to uprear a splendid abbey, worthy of the ecclesiastical architecture of Rome.

The Abbey, when complete, is said to have been, both in grandeur of design and exquisite in finish and detail, the most magnificent building in Britain, or even west of the Alps, and as such remained until early in the ninth century, when the Northmen began to ravage the country, and swooped down Tynedale devastated Hexhamshire, committing frightful outrages, and leaving the town and abbey a mass of blackened ruins. This was in the time of Bishop Tilfrith, who fled affrighted from the terrible atrocities committed by the Danes, and never returned; and from that period Hexham ceased to form a separate bishopric, after a rule of 136 years. It was consecrated in 678, and its first Bishop was Eata, Tilfrith being the last, in 814.

The city of Hexham, at this early period, according to the history of Prior Richard, who dwelt here in the twelfth century, was ample and magnificent, as the vestiges of antiquity testify, for, apart from the abbey, St. Wilfred also built two other churches, St. Mary's and St. Peter's. Relics of the former still remain ; of the latter not a vestige. 'Tis said that after the advent of the Danes, churches and houses lay ruined and roofless, and not a single human being was left to mourn over the havoc and desolation, and thus it remained for upwards of two hundred years, until Thomas, the second Archbishop of York, in 1113, restored part of the beautiful fabric, when it became a Monastery of Augustine canons. A few rare and antique relics of Wilfred's time still remain in the present abbey church, and also others of a people who dwelt here long anterior to the Saxon. Wilfred's career was a stormy and eventful one, for he was ever a stickler for the supremacy of, and obedience to, the power and usages of the Roman Church. At Rome he was a student under Boniface, the Archdeacon ; he daily visited the tombs

A Peep of Hexham.   EDMUND ROOD.

of the martyrs, and gathered together relics of the saints. Twice or thrice he was driven from his bishopric, and after a life of almost continual strife and wandering, seeking redress from the Church of Rome, he died at a good old age, at Oundle, in Northamptonshire (709). Acca, the companion and friend of Wilfred, was his successor to the bishopric. He was an accomplished scholar and singer, having been educated at Rome, where he was so charmed with the church music that he engaged an Italian (probably the first music master who had been brought to Britain). This man taught both the choir of Canterbury and Hexham to sing most heavenly. At the latter place Bishop Acca took the lead in the choir. It was he who gilded the walls of the cathedral with silver and gold, and added rich coverings to the altar, and beautiful candlesticks to illume the building. Bede the Venerable loved him dearly, and he tells us that he was a most heavenly man, a great soul, and a guardian angel over all good men. That holy, God-fearing man, St. John of Beverley, whose saintly character stands out so bright and luminous on the pages of history, and adds a halo of sanctity to it, was also associated with this place. Whilst here he daily retired to pray into a little oratory, or cell, a mile and a half away, on the north side of the river, still known as "St. John's Lee." The Venerable Bede was one of his disciples. John of Hexham and Prior Richard, two celebrated historians, were natives of this place.

Roman Altar.   GIBSON.

The memorable battle of Hexham, fought between the Lancastrians and Yorkists (1464), took place along the ridge of the hill, just on the outskirts of the town. Battle Hill, the name of a street leading on to the battle-field, is a memento of that fight, so fatal to the cause of the Lancastrians. "King Henry," says Hall, "was the best horseman of his company that day, for he fled so fast that no one could overtake him, yet so closely was he pursued that three of his body-guard, with their horses trapped in blue velvet, were captured, one of them wearing the unfortunate monarch's cap of state, called a boycocket, embroidered with two crowns of gold, and ornamented with pearls.

Some two miles south is the most beautiful ravine called Deepdene. Hidden in the deep recesses of this glen, overhung by sandstone banks and waving branch and luxuriant foliage, is Queen Margaret's Cave, where she and her child took refuge after the battle so disastrous to her cause ; and here also, when wandering forlorn in the woods, she was met by the robbers, one of whom so nobly befriended her. This incident is well known to all readers of English history, and as there is nothing improbable in this romantic story, why should we doubt the truth of it ? Everything points to its authenticity—situation of battle and the nearness of the forest, ravine, cave, etc.

It was a *fête* day on my first visit to Hexham, and the inhabitants from the surrounding district, dressed in their best attire, and radiant with smiling faces, were hurrying to the town, all boisterous with mirth, chaffing, and cracking of jokes, etc. The place re-echoed with merriment and revelry on that day.

A fine view of Hexham is obtained from a slight eminence on the south side of the Tyne. 'Tis a charming scene, pastoral garden and orchard intervening and surrounding it, the red roofs of the old town clustering beyond, above which loom mediæval relics, pregnant with historic memoies ; beyond rise tier above tier the billowy woodland hills, clothed with diversified foliage. 'Tis a unique and primitive little market town, being unpolluted by manufactories, having a Flemish aspect about it. The Market Place is approached through the gateway of a fine Edwardian Tower, thus imbuing the town with the military significance of the past. On the west side is the Market Hall and the Market Place, from which the streets radiate. This is still a very interesting square, and was, half-a-century ago, the most antique in Great Britain. The Abbey Church, though now shorn of its former grandeur, is still a magnificent and sublime building, impressing the beholder with the solemn, hoary sanctity which still seems to pervade it ; it comprises transept, 156 feet in length, and beautiful choir, now used as the church. Amongst many relics of an old world special mention should be made of the Saxon Crypt, a fragment of the original church built by St. Wilfred, and nearly similar to the one at Ripon, also erected by the Bishop. Ripon was the most beloved of his numerous places of residence. In the construction of the Crypt ample evidence has been found of the Roman Wall, and also the Roman town of Corstopitium (Corbridge), having been used as a quarry by the builders. The Roman Altar, now in the transept, is a rare piece of early sculpture. Prior Richard's tomb, or shrine, and the grotesque figure of a monk at the entrance, are curious examples of mediæval craft ; also the antique rood screen, which bears a Latin inscription, and, translated, reads : " Pray for the soul of Lord Thomas the Second, who caused this work to be made." But the most sacred and interesting relic is the Frid Stool Peace, or Sanctuary Chair. Four elaborately carved crosses stood at four different entrances to the city to mark the way to sanctuary and refuge, and once the fugitive was within the limit of the boundary he was practically safe from arrest, but once seated in the Stool of Peace the accused, whatever his crimes, was religiously protected by the laws and power of the church, and if his pursuers attempted to remove him from the stool by force, the offence of so doing was punishable by death. What scenes and incidents this hoary relic brings forth on the memory, connecting, as it does, the story of Biblical days, and the picture of the fugitive fleeing for safety to the city of refuge.

The abbey gateway, clad with ivy and lichen, is a fine relic of Norman work, and stands about a hundred paces to the north-west of the church. The old churchmen of Hexham were renowned for their sympathy and kindness to the people, and when the distressing edict was sent forth by the command of the Eighth Henry for the monks to deliver up their church, lands, and belongings, the people rose, fully armed, and gathering around them, vowing to protect them from such pillage and insult. This was the first symptom of the insurrection known in history as the Pilgrimage of Grace, which ended in disaster and ruin to many of the participators, amongst others, the last Abbot, Edward Jaye, who was hanged beneath the abbey gateway.

Two and a half miles east from Hexham, and just south of the road leading to Corbridge, the ruins of Dilston Castle peer from its leafy surroundings down the

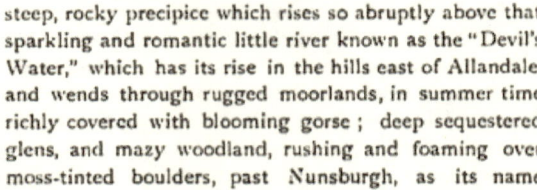

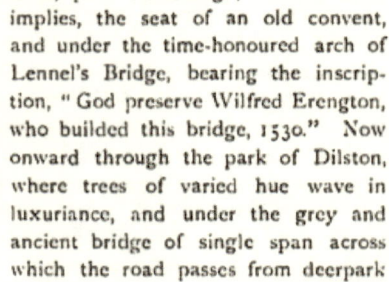

steep, rocky precipice which rises so abruptly above that sparkling and romantic little river known as the "Devil's Water," which has its rise in the hills east of Allandale, and wends through rugged moorlands, in summer time richly covered with blooming gorse ; deep sequestered glens, and mazy woodland, rushing and foaming over moss-tinted boulders, past Nunsburgh, as its name implies, the seat of an old convent, and under the time-honoured arch of Lennel's Bridge, bearing the inscription, " God preserve Wilfred Erengton, who builded this bridge, 1530." Now onward through the park of Dilston, where trees of varied hue wave in luxuriance, and under the grey and ancient bridge of single span across which the road passes from deerpark to the castle. Thence, turning in a semicircle, flows beneath giant ancestral trees, which here rise in grandeur, and canopy the scene with their beauty. Now, smooth and silent, it flows, brown with the tint of its moorland source, nature exquisitely reflected in its bosom ; again, bursting from all restraint, it dances and sparkles into foaming riplets past mills of olden time, picturesque in their half-ruined confusion, adorned with a robe of moss, lichen, fern, flower, trailing wild plant, and the roots of ancient trees, from whence the water, in its fury, at flood time, has swept away the soil—such is the beauty of " Devil's Water," as it sparkles past Dilston Hall, and winds through an avenue of foliage to the Tyne a few hundred paces beyond.

And here, on this commanding eminence above the little river, with the delightful vistas of Tynedale spreading far and wide beneath, the old Norman family of Dyvelston reared their baronial keep. History mentions a Robert de Dyvelston, a William, Thomas, and Simon de Dyvelston, and the name of the little rivulet still preserves the memory of this old Border race. In course of generations the estate passed into the possession of the Tyndalls, so called from their domain, which stretched for several miles along the course of the South Tyne. Langley Castle, then the baronial residence of the Tyndalls, stood majestically on an eminence, which

commanded the southern banks of the Tyne, two miles west from Haydon Bridge. The castle was in the shape of the letter H, and was defended by a moat and four noble towers, standing in position north and south, the walls of which were seven feet thick. Two Adams de Tynedale, father and son, held possession of Langley during the long reign of Henry III.

> " That castle rose upon the steeps of the
> Green vale of the Tyne,
> While far below, as low they creep,
> From pool to eddy, dark and deep,
> Where alders bend and willows weep,
> You hear her streams repine."

Dilston Hall Bridge.   EDMUND BOGG.

Sir William de Tyndall married Alana, daughter and heiress of Margaret of Silesia, a niece of Wincesslaus the Good, and almost the last of the ancient Kings of Bohemia ; her paternal ancestors had occupied for ten generations the throne of Poland. Margaret came as a companion in that courtly train of her cousin, fair Anne of Luxemburg, the beloved wife of Richard II. Such is a brief outline of the Tyndalls, who became possessed of Dilston, and were ancestors of William Tyndall, the Apostle of the English Reformation. From the Tyndalls it passed to the Claxtons, and from them, by marriage, to John Cartington, of Cartington Tower ; and his daughter and heiress, Anne, married Sir Edward Radcliffe, of Derwentwater, whose castle stood on an island in the beautiful lake, whose natural charms can scarcely be surpassed.

---

* Devilstone so called from its situation on the high banks of the Stony Brook Devil.

> " A land of vale and mountain,
> Isles of the Derwent lake ;
> Stream of a thousand fountains,
> Mists on the mountain's peak."

By this marriage, which took place towards the end of the fifteenth century, Dyvelston was added to the possessions of the Radcliffes of Derwentwater.

Who is there that hath not heard of the dismal tragedy which overtook the scions of the Radcliffes for their adherence to the lost cause of the ill-fated Stuarts ? There is a melancholy and pathetic interest attached to the noble-hearted, yet unfortunate, Earls. Of James, the first Earl who suffered, a writer who knew him, says :—" The sweetness of his temper and disposition, in which he had few equals, had so secured him the affection of all his tenants, neighbours, and dependents, that multitudes would have lived and died for him ; he was a man formed by nature to be generally beloved, and was in the habit of continually visiting the cottages of the peasantry, so that he might see their wants, and with his own hands relieve the poverty and distress of the poor, be they Romanists or Protestants. He kept a house of generous hospitality and noble entertainment." Such was the disposition of the ill-fated Earl. There were numerous north-country ballads respecting him ; one says :—

> " Oh, Derwentwater's a bonnie lord,
>   He wears his gowd in his hair,
>   And glinting is his hawking eye,
>   Wi' kind love dwelling there.

> Yestreen he cam to our lord's yett,
>   An' loud, loud would he ca'—
> ' Rise up, rise up, for good King James,
>   And buckle, and come awa' !' "

He was beheaded on Tower Hill, February 24th, 1715, in spite of the earnest supplication of his wife, and the efforts and entreaties of his numerous friends. 'Tis

said that the instant the noble head was severed from his body, a strange moaning sound of agonised sorrow was uttered by the vast multitude of spectators, and far and wide across the northern counties bitter tears were shed, and expressions of horror and grief uttered for the hapless fate of the winsome young earl.

" The Tyndale peasants wake and weep,"

says one ballad, and round the blazing fires, on dark winter nights, tales were long told of how the spouts of Dilston Hall ran blood, and the new corn which was ground at the mill on the day of execution was tinged with crimson. The Aurora Borealis, since that time known in this district as the Derwentwater lights, shone with unwonted brilliancy on that night ; and " Devil's Water " ceased its prattling music, and became sombre and mournful, changing to a crimson hue. There is a beautiful tradition which records that in the park and woods, the spirit of the unhappy Lady Derwentwater has often been seen, gliding, ghost-like, as if in search of her husband ; and again, in the night-time, she has appeared on the turret, holding lamp or torch high above her head, as if to guide the way to the castle. It was from this place she was wont, in the happy days, to watch for the coming of her lord.

The body of Lord Derwentwater was brought to Dilston, and, without any ostentation or display, sorrowfully deposited in its family vault within the chapel. His lady and friends, and the tenantry, gathered round the vault, some loud in their lamentation, others silently weeping, for they remembered how kind he had been to them. But who can tell the utter desolation which swept across the heart of the bereaved lady. For a short time she remained at Dilston, where she was courteously treated with compassion by the people, for they knew how holy was her affection for her lost lord ; but her cup of sorrow was filled to the brim on making a last visit to Derwentwater lake, where the peasantry actually rose and insulted the unhappy lady. Once she is said to have hidden herself from their fury in a hollow of Wallow Cragg, still known by the name of " Lady's Rake." Story says that, had it not been for her earnest persuasion, the Earl would never have embarked in that ill-fated rebellion, which ended so tragically. The unhappy lady seems never to have been at rest, for she was constantly changing her place of residence, dying at the age of 30, August 30th, 1723. Her son survived his mother eight years, dying in 1731 ; and whatever possessions the son had not been deprived of by the attainder of his father, fell to his uncle, Charles Radcliffe, as gallant a soldier as ever drew sword or buckled on armour, who, 30 years after the execution of his brother, also suffered for his loyalty to the Stuarts. He was executed on Little Tower Hill, 1746, and his body is supposed to have been interred in the Church of St. Giles, in the Fields, but his heart, according to his own request, was embalmed, and deposited in the coffin of James, his brother, in the vault, of the family chapel at Dilston. Such is a brief outline of the sad tragedy which overtook the gallant lords of Dilston and Derwentwater.

Beautiful indeed is the position which the solitary relic of Dilston Castle occupies, just above the verge of the precipice, overhanging "Devil's Water," its exquisite

loveliness blending with story and romance. Many interesting chapters might be
written anent its days of strife and Border feud, and the tragical ending of its noble
owners. There is a tradition of a subterranean passage, and unearthly sounds have
often been heard issuing therefrom, and the forms of ghosts and goblins have also
been seen in the dreary vaults beneath the castle, where many an unhappy captive has
fretted and pined in solitude and utter darkness, far from friends and relations.
Adjoining, on the south side, is the little Catholic Chapel of the Radcliffes, with its
flagged roof, modest tower and bell gable, mellow with time. Within its hallowed
precincts is the family vault of the Radcliffes, and here rests the body of the unfortunate
James, the first Earl, who was beheaded, and the heart of his brother, the gallant
and noble Charles. Patriarchal trees of vast growth abound, and the remains of the
noble avenue of chestnuts is still to be seen.

Regretfully we turn from Dilston, and follow the road leading to Corbridge, once
the largest Roman town in the north of England. Here the Tyne, broad and
beautiful, sweeps under the noble bridge, built on Roman foundation, and which has
proved to be a most remarkably strong structure, its resistive power, owing to its sure
foundations, being very great. It was the only bridge which escaped being swept
away between Alston Moor, the source of the South Tyne, and the sea, during the
awful fury of that tremendous flood, November, 1771. Those who have stood on this
bridge will know the great height of the parapet above the water when not at flood,
yet on that night persons leaning over washed their hands in the rolling waters.
Fearful was the catastrophe which overtook many of the inhabitants' dwellings along
the banks of the Tyne on that memorable night. Part of the old bridge at Newcastle, with the shops, one of which was built on every pier, were swept away, and
many of the occupants therein drowned.

Corbridge, being the site of the Roman Corstopitium, has yielded a wealth of
treasure appertaining to those people. The little River Cor, from which the town
receives its name, runs into the Tyne a few hundred yards to the west ; here a huge
skeleton was found in the 17th century, its measurements, according to tradition,
being indeed fabulous. The name Bloody Acre, just on the south side of the Tyne,
marks the site of a battle fought between the English and Scotch during the invasion
of King David, 1138. "The Angel," an old hostelry, is still standing ; and built
partly in the churchyard is a fine example of an ancient peel tower, 13th century period.
In former times it was the residence of the vicar, and afterwards used as the town
gaol : the entrance door is still protected by bands of rare ironwork. The north
aisle of the church contains numbers of sculptured stones, fragments of altars, etc.,
and a broken figure of Hercules, found in the churchyard ; also examples of Saxon
work, and tomb covers, etc., of mediæval times. The church, with its tower and the

peel castle adjoining, form a very interesting picture, and are also types of interesting architecture.

Half-an-hour's tramp north of Corbridge, past Beaufront Castle, charmingly situated, where the ill-fated Radcliffe visited his friend and kinsman on the eve of the Rebellion ; with the beautifully wooded valley of the Tempe stretching away to the west, we reach *Aydon Castle, an interesting mediæval structure, more akin to a fortified mansion than a Border peel, probably dating from the days of the Norman kings. It was the seat of Emma de Ayden, a rich heiress in the reign of the first Edward, who disposed of her in marriage to Peter de Walles, or Wallace, from Walls, in France. A deep, well-timbered ravine, down which babbles a turbulent stream, half encircles the structure ; on the opposite side a ditch completed the circle of defence. On my visit an immense colony of rooks made noisy clamour to the otherwise peacefulness of the spot. From the walls you look sheer down into the abyss. In Norman times it was in the possession of the Baliols, from whom it passed to the Aydons. The house, as it now remains, is supposed to have been built by Peter de Vallibus towards the end of the 13th century. A rock overhanging the ravine is said to have received its name, " Jack's Leap," from a Scotchman, who leapt

Doorway, Corbridge Peel Tower.   r. 6006.

from the precipice and escaped his pursuers, whilst his companions were captured, or hurled into the glen and killed.

A few hundred yards still further north is Halton Peel Tower, a massive square structure, with Jacobean farm-house and a chapel adjoining, the seat and manor of the ancient family of the Haltons.† There was a John de Halton in the reign of

---

* Aydon, so called from its situation on the brink of a deep ravine—The High Dene.

† From the Halton family the manor passed to the Carnabys, one of whom appears to have been a warden of the borders, for we are told that on one occasion, whilst he was deeply engaged on the trial of some of them, a very notorious and desperate villain was seized by his son, who asked his father what he should do with him. " Do with him," said the father ; " why hang him !" As soon as the trial was ended, he ordered the man to be brought before him, but was told he was hanged instantly, according to his order. On complaint being made to the Crown, a fine of £4 per annum was laid upon the Halton estate, which was still paid at the end of the eighteenth century."

Henry III., and a William de Halton was High Sheriff of Northumberland in the following reign. The interior of the latter is very plain ; one interesting feature is the Norman chancel arch. Very droll were the remarks of the aged sexton, who could not give us any information. He only knew it to be "ah varry oad consarn ; it's been here," said he, " iver sin ah remember how't, an' ah'm 76." An ancient altar table, standing on arched pedestals, is in the graveyard. The place is delightfully rural and picturesque, seen from the road, with huge arms of massive trees reaching into the burial ground, and the lowly chapel, with machiolated walls to match the castle, in the background, form a very interesting subject.

A little to the north of Halton is the site of the Roman station of Hunnum. To our astonishment, on asking a native to direct us to the site, he answered, " I've lived in this hoose 40 years, but it's the first time I've heard of a Roman station in this vicinity." Such indifference to the interesting relics abounding in his own locality appeared most strange to us, considering the many miles we had tramped to visit the spot. An up-to-date city was, no doubt, more to his taste

Now turning west, with our backs towards Newcastle, we follow the site of the Roman Wall for several miles. Passing Cocklaw Tower, an ancient hall of the Erringtons, we reach St. Oswald's Chapel, a place of holy memories, standing on the rising ground above the Tyne valley. It was here, in 635, that King Oswald, a man beloved of God, gave battle to that celebrated Pagan warrior, Ceadwalla, King of the West, who had previously slain Oswald's brother, King of Bernicia, and nearly destroyed his army. This good King Oswald had been taught by Aidan at the monastery of Iona, and the seed there sown in after years bore good fruit. The story of the vision which had appeared to the Emperor Constantine just before the battle of Milvian Bridge flashed on his memory, so hastily raising a wooden cross in front of his army, he called to his soldiers to kneel around it, and lifting up his voice to heaven, he prayed to be delivered from the power of the enemy. It was a battle between the Cross and Paganism, similar to the great fight at Arthuret, half-a-century earlier. Placing his men in a most advantageous position, on a plateau behind the Roman Wall, protected on the north by a ridge of rocks, he calmly awaited the coming of the foe, who could be discerned in the distance marching along the east bank of the North Tyne. It is said that the Pagan Prince laughed in mockery when he saw the smallness of the force gathered there to oppose him. Fully confident of victory, his forces flung themselves with fury against the strong barrier of defence, and were thrown back, scattered and broken. Again and again the advancing wave of Paganism was sent reeling backward by the gallant little army of Oswald's, who finally triumphed, scattering and chasing the Pagans across the Roman Wall and over the Tyne river, the discomfited chieftain being slain some seven or eight miles from the battlefield. The success of Oswald was so far above all human expectation, so they named the site of the battle Hefenfelth, or Heaven's Field, *i.e.*, the Holy Dene. To this spot the monks of Hexham repaired yearly, on the anniversary of Oswald's death, to offer up prayers for the repose of his soul ; and soon after a church was built on the site of the battle, and was named Saint Oswald, after the sainted and victorious King.

Crossing the bridge at Cholleford we pass forward to the Roman station of Cilurnum, which occupies some five and a half acres along the south bank of the North Tyne, situated in the grounds of the Claytons (the Chesters). The walls of the station are in many places several courses in height, and the exact position of the

Ruins of Cilurnum.   EDMUND ROGG.

different departments can be distinctly traced—the rooms occupied by the soldiers, the entrance, and sanitary arrangements, the forum, pretorium, treasury, baths, etc. What scenes of war, tumult, and building and making of roads, this valley has witnessed.

About the dawn of Christianity men of various nationalities were marched hither from all parts of the known world. The Carthaginian and Numidinian from Africa ; men from the banks of the Tigris and Euphrates ; the Armenian and Syrian ; uncouth warriors from the wilds of Tartary, the banks of the Volga and

D

the Caspian, in Asia; Cretans, Thracians, Tungrians, Galatians, and Dacians; and the Cymbrians and Teutons; formidable warriors from the shores of the Baltic; the Huns and Goths from the Danube; the Gaul; the Spaniard; men of Sparta, Athens, and other cities of ancient Greece and Rome, the latter well cultured and civilized; also people from the conquered provinces along the shores of the Mediterranean, veterans in war, trained with a stern discipline by their leaders, were there gathered to protect this frontier of the Romans.   Mighty indeed are the changes which have come to pass since the mistress of the world ruled here, and with strength and splendour raised that line of defence, the frontier wall, from coast to coast, built city, town, and station, and formed those far-extending military roads, along which courier and gaily painted chariot sped, bearing onwards the proudest blood of ancient Rome;

A Bend of the Tyne.

and stately galleys were then to be seen ascending or descending along the bosom of "Father Tyne." Her strong-handed rule to be succeeded—when the legions were withdrawn to save her own capital from the spoliation of the invader—by the influx of wild men from beyond the Wall, leaving in their train havoc, wreck, riot, and ruin, and the oppression of the old British race, who invited the Saxons from over the sea to their aid; the latter, in turn, also became their oppressors.   Then came the final attempt of the down-trodden nation to hurl back the invader who had stolen in under the guise of friendship, the uprising, tottering, and falling of petty kingdoms and states, until, in the fulness of time, came that cohesion, and the formation of a mighty people, whose empire stretches far beyond the dreams of Roman conquest.

As we stood thus musing amidst the treasures of antiquity, imagination re-peopling the spot with the activity and splendour of military life; the muse of the magic mirror revealing the stately tramp of legions, the fluttering of triumphal banners, the echoes of war, the roll of chariots, the struggle on the battlefield, the flight of the vanquished, the return of the victors, bearing aloft the eagle-crested banners, and in their train, to swell the glory of conquest, are captive princes and shaggy unkempt warriors, of grim and fierce aspect, from the unknown Pictish regions, which the Roman Eagle seemed afraid to penetrate, and which she never thoroughly subjected.

Before leaving this beautiful and historic region, we note the remains of the Roman bridge which here crossed the river, fragments of the piers being still to be seen. A little higher is the fine bridge at Cholleford. About twenty years ago a medical man from Newcastle, who had been called to Cholleford on urgent business, was crossing the narrow bridge in fine style, when his trap collided with a large stone placed to keep the carts from damaging the parapet. The doctor had a very narrow escape, his groom not being so fortunate, for a stifled cry and a heavy splash in the river, far below, told him of his servant's fate. Rushing to the "George," which stands at the foot of the bridge, the doctor procured a light and assistance, meanwhile fearing they would be of no avail ; but what was his astonishment, on nearing the bridge, to meet the man, dripping like a half-drowned rat, otherwise none the worse for his immersion.

After a halt at the "George" for refreshment, we still follow, for some distance, the highway which runs on the side of the Roman Wall, at a grand elevation above the river for about twenty miles west from Newcastle. But before proceeding we will make brief mention—for our space forbids anything more—of the interesting places lying between Haltwhistle and the junction of the North and South Tyne, as, for instance, Fourstones, a name derived from that number of stones, which probably marks some ancient boundary. In the cavity of one, the Earl of Derwentwater, when hiding from the warrant which was issued for his arrest, was wont to deposit his letters, which, story says, were collected by a boy clad in green like a fairy, and as such believed to be, to the astonishment and wonder of the natives. From hence to Haydon Bridge the Tyne flows on calmly and tranquilly, through exquisite scenery. The last-named place received its name from the steep bridge which crosses the river at this place ; and the old cemetery, from its sorrowful association with a wild border foray, is known as the "Cruel Syke." This is also the birthplace of Martin, the artist.

Further west, before we reach Bardon Mill, Langley Castle is passed to the south, and the beauty of the river flowing through charming woods claims our admiration. Ridley Hall, a noted place, stands between the Tyne and the Allen. The Ridley family were noted borderers, and took part in many a wild adventure. The walks in the vale of the latter river are most delightful. The little River Allen, which joins the Tyne below Ridley Hall, takes its rise on the moors to the east of Alston, and wanders in its twelve miles course through a rich profusion of nature's loveliness, most notable at Monk's Wood, near Whitfield, and the charming scenery at Stanard-de-Peel, where the river passes through the hills, beautifully clothed with rich and variegated foliage of waving woods. Reverting to the Tyne again, further west is Willimoteswick (*i.e.*, the mote or keep), formerly a place of great strength, and Unthank Hall, both residences of the Ridley family—a member of whom was the famous Bishop Ridley, who suffered martyrdom. Several of the Ridley family were eminent divines, and others celebrated in literature. For their adherence to the Royal cause, the Parliament confiscated some of their estates in 1652.

> " Thus fell the Ridley's martial line,
>   Lord William's ancient towers ;
> Fair Ridley on the silver Tyne,
>   And sweet Thorngrafton's bowers."

Arms of the Ridleys.

Continuing our ramble from Cholleford, we leave the highway, where it separates from the Wall, and follow the course of the great military barrier over hill, dale, and barren upland, crossing a wide range of basaltic rocks. It is a rough tramp, but most enjoyable and interesting. At Sewinshields, traditions of King Arthur lend a zest of romance to the stern relics of old Rome. To the north of the Wall formerly stood a strong Border castle ; beneath was an enchanted cave, where the king and his court lay entranced, as the bard says they do under the Eildons, waiting for the spell to be dissolved by the magic sound of the bugle.

As we proceed the land becomes more wildly picturesque. In several places we walked along the surface of the Wall, and our imagination depicted the Roman sentinel pacing to and fro in the darkness, keeping watch and ward, scanning eagerly across the wild waste to the north, or, peradventure, thinking of his own beloved home away in the sunny south, maybe contrasting that home on the banks of the Tiber, or the sunny shores of the Adriatic Sea, with the black sterile hills where he was doomed to spend many weary months, or even years. Past " Cat Gate," so named from a hole made by the Scots large enough to admit the body of a man, and " Busy Gap," a place notorious in olden time, and the rendezvous of moss-troopers and border-thieves. Now we reach Borcovicus, the most important station on the Wall, and defended in Roman times by the first Tungrian Cohort, or Belgic Gauls. The Temple of Mithras and Mithraic Cave bespeak memories of the eastern world. Just before we reach the highest part of the Wall we drop into a sheltered hollow in the hills, near the foot of the Northumbrian lakes. Hot Bank, the name of a farm, is tenanted by an old Border family of the name of Armstrong. 'Tis a strange and pathetic sight, says one, to watch a funeral cortège pass over the moorland from such out-of-the-way places. One of the Armstrongs who died many years ago, a character in his way, was followed by two hundred mounted borderers across the moor to his last resting-place. Here we rested awhile, partook of refreshment kindly provided by the good lady at the farm, and after a chat with the farmer, who was busy mowing the little plot of grass by the lakes, we followed the barrier line over the most wild, rocky, and inaccessible part of the Wall, which in many places follows the brink of abrupt precipices, rising sheer from the Northumbrian lakes, or lochs, as they are here called. In such places, where there is a natural bulwark, the ditch or vallum, which generally runs parallel with the Wall, has been dispensed with. The view from the highest point of land, over a thousand feet above sea level, at sunset is magnificent—east, west, north, and south, the view extends far, far away across mountain, moor, and lake, the wall line cutting this panorama of wildness and beauty. The Cumberland hills rise dim and shadowy, tier above tier ; westward, the crest of the waves on the Solway glitter and sparkle like a myriad of rubies ; to the north, Scotlandward, stretches an inhospitable region of dreary moor and rock ; bosomed in such scenes are the lonely lakes, flushed, on this eve, with the roseate hues from the setting sun. How strangely quiet—no sound of human life here, only the startled cry and flutter of

The Roman Wall

wild fowl on the lake, which have been disturbed by the splash of a stone falling into the water, or the distant bleating of sheep, the wail and shriek of curlew and snipe.

Long we stood musing on the memories and associations connected with this landmark of the world's history, the remnants of crumbling walls, mouldering ruins, and palaces, stretching away from our feet, ruled over by the mighty Cæsars of the eternal city, the centre, at that period, of the world's vitality. Unchecked in her conquest she became haughty in pride and power ; a hundred nations were trampled in dust before her ; she was the law-giver to the world, even our Saviour said, " Render unto Cæsar the things that are Cæsar's." The name, Eternal City, proved to be a misnomer, for at length the spark of her vitality was crushed out, her mighty strength and energy waned, her vast buildings, walls, and cities were thrown down and trampled into dust and ashes. "And as we trace," says one, "Rome's remnants and memorials, crumbling walls and fallen bulwarks, remaining only, as it seems, in mockery of man's boasted strength, wherein can be read, in plainer and more impressive character than any printed page could show it, the vanity of earth and all that rests upon it."

Further along the Wall is a house known as Burnt Deviot, formerly a resort of smugglers and reivers. Many a fierce fight has taken place in this vicinity, which the numerous skeletons discovered from time to time testify.

The Roman Wall.   GIBSON.

Now for the present we leave the Wall, and drop down the steep declivity. Looking back, the sun's rays were tipping with a golden thread the Roman bulwark, throwing into fine relief miles of that ancient landmark.

Haltwhistle, a long straggling market town, stands on the north bank of the South Tyne, and still retains many curious features of domestic architecture of the sixteenth century period. Here many primitive customs and superstitions still linger. In the days of feud and foray it was a place of resort for outlaws and moss-troopers. A feud long existed between the Armstrongs of Liddlesdale and the Ridleys of Tynedale, ending in the death of at least two of the Armstrongs. Castle Hill, an artificial mound, and the Church of Holy Cross, containing an altar tomb of the Ridleys, and an incised gravestone of the Blenkinsops, are objects of great interest. Bellister Castle, once the residence of the Blenkinsop family, stands on a small plateau, a few hundred yards to the south of Haltwhistle, and just to the east of the river, which here changes its course from south to north, to east and west. The walls of the ruin are of immense thickness, and sheltered by large sycamores. From appearance it has only been a strong Border peel of the same type and character as those nearer the Border line. Part of the ruins have been restored, and additions made, and it is now inhabited. Half-a-mile south-west is Wryden Scarr, where the river washes and wanders around a beautiful wooded cliff. From the summit fine views of the country west are obtained, further up the river flows through a scene of exquisite loveliness. Passing Sunhill and Rowport, old-world hamlets, we reach Lambley, where, previous to the thirteenth century, was a Benedictine convent, but the Scots, under Wallace, says Knighton, "consumed the house of the holy nuns of Lambley, and all the country round, in horrible fire." The ruins, which stood by the river's bank, have been washed away by furious floods.

To the south the fells rise boldly into the sky, and the glens sink deeper, and the scene grows more wild and lonely. 'Tis a beautiful June day, flowers carpet the brink of the river and the edge of the woodland, cloud packs like huge rocks and mountains float across the heavens, trailing shadows over the brown sunlit moor ; humming bees flit from flower to flower, birds carol, and trout and other fish glitter in the infant Tyne. Here, in the solemnity of the everlasting hills, we are hidden away from the noise and din of the busy world. Around us are scenes teeming with loveliness and wildering in beauty. Turning our faces north we follow the windings of the meandering Tyne, and pass the place where Nicholas Featherstonehaugh was murdered, October 24th, 1530. He was slain by William Ridley of Unthank, Hugh Ridley of Howden, and other members of this family.

The old ballad, which was alleged by Suretees to have been taken down from the recital of aged women upwards of one hundred years ago, says :—

```
" There was Willimoteswick,                And afore they were done gat sic a stun
    And Hardriding Dick,                   As never was seen since the world begun ;
    And Hughie o' Hawden, and Will o' the Wa' ;   I canno' tell a', I canno' tell a'.
    I canno' tell a', I canno' tell a' ;   Some gat a skelp, some gat a claw,
    An' mony a mair that the devil may knaw.   But they gar'd the Featherston's haud their jaw,
    The auld man went down, but Nichol his son   Nicol and Alick and a'.
    Ran away afore the fight was begun ;   Some gat a hurt and some gat nane,
    And he run, and he run.                 Some had harness and some gat sta'en."
```

Following the banks of the Tyne we approach Featherstone Castle, which stands on a level haugh, or meadow, delightfully secluded by fine trees, and hidden by the land which rises immediately above. Thus encircled by its native hills and the windings of the Tyne, it remains a perfect gem of romance and baronial glory in a rich setting of nature ; its mediæval towers, still perfect, ivy-clad and grey, carry back our thoughts to the rude age of strife and Border warfare, and fancy almost hears, borne on the breeze, the jingle of armour and the neighing and curvetting of war-steeds. Story says the castle received its name from the fact of its having formerly stood on the high ground to the east, near two large stones, known by the name of Fether-stones, the latter syllable, "haugh," being added to the name on the removal of the castle to its present site. The Fether, or Featherstonehaughs, were a noted Border family during the Norman and Tudor dynasties. From the castle we wander back to the Tyne, and over the remarkable bridge, of one bold arch, like Twizel on the Till, worthy of preservation. Here is a glen, and a delicious little waterfall. All is beautiful—overhanging trees, delightful glades and shadowy pools, where the fish love to lurk.

Featherstone Castle, South Tyne.

Passing west from the river we approach Blenkinsop Castle, situated on the slope of a steep bank, near Greenhead. Little of the original structure remains, extensive alterations having been made about 1880. The position of the castle has been well chosen, commanding, as it does, the vale country east and west. There is a tradition, grim and significant, relating to one Bryan Blenkinsop, who rode far and near in search of a wife possessed of a chest of gold so heavy that ten men would be required to carry it, and at length he found a lady who owned a chest of gold according to his heart's desire; he married her, but instead of love she soon learned to hate him. She hid her gold away in some secret chamber, and the knowledge of its hiding-place dying with her has caused her troubled spirit to wander. A lady, clad in white, has oft appeared at unearthly hours, vainly seeking for some mortal to whom she can disclose the secret of her golden hoard. Another tradition concerning this family is of a huge black hound, which is said to always appear a few days previous to a death, and again passes through the chamber of sorrow immediately the spirit leaves the body.

About a mile west of Greenhead, and built on a commanding site on the high rocky bank above the little River Tippal, a tributary of the South Tyne, are the sombre ruins of Thirlwall Castle, surrounded on three sides by dark firs, and, seen in the twilight, the place presents a strange, eerie picture of gloom and loneliness. It was guarded on the east by the deep ravine, and on the south and west by the Roman Wall and vallum. A deep silence of awe and mystery broods over this hoary relic, disturbed only by the fretting, foaming, and tumbling of the burn below. It would seem as if the spirits of all the warriors who have been slain in this district, during the centuries, might at any moment reappear on the scene, so impregnated is this spot with the glamour of the past. Only shattered fragments remain to bespeak its former glory ; the walls in many places measuring fully nine feet in thickness. The castle was formerly in the possession of the Thirlwalls, whose gathering cry in olden time resounded through the vale—" A Thirlwall! A Thirlwall!! A Thirlwall!!!" There was a John de Thirlwall in the reign of Edward III., and a Robert de Thirlwall, *tempo* Elizabeth. The last sole heiress, Eleanora Thirlwall, died towards the latter portion of the eighteenth century, when the castle came into the possession of the Carlisles. As a proof of its importance, Edward I. rested here a night in September, 1306.

Between here and Brampton the country is sparsely populated, and consists of farms, etc., generally standing on a small hill, intersected with knolls and fells, babbling brooks, and moorish meadows, where range herds of black, hornless cattle.

CHAPTER IV.

⚬ IRTHING VALLEY. ⚬

MILE west from Thirlwall we pass out of the eastern watershed into the valley of the Irthing, which takes its rise in the Tarnbecks, north of Bewcastle, and flows through a wide stretch of moorland called the Wastes, crosses the Roman Wall at Gilsland; thence, for the greater part of its course, it murmurs through scenes remarkable for beauty and historic significance, joins the waters of the Eden, and finds its way into the Solway, on the Cumberland coast. Gils-Land is a very ancient, interesting spot, and the healing virtues of the holy well had a great reputation in pre-railway times; but the situation was lonely and laborious to reach, and the district was so infested with moss-troopers and highwaymen, even down to the latter part of the eighteenth century, that people in search of health feared to travel to this shrine so famed for mineral virtues. The name Gilsland, from Gils or Gilles-Beuth, is said to receive its name from a Celt owing the allegiance of the Saxon, and who was possessed of this Barony in pre-Conquest days, stretching between the Irthing and the Liddle, and Beuth's Castle—the Bewcastle of our day was his original stronghold, a place difficult of approach at that date, situate in a lonely wilderness of heather. For affecting the cause of Gospatric, the Earl, the Conqueror stripped him of his lands, which were given, in turn, to a Norman adventurer, a De Vallibus or Vaux. Gilles, the son of the above-mentioned Beuth, is described in the Abbey of Lanercost as Lord of Gilsland, yet he never really ruled over the possessions of his ancestors. He joined with the disaffected Saxons who, with the assistance of the Scots, made repeated incursions over the Border, hoping, no doubt, to win back his heritage. At length a Tryst was arranged between Beuth and De Vallibus, whereby they might come to some final settlement and mutual understanding regarding the estates. But tradition records that, in violation of the rules

Waterfall on the Irthing, Gilsland.

of Tryst, Robert de Vallibus shamefully slew Gilles Beuth, and as an atonement for that guilty act, the Norman built and endowed the Priory of Lanercost (1169).

Camden says : " Gillesland Barony is a tract so cut and made with brooks, which they call gilles, that I should have thought it had taken the name from them, if I had not read in the Lanercost Book of one Gilles, son of Beuth, who was possessed of it, so that probably its name came from him." The same idea, I am sure, will occur to any interested observer, when looking into the vale of the Irthing at this place, so numerous appear the gills and becks, and tortuous windings of small watercourses, amongst the shrubby brushwood and numerous dwarf hillocks, seeming to point out, as an appropriate name, Gillesland, or the land of gills. The village is not by any means striking or picturesque, and the old-time cottages have been superseded by numerous small villa residences, without any pretension to architectural art. Yet the vale of the Irthing is beautiful, and possesses a character entirely its own. It was here that Sir Walter Scott, in the summer of 1797, first met Miss Carpenter, whom he married in the following year. The natives tell that he proposed to the lady of his choice at the famous popping-stone yet to be seen in the bed of the river, a spot where many love-sick swains make those vows which are only to be severed by death. "Guy Mannering," and the "Bridal of Triermain," have done much to make the visitors interested with this district.

Mump's Ha', which, Scott says, had an evil reputation, was formerly an alehouse. The front of the house has been altered, but the interior still retains most of its original features. It was here that Dandie Dinmont told Meg Merrilees of the death of Ellangowan, and it was here also that Fighting Charlie, an Armstrong of Liddlesdale, stayed to refresh himself when returning from Stagshawbank Fair. Meg was usually kind and gracious, and played the hostess well; watching her opportunity, however, she adroitly withdrew the charges from his pistols, and re-wadded them with tow; but all her blandishments and smiles could not prevail on Charlie to stay for the night, for he had been warned of the evil reputation the innkeeper and his wife bore. So he mounted and rode off at a sharp trot in the darkness; but suddenly remembering that under Meg's bland face there had lurked a sinister smile, he felt for his pistols, and, to his anger and astonishment, found the charges had been withdrawn and the space filled with tow. Fully convinced that he was to be waylaid, he carefully reloaded his pistols, and spurred his steed over the wild waste, scanning the moor in every direction. Suddenly two mounted fellows, disguised, and armed to the teeth, confronted him, and a glance over his shoulder proved that two other men had taken up the rear. The men in front called on him to stand and deliver, but Charlie, spurring his horse, went boldly onward, and covered the robbers with his pistols. "D—n your pistols," shouted one of the robbers; "aw care not a curse for it." "Aye, lad," said the deep voice of Fighting Charlie, "but the too's oot noo." This was enough for the highwaymen; they had oft heard of Charlie's prowess, but had never expected to meet a man so cool and daring. They turned and fled over the moor, and Armstrong reached home without further molestation. But he always swore that the robber who challenged him was no other than the landlord of Mump's Ha'. Meg lived to the good old age of one hundred years, and her grave can be seen in the churchyard of Upper Denton. On her tombstone is the following :—

" Mump's Hall.
Here lies the body of Margaret Carrick,
Who departed this life ye 4th of December, 1717,
In the 100th year of her age."

Another stone records the age and death of her daughter :—

" Here lieth the body of Margaret Teasdale,
Of Mump's Hall,
Who died May 4th, 1777, aged 98 years."

Truly great ages, and to have lived through such evil repute.

Three miles to the north of Gilsland stood the castle of Triermain ; all that now exists is a part of one of the walls. It was a place of vast strength, and was the earliest Norman structure built in this district after the Conquest, and stood the brunt of many a fierce fight before the castles of Askerton and Naworth had an existence. Centuries have rolled away since the warriors, attired in chain mail, passed beneath the barbican, and the banners which waved on the high keep have long since mouldered into dust. Sir Walter, in his " Bridal of Triermain," graphically describes the fierce fights and forays of the lord of the castle, and also tells how

*Crest of Vaux
of Triermaine
Gilsland*

" There the main fortress, broad and tall,
Spread its long range of bower and hall
And tower of varied size,
Wrought with each ornament extreme,
That Gothic art, in wildest dream
Of fancy could devise."

The Wizard of the North has rendered the names of Vaux and Tryermain immortal.

" Thou shalt not die, O Tryermain ;
Thou hast a glory greater far
Than any Border chieftain's reign
O'er land and men. Such glories are,
And fade, and these few stones remain.

But Walter Scott, he of thee sings,
And Coleridge, e'en, in 'Christabel,'
Throned thee in music. These the things
That make earth loveliest. Such a spell
Lasts longer than the ivy clings."

Seven miles to the north of Triermain is Bewcastle, remarkable for its unique monument, which stands fifteen feet in height, and is two feet square at the base. There is no definite opinion by whom, and for what purpose and what date, the stone was raised. Bewcastle thieves were the most renowned on the English side of the Border. "Once," says Sir Walter, in notes to the "Lay of the Last Minstrel," "the captain of Beweastle, having made a raid over that border, was defeated by one Wat Tinlinn, a noted Liddlesdale archer, and pursued through a dangerous morass, in which the district abounds. The captain reached the firm ground in safety, and seeing Tinlinn dismounted and floundering in the bog, sarcastically called out, 'Sutor Wat, ye cannot sew your boots; the heels rish and the seams rive.' Wat was a sutor, or shoemaker, by trade. 'If I cannot sew,' retorted Tinlinn, discharging a shaft which

BEWCASTLE CROSS

nailed the captain's thigh to his saddle; 'if I cannot sew, I can yerk.'" Hobby Noble, so celebrated in Border ballads, was born at the Crew, a peel tower in the vicinity.*

Now westward along the vale of the Irthing, and across the river at a shallow part, and a climb up the steep bank to Burdoswald, the Roman station of "Amboglanna," the glen, the brink or bank of a river. We need not describe the remains of the station, as Mr. G. T. Lowe has very faithfully portrayed this and the other stations in his chapter on the "Wall"; but as I am writing, a friend who has just returned from the confines of the Sahara desert describes to me the numerous Roman camps, and even cities, mouldering there in ruins, similar to those on the Wall, raised and inhabited by these conquerors of the world, anterior to the conquest of Britain. The camp is situate on a precipitous rock, and overlooks the river, which forms a natural rampart from the south. Few spots are more strikingly beautiful than the vale of Irthing, seen from this spot. The soothing music of the murmuring river, winding far below in half circles, falls on the ear; gleams of silver, sandy margins,

* A farmer, a native of the district between Beweastle and Cannobie, a great original in his way, and remarkable for his fondness of a "big price" for everything, attended at Langholm Fair, and notwithstanding his parsimonious habits, actually sold his lambs to a perfect stranger upon his simply promising to pay him punctually at the next market. On his return home the farmer's servants, who regularly messed at the same table, and seldom honoured him with the name of master, inquired, "Wee'l, Sandy, ha'e ye sel't the lams'?" "Atweel ha'e I, and

rock and pebbled shore, rich green verdure, hill, furze, and woodland, and the beautiful perspective enhanced by the twinings of the river. The Earl of Carlisle says that this scene wonderfully resembles the view of Troy from the plain of Troad. For some little distance further we follow the Wall, and then drop down into a green haugh on the north side of the Irthing river, and here, in a flower-decked vale and wood, glade and river, stands the Priory of Lanercost. The entrance is under a

The Priory of Lanercost, from the Gateway.

picturesque Norman gateway, through which the abbey is seen to fine advantage in the immediate perspective. The priory farm buildings, ancient barn, Edwardian

---

I gat a saxpence a heed mair than ony ane else in the market." "And a' weel paid siller?" "Na, the siller's no paid yet, but it's share (sure) eneuch." "Wha's yer merchant, and what's yer sakeritie (security)?" "Aye, aye, I ne'er fashed mysel' ta speer, but he's a weel fae'd mon, wi' muckle tap bits (top boots) and a bottle-green coat."

The servants at this laughed outright, and tauntingly told him he would never get a farthing. Sandy, however, thought differently, and having hurt his leg so as to prevent him from travelling, he sent a shepherd to Langholm, with instructions to look for a man with a bottle-green coat, whom he was sure, he said, to find standing near a certain sign. The shepherd did as he was bid, and strange to say, discovered a person standing at the identical spot, who, on learning his errand, inquired kindly for his master, and paid the money to the uttermost farthing. Sandy, who piqued himself on his skill in physiognomy, heard the news without emotion, and merely said, "I wad ony whiles lippen (trust) mair to looks than gabs (words), and whan I seed Colly smirking sa blithely and kindly aboot 'm I ken't weel eneuch he couldna' be a scoondr'l."

tower, and vicarage, are on the right—a confused mixture of antique architecture, mellow and grim with time.

> " The spirit of the spot shall lead
> Thy footsteps to a slope of green access.
> Where, like an infant's smile, over the dead,
> A light of laughing flowers along the graves is spread,
> And grey walls moulder round, on which dull time
> Feeds like slow fire upon a hoary brand."

The entrance portal at the west consists of numerous mouldings, supported by pilasters, with plain capitals and bases; immediately over the doorway is an arcaded

gallery, which formerly held figures, supposed to be those of Our Saviour and the twelve Apostles. A niche in the gable above the three lancet windows contains the sculptured figure of Mary Magdalene, and a monk kneeling before her. Services are held in the nave, which has been thoroughly

Lord Dacre's Tomb, in Lanercost Priory.   EDMUND BOGG.

renovated, and now does duty as parish church. But the most absorbing interest is centred in the choir and transepts, which are roofless. The associations connected with the exquisite altar tombs, linking the abbey with the great historic Border families—the De Vallibus, Roland de Vaux, the Dacres, the Howards—seeming to me like some enchanting page of Gothic legend from old romance.

As I stood on that holy ground, in the fading twilight of a summer's eve, in company with the venerable and kindly vicar, who was soon to be numbered with those already sleeping beneath our feet, and wandered from one decaying tomb to another, like the roofless choir, eloquent with lessons on the mutability of all things on earth, he, reverent and aged, with silver locks, never seeming to weary of pointing out and explaining the many interesting and artistic portions of the fabric ; I have often looked back on that witching hour of twilight we spent amongst the tombs, associated as they are with men famous in the annals of chivalry of the north, whose lives were adorned by noble deeds, high resolve and emprise; perhaps it may have been the soft, pensive glamour of the evening hour, for there was a spell of mystery, blending with romance and art, that did not mingle freely with the stern realities and harsh surroundings of the outer world. The tomb of Roland de Vaux is in the wall of the north transept. The fragments of the effigy of a knight, in red sandstone, supposed to be that of Roland, were, a few years ago, discovered in the crypt, and are now placed on the tomb. How finely descriptive are the following lines of the Bard :—

Tomb of Roland de Vaux.   EDMUND ROSS.

" Sir Roland de Vaux he hath laid
   him to sleep ;
His blood it was fevered, his
   breathing was deep,
He had been pricking against the
   Scott,
The foray was long and the skir-
   mish hot ;
His dinted helm and his buckler's
   plight,
Bore token of a stubborn fight."

In the north chapel of the choir is the tomb of Humphrey Lord Dacre, Warden of the Marches in the reign of Richard II., and also that of his wife, Mabel Parr, great aunt to Queen Catherine ; and tombs of the Howard family. But the most magnificent altar-tomb is that of Lord Dacre's, which stands in the centre of the choir, emblazoned with armorial bearings, a perfect source of delight to all lovers of heraldry. Beyond this, in the south transept, are effigies, presumably of the Edwardian period ; the whole choir is a shrine, or a valhalla, crumbling with memorials of the great.

Lanercost was the favourite resting-place of the First Edward, for on three occasions he stayed here during his northern expeditions. On his first visit, in 1280, he was accompanied by his good Queen, Eleanor, on which occasion an altar cloth of silk was presented to the priory. During this visit a magnificent hunt was proclaimed, and, attended by his barons, he rode forth and chased the wolf, wild boar, and red deer, in the adjoining forest of Inglewood ; apart from other royal game, we are told two hundred stags and hinds were killed. At Lanercost Edward spent the

E

last six months of his life, from Michaelmas, 1306, until the spring of 1307. Here the stern old warrior, victor in many a fight, may have felt the near approach of his victorious enemy—death ; for at no period of his life was he so impatient of restraint, or more determined to trample underfoot and subjugate the liberty of Scotland. Had he not, at the great Feast of Pentecost, in the old Abbey of Westminster, before marching north, sworn that he would avenge " The contempt done by Robert Bruce to God and the Church," after which he would never more bear arms against Christians, but would spend the remainder of his days warring against the infidels in Palestine, for the possession of the Holy Sepulchre ? No doubt this would be the most brilliant period of the priory's existence, gorgeous ceremonials and processions of monks, high mass and prayers for the welfare of the expedition, when the aged King, with his young and handsome Queen, Margaret, and his noble train of attendants and warriors, would often be present. Hither, with a splendid retinue, came the Pope's legate, Peter, Cardinal of Spain, on some temporal errand, yet adding his maledictions to the terrible curse of excommunication that hung o'er the devoted Bruce. Hither before the stern King were brought, covered with wounds, more dead than alive, Thomas and Alexander, brothers of Bruce, who had been captured in battle by Duncan Macdoil, a Galwegian chief. But there was no mercy in that insatiable thirst for revenge which burned within the breast of the monarch, for we are told how they were hurried to Carlisle, dragged by horses round the city, hanged and quartered, their heads placed on spikes to adorn the city gates. But the end was not afar—a light was soon to illumine that dark, dreary night of Scotland.

In the early summer of 1307 the King left Lanercost, borne on a litter, to Carlisle, and by easy stages followed the army to Burgh-on-Sands. Still stern, indomitable, resolute, and with his face fixed on Scotland, he died July 7th, 1307. We are not surprised at the actions of Bruce, who in after days swooped down on Lanercost and imprisoned the monks, and did other mischief—no doubt bitterly remembering the small mercy bestowed on his brothers. Thirty-five years later, King David, in his wrath, again bore down and despoiled the priory, burning and plundering, and reducing, says the chronicler, in expressive words, " In Nihilum, all they attacked."

Continuing our journey, we cross the river by the stepping-stones, a little to the east of the old bridge, and follow the path winding through the woods. Looking back through the trees we obtain a most bewitching peep of Lanercost Priory. Through Nature's temples we wander by the loveliest of paths, trees and flowers breathing perfume ; now we descend into some attractive glen, and the path, alluring us onward again, rises high over the limpid brook, whispering tuneful melody ; stray glints of sunshine pierce the sombre depths of the woods, tints of emerald, gleams of gold ; the beauty of nature joining with birds and stream in one universal song of praise.

Through this arcadian woodland we approach Naworth Castle, standing high, stately, and grand, holding sentry over the vale. The approach from the south is very majestic, the front being strengthened by a curtain wall, strong corner towers, and emblazoned gateway, over which are the arms of the Dacres and the Howards. The Dacres of the north, Barons of Greystock and Gilsland, received their name from an ancestor who greatly distinguished himself under King Richard at the siege of

Lanercost Priory. from the North.

Acre. From the Dacres it passed by marriage to William Lord Howard, known for his Border exploits as "Bauld Willie" and "Belted Will." He was the ancestor of the Earls of Carlisle. It is in quadrangular shape, defended on three sides by deep ravines ; to the south, across the neck of land, ran two deep moats, and the ingress protected by drawbridge and barbican. The south front measurement is 208 feet. Sandford, writing in 1695, says : "Around it were pleasant woods and gardens ; ground full of fallow deare feed on all somer tyme ; brave venison pasties and great store of reade deare on the mountains ; and white, wild cattel with black ears only on

E 2

the moors, and black heath-cockes and brone moor-cockes and their pootes, etc."
An arched passage leads into a spacious courtyard.   The large banqueting-hall is
reached from the court by a broad flight of steps.   The north end of this room
contains a fine portrait of Charles the First and his Queen, Henrietta, by Vandyke,
and other rare portraiture.   There is also a fine suit of armour worn by Belted
Will.   The walls are hung with tapestry and ancient armour.   Meditating within
this banqueting-hall, fancy easily conjures forth the scenes of olden-time feast,
revelry, and song, in the rude days when "might" was "right."   The music-room also
contains some very fine pictures by the old masters.   The private apartments of
Belted Will were in the south-east corner of the castle, and consisted of his oratory or
private chapel, library, and bedroom ; these are kept intact, and are much the same as

Armorial Ceilings in the North Side of Lord Dacre's Room.

during his lifetime.   During the great fire which took place at this castle, a secret room
was discovered in this chamber ; also a secret passage, which is said to connect the castle
with the priory of Lanercost.   The view from the turrets of the castle is most entran-
cing.   The approach to Belted Will's rooms is by a staircase only wide enough to
admit the body of one person, and the several doors, of immense thickness, were plated
with iron and secured by huge locks and bolts.   His body-guard consisted of one
hundred and forty well-mounted troopers.   During his wardenship his firmness and
high courage did much to repress the pillaging on the Border, and his name became
a terror to the moss-trooper and evildoer ; yet he was renowned for learning and
for courage, and still pious withal.   One story says that, once, whilst deeply engaged
in his studies, he was disturbed by one of his officers, who had brought in some
prisoners, and wished to know his orders regarding them.   " Hang them, in the devil's

name," he answered peevishly, angered at the fellow's intrusion. This reminds one of the Jedburg's and Lydford justice :—

> " I oft have heard of Lydford law,
> Where, in the morn, men hang and draw,
> And sit in judgment after."

When he had finished his studies he remembered the prisoners, and inquired after them. He was both surprised and grieved to find that his hasty orders had been literally fulfilled. Scott, in the "Lay of the Last Minstrel," in descriptive verse,

The Banqueting Hall.

graphically depicts the appearance of Lord Howard at Branksome, to witness the fight between Richard of Musgrave and William of Deloraine :—

> " When for the lists they sought the plain,
> The stately *Ladye's silken rein
> Did noble Howard hold :
> Unarmed by her side he walked,
> And much, in courteous phrase, they talked
> Of feats of arms of old.
> Costly his garb—his Flemish ruff
> Fell o'er his doublet, shaped of buff.
>
> With satin slashed, and lined ;
> Tawny his boot, and gold his spur,
> His cloak was all of Poland fur,
> His horse with silver twined ;
> His Bilboa blade, by Marchmen felt,
> Hung in a broad and studded belt ;
> Hence, in rude phrase, the Borderers still
> Called noble Howard ' Belted Will.' "

Lady Scott of Branksome.

The tree which served as a gallows was an aged oak even in Belted Will's time, yet it survived this rude baronial tenure by three centuries, but at length became dangerous, the top being too heavy for the trunk, and it fell in 1896.

> " Straightway he taketh the moss-trooper,
>   He taketh him to the tree ;
>   No trial was there, nor given a prayer,
>   He hanged him speedily !
>
> Lord Howarde thought of that hasty word,
>   Whenever he passed the tree,
>   For ever was heard a raven bird
>   Croaking most piteously."

It is here opportune to express our admiration and appreciation of the extreme kindness of the Carlisle family. We were permitted to walk about the vast range of park, gardens, and the fine baronial residence, and view the splendid works of art, and other antiquities, at leisure, and without any hindrance, interruption, or formal

Naworth.

permission ; in fact, we were allowed to go wherever we pleased. We are indebted, further, to Lady Mary Howard for her voluntary permission of a view of the drawing and several other rooms, in which we were very greatly interested. Unlike many other noble families, the wish of the Howards seems to be not to reserve all the splendour of their vast estates to themselves, but freely to allow others to enjoy the objects of art and antiquities, and to ramble at will. Their motto, if we may say so, seems to be, "Enjoy yourself rationally, and destroy nothing."

Across the park, and along the beautiful avenue crowning a ridge, we wander to Brampton, the capital of Gilsland, a small market town of two or three thousand inhabitants, a place of some pretence, yet withal quaint and rustic. The houses are chiefly of brick ; a large hill rising from the edge of the town is called the Moat. Near the summit are evident signs of its having been in a state of defence in bygone days. On the surface of the hill, from whence is a fine view of Brampton, is a statue erected to the memory of George William, the seventh Earl of Carlisle.

Now we enter the valley of the Gelt, a charming little river of that name, which joins the Irthing near Lanercost. It is a delightful walk, streams flashing and gurgling, miniature waterfalls, sombre aisles and sylvan paths winding and wandering by stream and towering fell, clothed to their very summits in the green grandeur of early spring ; tapering firs shooting upwards like pinnacles ; silvery birch, stately oak, and supple ash clothed in the refreshing and varied tints of foliage, forming sweet bowers for the little twining Gelt flashing onwards, its trembling murmurs borne on the breeze, adds a charming witchery o'er the scene.

How Hill, a place of meadow nooks, footpaths, and stiles, stands, as its name implies, on a how, or hill, crowned with the light green larch, and the darker canopy of Scotch firs, whose trunks have roseate hue in the waning sunset. The place is very picturesque and rural. The ducks are disporting in the village pond, and the silvery laughter of children at play upon the green, awake pleasant memories of boyhood days ; the undulating distance of fair pasture lands, cornfield, and wood, stretch away over the vale of the Irthing to the upland moor above Liddlesdale, displaying such vistas and effects of colour, when the gloaming deepens, which makes a man's heart leap with joy.

At Hayton, resting in a richly cultivated district, is another How Hill. On the surface is a level plateau, now covered with trees of giant growth ; the spot is still known as Castle Hill, and is said to have been a fortified residence in the days of Belted Will. Cannon balls and other relics of war have been found here. It was a Sabbath eve when we entered the churchyard and rested under the branches of a beech tree, and listened to the sound of the organ, with the sweet voices of children blending in praise to their Maker. Outside, on the trees, the choristers of nature mingled their rich melody with the songs of the children, as if enraptured with the soothing strains from within ; and on the cross over the roof of the chancel, a blackbird perched, and poured out a melodious cadence—a deep spiritual ecstasy—as if he, too,

The Eden at Corby.   EDMUND BOGG.

would fain add his praises to a bountiful Creator. The district between Hayton and Warwick Bridge is very pleasant, soft, hazy, blue vistas, stretching far away. The lanes are sweetly wooded, and afford delightful shade to a tired traveller.

We have now reached the banks of the Eden, which we shall follow for some considerable distance before crossing to the Tees valley.

Little Corby is a quaint hamlet, with many features of a bygone century remaining : the group of old thatched cottages, with garden and orchard, trees overhanging the Eden, help to form one of the most artistic groupings of meadow, cottage, and river, scarcely to be surpassed ; and the beautiful twining of the river at this place, forming true lines of beauty, is picturesque in the extreme. The pastoral charm of Warwick Bridge is sadly marred by several ugly mills, which, during our visit, were not in a very flourishing condition, judging from the tenantless houses adjoining. Warwick village, and its ancient kirk, crowns the eminence about a mile west. Crossing the fine bridge over the Eden, we pass through the meadows. Holme-Eden mansion and Holme-Eden church, with its graceful spire, is on the east bank. The pretty church, built of sandstone, harmonises sweetly with the green ivy which embraces its walls. 'Tis a beautiful picture, the rich green of cattle-flecked meadows, the river winding through overhanging woods, and brown waters eddying over rock shelves of red sandstone. The bank, strewn with *debris*, bespeaks of the angry river at flood time.

CHAPTER V.

THE EDEN COUNTRY.

ANDERING on, we soon reach a scene of surpassing loveliness, a perfect El Dorado of delight, the river, flowing deep down through the red sandstone hills, forming a series of pictures, perhaps the most exquisite in the north of England. The village of Wetheral is chiefly scattered around a large green, and is built on the high bank just at the entrance to this charming region; but the most interesting parts are the church, abbey ruins, old hostelry, and white-walled cottages below the village, on the low shelving bank adjoining the river, whilst the huge railway bridge spans the stream just beyond. The line, stretching from Newcastle to Carlisle, was opened for traffic early in the "thirties." A lady acquaintance of mine who remembers the occasion, told me of the great excitement which prevailed on the approach of the first train, crowds of country folk having travelled miles to witness the novel and strange sight. Unfortunately an accident occurred, by the bursting of the boiler; the spectators became panic-stricken, and a stampede of women and children was the result; and we are told that even men fled, helter-skelter, across the fields, fearful and trembling, anxious to place as much distance between themselves and the hissing, "panting fiend" as possible.

The surroundings of the church are extremely lovely, the edifice being delightfully sheltered by trees, and the soothing music of the stream falls on the heart in witching melody. From the number of tombstones, we should imagine it to be a favourite place of burial. Near the west doorway is an ancient yew, remarkable for its vast growth. The entire population of the village might find shelter under its ample boughs and branches, which embrace thirty-six tombstones.   An inscription on one tombstone records :

> " In this vain world short was my stay,
>   An' empty was my laughter ;
> I go before and lead the way,
>   And thou comes jogging after."

The church contains an effigy of Sir Richard Salkeld, Knight, and the inscription says :—

> " Here lies Sir Richard Salkeld the Knight,
>   Who sometimes in this land was miche of might ;
> The Captain and Keeper of Carlisle was he,
>   And also the Lord of Corby.
> And now he lies under this stane,
>   And his lady and wife, Dame Jane.
> In the Year of our Lord God one thousand
>   Five hundred as I understand,
> The eighteenth of February.
>   That Gentle knight was buried here.
> I pray you all that this does see.
>   Pray for their souls for charity,
> For as they are, so mon we be."

At Sir Richard's feet is a lion and a helmet under his head.   There is a beautiful marble group in the side chapel to members of the Howard family, by Nolkins.

    The gateway tower of Wetheral Abbey is all that remains of that old-time edifice, and forms the entrance to an adjoining farm.   In the meadows, however, the foundations are easily to be traced.   The roof of the tower, which is battlemented, can be gained by a newel staircase. From the top fine views are obtained of the woods around Corby, which are adorned with statues and classical sculpture, access to which is gained by the ferry. The ferryman's rural cottage can be seen on the opposite bank, resting 'neath the woods. Midway between Wetheral and Carlisle is the pleasant village of Scotsby, with its new church crowning the eminence on the verge of its fine village-green. Cumwhinton, resting in a small hollow, is further to the south, and is ex-

tremely rural, with several thatched cottages, whose walls seem to be composed of red rubble, but the black mullions and door frames add rather a gruesome aspect to the scene. Still further to the south-west is Brisco and Wrea, in the vale of the Petteril, a beautiful stream rising in Greystoke Park. Along its banks a lover of nature, or a peaceful angler, may muse away many a quiet summer's day.

Brisco is a very ancient spot, with white and yellow-washed cottages, ivy-clad, with overhanging thatched eaves, and is one of those dreamy places where the life of the inhabitants seem to run evenly onward—toil and rest succeeding day by day. In one of the oldest cottages we partook of our

The Eden at Wetheral.   EDMUND BOGG.

tea ; the roof was spotless with whitewash, and the rough beams on which the roof has rested for three hundred years are bent and twisted with age. Such old cottages add art and poetry to the landscape. How sweetly the chimes of the "grandfather's clock" sounds, bringing forth memories and glimpses of our childhood, the old clock and pictures in the parlour, and familiar voices which have long been silent. Brisco Post-office is a model of bygone village architecture.

Retracing our steps to Wetheral, we follow the windings of the Eden through the woods to the caves, or, perhaps, a better term would be the cells, of a hermit.   Legend relates that they were hewn out of the rock by a younger son of Constantine, a King of Scotland—Cumberland and Westmoreland at that date being part of Scotland.   Here the Prince took up his quarters, and lived and died a hermit.   The cells were afterwards used as a place of refuge during the Border wars.   They are divided into three distinct apartments, and a battlement terrace runs in front and impends over the river, shut in by thick woods.   The spot would be a secure hiding-place.   Access to the caves must have been by a ladder from the river-side.

The path now runs through deep clustered foliage, forming Eden-like bowers. We rest from the glare of the sun under the shadow of an immense elm ; deep down the river flows sweetly.   How beautiful and holy are the solemn woods, and how graceful is the motion of the water, now bubbling and fuming, anon calm and noiseless as sleep, or giving forth a subdued slumberous song, until there steals over us a rest in which the stern realities of life are dispelled.   It is the voice of nature lulling us to dreamy slumber and into a reverie of bright vision.   A heavy-ladened bee, seeking its hive, murmurs past ; birds of beautiful plumage, and sweeter song, are carolling overhead, and from myriad insects steals forth that continuous humming sound.   A kingfisher shoots past like a sunbeam on the surface of the water, and ousels shriek angrily as they flit from rock to rock in shallow stream.   Shadows dance, and light flickers on the woodland path ; monster roots and far-reaching arms of trees of giant growth stretch across the shimmering water, and are mirrored therein.   Trunks, torn and twisted by the hurricane, lay across the path.   The one feature which arrests the attention of the observer is the richness of the luxurious vegetation, which thrives so abundantly along the course of the Eden.   Such are the beautiful banks of the Eden above Wetheral.

Some five or six miles further up the river, Armathwaite reposes dreamily in the bosom of the vale.   The church is a most primitive structure, standing on the sloping hill side, above the village street, and is almost hidden by yew and evergreen trees. One curious feature is the bell, which is rung from the outside, and a cover is raised to protect the ringer during stormy weather.   The woodwork of the interior is very barn-like in character.   Strange to say, the first marriage ever solemnised in this sacred edifice since its erection, over two hundred years ago, took place so recently as the 18th of February, 1897, the contracting parties being Dr. E. G. Walls, son of the late Rev. R. G. Walls, of Boothby Hall, Lincolnshire, and Miss Alice Blanche Dixon, third daughter of Mr. G. H. Dixon, D.L., of Armathwaite Hall.

The bridge, of three arches and long angular buttresses, is most charmingly situated.   The water above and below the bridge is a famous fishing length, and many salmon, and also trout, of fabulous weight, have been captured here. Proceeding along the west bank of the Eden, through park-like meadows, a more lovely place in which to wander cannot well be imagined ; 'tis a scene long to be remembered. The deep sound of the river falling over the weir ; salmon leaping out of the stream in their attempt to scale the fall, for a moment lay shimmering, only to be hurled back by the glittering water ; the deep woods which clothe the hills on the east bank, the old water-mill and wheel, the rustic wooden bridge over the mill-race, and the moss and lichen ; the rural farm, with its curious corners and angles, where fowl and beast run riot. The miller's wife is feeding the poultry and pigeons from a large skip ; there is a rush, a flutter and scramble, and a hurried feed and many a skirmish. Still south, across the wide moor, on the west side of the river, the heather is in full bloom, and the moor appears gorgeous in colour.

Armathwaite Mill. EDMUND BOGG.

A five miles' walk brings us to Lazonby. It is a large, scattered village, with no special features. The situation is most beautiful, clean, and healthy, standing high and dry above the west bank of the Eden. There is a new church, and a typical old Scotch fir in the graveyard. Between this place, of Danish occupation, and Kirkoswald, a mile away, on the opposite bank of the river, of Saxon occupation, there has been a feud for centuries, and the rivalry has not yet entirely disappeared. The bridge, midway between the two villages, is the rendezvous for the young people. The road now passes beneath a beautiful avenue, the river winding on one hand through a most fertile vale.

At the entrance to Kirkoswald stands the kirk in rather a singular situation, being entirely hidden from the village by a large hill, rising immediately from its walls. The path to the church is through a most beautiful avenue of trees, of patriarchal growth—nature's cathedral aisle (God's Gothic)—the branches interlacing in such picturesque combination and loveliness, the lofty trunks, like columns, shoot upwards, clean and shapely, and the thriving branches rise and spread, as if to seek communion with heaven. Surely such scenes suggested to the monks of old a cathedral aisle. How beautifully shadow and gleam chequer the path, and how loudly the rooks clamour in the tree tops on this sunny morn. Through such gifts of nature we approach the holy ground where the villagers have worshipped, and the dead have rested, through the centuries. Near to an ancient yew are two tomb slabs, incised with floriated crosses ; another, evidently the tomb of a priest, with crosses and sword,

A Glimpse of the Eden Country.   c. 8060.

and the dragon of superstition and paganism darting the sting of venom on the symbol of true faith. Immediately under the west end is a well of pure crystal water. The stream which feeds the well, which is known as St. Oswald's Well, flows beneath the foundations of the church, typical of the living water. In the early days of the Saxon kings the holy fathers baptised the people of the surrounding district at this fountain. Outside the edifice many relics abound, which attest to the antiquity of the spot. The interior has been judiciously restored, and retains many interesting features. The font is Norman, and at the entrance to the chancel, the base of the early church has been left, which affords a study for those interested in ancient structure. On the old glass in the windows are the shields of the Howards, Musgraves, and Baron's Dacre. Within the altar railings is the mutilated effigy of a lady, cut out of red sandstone, and on the opposite side the tomb cover of a warrior priest, with sword and crozier. The church is dedicated to St. Oswald. As we have remarked, the sacred edifice is entirely hid from the village by a large hill, on which is built a bell tower, which can be descried for miles around.

A few hundred yards to the south-east, and built on another eminence, are the ruins of Kirkoswald Castle embedded in trees. Its position, remains, and the moat all point to its importance in early Norman days. " This great castle of Kirkoswald was one of the fairest fabrics that eyes ever looked upon. The hall I have seen is one hundred yards long." It was erected by Ranulph d'Enjain, and afterwards came into the possession of Hugh de Morville, and thence to the Miltons, the Dacres, and the Musgraves. Most of its interior adornments were removed to Naworth, on the building of the latter. The place is now silent and deserted save by the birds, who still sing as sweetly, peradventure, as when harp and revelry sounded within the walls.

Kirkoswald we might describe as an ideal village, and is situate on the ground rising from the foot of Tower Hill. Here is an old Tudor mansion, which will amply repay a visit. At the bottom of the village a turbulent stream, the Raven, crosses the street, and renders the scene more pleasing and beautiful. Higher up the street is the Square or Market Place, with the cross and part of stocks remaining, and the whole appearance bespeaks a town of the last century. Several houses of better class architecture still remain, and have evidently seen more prosperous days.

About two miles north from Kirkoswald, the little river Croglin passes through a glen of great depth and beauty, called the Nunnery Walks, from a Nunnery at one time adjoining, but now demolished.

On either side of the glen are romantic walks, under majestic cliffs and over-hanging trees. At flood time the roar of the waters creates a solemn and profound impression upon the visitor. The woodland banks rise on either side from one to two hundred feet above the river. At the entrance the water falls down a great depth into an immense cauldron-like hole, seething and roaring over huge shelves of rock, and immense boulders lay athwart the stream ; moss, lichens, ferns, and hearts-tongue pro-trude from every niche and cranny. Monstre trees, uprooted long ago, bridge the stream in several places. In the solitude of this ravine, on a September evening, we are resting by a gurgling waterfall ; deep shadows are fast creeping o'er the scene. The only signs of life are trout leaping, and trying in vain to scale the water-fall,—again and again they shoot out of the water, only to be hurled back by the force of the current. An ousel dives into the river at our feet, and other birds, only to be seen in these secluded places, fly past. A few hundred yards lower down, where the Croglin joins the Eden, we emerge from the deep sombre woodland into the open moor, and the hue and glory of the waning sunlight, reflecting in the Eden the vermilion sky and all things on its banks, appears, as our eyes follow its windings, like a trailing pathway of gold stretching to the shores of heaven.

A sweet Sabbath morning, and we are strolling by the side of the Eden, which flows onward with calm, unruffled tranquility.   On either bank are the villages of Lazenby and Kirkoswald   The sun shines brightly, gentle breezes are wafted from the hills, and rustle among the leaves, and the green of woodland and meadow are showing signs of approaching winter.   It is the time of harvest, and the yellow corn-fields are dotted here and there with sheaves, blending sweet contrast.   High above yonder can be seen Crossfell, like a solitary sentinel, looming dark and threatening in the background.   At our feet the waters murmur out tuneful melody, and the sweet chime of Sabbath bells from the two churches float down the bosom of the river, and lull our souls into reverie and peace.   That lone glen, which reaches down to the Eden,

is the Del-Raffen, a stream flowing through a winsome little glen, which here enters the Eden.

It is one of those out-of-the-world and unknown spots which amply repays the tourist for exploring. You can trace its varied windings from Crossfell by the line of trees which thrive along the banks of the stream ; every line and curve is beautiful, and suggests a picture.   It is up these se-cluded becks that the salmon and large trout force

The Del-Raffen.   BOWEN.

their way in the autumn to spawn.   At flood times the ascent is particularly easy, but the small streams, which the fish love to penetrate, fall as rapidly as they have risen, and imprison the fish in the deeper pools.   The poacher is well aware of this proceeding, and with the aid of his bull's-eye lantern in the night-time, can easily secure as many fish as he could carry home, and none but his wife the wiser for his adventure.   To the right is a very ancient pack-horse track, in use long before the moor was enclosed.   Just above the vale, to the south, is the village of Glassonby, with no particular feature except its sweet rural seclusion.   About half a mile south-west is Addingham Church.   A primitive air and solitariness pervades the spot, standing in holy meekness guarding the moor with its sacred presence, the nearest house being about half a mile away ; its very solitude soothes the soul, and impresses us with peace and sanctity as we meditate amongst the tombs.

The churchyard contains the upper portion of a fine Saxon Cross, and also the base of another is in the chancel, and a portion of a shaft in the porch. This goes far to prove the existence of an Early Saxon church, which would be destroyed, or taken down on the rebuilding of the Norman structure. The church has been restored within the present century, and apart from those features already mentioned, the piscina, and a fine old parish chest, with two locks, there is nothing of interest—the chancel arch is only a wretched imitation of Norman style. There is a deep-rooted tradition prevalent that this church once stood lower in the vale, somewhere by the Eden side. We have carefully thought over this curious supposition, and can only account for it in this manner:—

Long Meg, the immense Druidical circle, is only half-a-mile distant south-west, and before the advent of Christianity in those parts (say up to the sixth century), would be the great temple for the Druidic worship, on which mysteries the people would gaze with strange and mingled feelings of superstition and awe—grand, solitary, and savage, yet impressive in its sublimity. Fourteen centuries have effaced most things off the face of the earth—Woden and Thor, the gods and temples of the Saxons, have perished and become forgotten, but the rock temples of the Druids still live on as if imperishable, and this tradition of the church, or temple, having once stood some distance from its present site, we should imagine is neither more nor less than memories, which have come floating down the aisles of time, handed from father to son, of that great heathen temple, whose High Priest once held the children of the Vale shackled in pagan mysteries. From the remains of crosses and other visible signs, the church evidently stands on the ground where it was originally founded. It is dedicated to Saint Michael, and churches dedicated to this Patron Saint, usually stand on high ground ; in this instance, it is the highest in the vicinity.

Half a mile across the fields, to the south, as we have already mentioned, stands the largest Druidical Temple in Britain—Long Meg and her daughter. It is formed of sixty-seven or eight large stones of three hundred and fifty yards in

F

circumference. Long Meg is a much larger stone than the rest, and is composed of granite, and stands a few paces apart from the rest, and out of the circle. Four other stones are in position, as if meant to form a huge altar.

Wordsworth writes thus :—" When I first saw this monument, as I came upon it by surprise, I might overrate its importance as an object ; but though it would not bear a comparison with Stonehenge. I must say I have not seen any other relic of those dark ages which can pretend to rival it in singularity and dignity of appearance."

When we look on this array of stones, grey with the lapse of ages, and furrowed by the storms of two thousand years, standing in silence on the moor, the curlew and lapwing flying over them, giving forth their spirit-like cry—the wind moans, and

Long Meg.

the helm storm raves around, but nothing pierces the veil of mystery which enshrouds those silent rocks, mute witnesses of strange scenes and ceremonies, and sacrificial offerings, long centuries since vanished with the sphinx, enshrouded in mystery, that veiled those sacred rites. The British Isles were the great centre of Druidic priest-hood, and in Britain was celebrated the most secret of their mysteries. A few hundred yards to the east there is a smaller circle, composed of eleven unhewn stones, and about eighteen yards in circumference. This smaller circle is very rarely visited.

A mile and a half still south is the extremely rural village of Hunsanby, serenely encircling a small green, nestling in pictorial charm on the lowest tier of the Cumberland Fells. A large stream passes the foot of the village. There are two bridges—one for heavy traffic, and the other, a rude one-arched structure of pack-horse style, forming a picture replete with bygone association. How pleasant it is to watch the ducks of spotless hue disport, and geese and gander patiently cleanse every stain from their downy covering, and hiss and screech as if in delight ere they marched, in stately file, to hold solemn conclave on the green. Near the low bridge formerly stood the Pound; the generation of its use has departed, and the walls are consequently in ruin. Less than half a mile west is the small hamlet of Winskill, with no particular feature of interest in its one long street. In the centre is a large pond, or mere, of filthy-looking stagnant water—its very appearance seems suggestive of fever.

But as we passed over the meadows towards Langwathby, a very sweet series of pleasant pictures, suggestive of country life of the olden time, came under our notice. The water for household purposes, to drink, etc., had to be obtained at a well, a large meadow's length from the village, some three or four hundred paces distant. The stream, or well, issues from a sandstone bank. It is a most secluded spot, and from the fountain, which is overhung by the branches of a large elm, not a vestige of house or habitation can be seen. It was spring time on our visit, and the little dell, being protected from the biting east winds, and opening to the south, daffodils, primroses, and cowslips were in full bloom. Many a scene of childish fun and frolic has this spot witnessed. It is also the meeting-place of lovers ; youths and maidens have met here for centuries to whisper the old, old story, and plighted their troth, to walk hand in hand together in good or evil repute the rest of their lives. Countless generations,

At the Well.   EDMUND BOGG.

passing to and fro, has this old tree witnessed, and children have sheltered, playing beneath its boughs, or resting on the green sward. The old men bent their weary steps thither to rest and muse on days long gone by, and recount stories to the young children, how the water sprite and elfin people were wont to visit this spot in the moonlight and career in circles, and dance to the melody of elfin music ; but in this matter-of-fact age of steam and electricity, the fairies have fled, yet as a proof of their former existence, the aged men point to the deeper green of the fairy circles, still

to be seen, thus testifying to their nocturnal visit.   Now the smiling faces, and troops
of village girls with hoop and pail, will soon cease to congregate at this spot, for this
is an age of waterworks and reservoirs, and the small village of Winskill is to have
a constant supply of water brought to their doors, and the old-time trysting place will
be a thing of the past.   But as an elderly native remarked to the writer : "When we
du hev't watter brow't et toun, we sall still gan dune to fetch et frae t'well ; hisen't
it a vast mure nataral te hev t'watter pure hout et grund, than te hev it out et lead
pipes," and he grumbled sorely about this innovation of the Waterworks Committee.

A hundred paces to the west, Briggle Beck, a large stream from the East
Cumberland Falls, flows past, in noisy prattle, to join the Eden near Salkeld.   The

A bit of the Green.   EDMUND BOGG.

path leads across this stream to Langwathby.
A circular mound of earth, evidently a tumula
of some old-world chieftain, is to be seen by
the path.   In it was discovered, some twenty
years ago, a large skeleton, also a vase full of
coins, said to be Roman.

Over the brow of the hill we drop down
into that most rural of villages, Langwathby.
The Langwath, or Meadow, before the enclosure of the common—a long stretch of
meadow, reaching by the east side of the
river, was so called, in the centre of which
stood, as it does to-day, the Shepherd's Inn,
in old days a resort of drovers and shepherds.

Langwathby is one of those pleasant
spots so dear to the soul of the true artist,
where everything is so delightfully irregular,
curious nooks the most primitive, and ancient
gables, broom-thatched cottages, with deep
overhanging eaves.   What sweet rustic scenes can be witnessed on the large green on
a summer's day ; children whooping at play, flocks of large grey old geese cackling
and screeching, and the old patriarch, the gander, hissing and fuming at every passer-
by ; a little terrier yelps angrily from behind a farm gate, ducks nestle drowsily on
the green, or wander down the alleys, where a kitten is seen disporting with the tail of
its angry dame.

The church, which has been restored of late years, is of no architectural
importance, and possesses few features of interest.   In a chest in a room under the
belfry we found a helmet and cuirass, probably worn by some ancient squire at
Flodden Field.

On an autumn day we have wandered by the river to where Bryggle beck meets the Eden. Little Salkeld, with its cool green lanes, is just to the east, whilst over the river, on the brow of yonder hill, is the more important village of Great Salkeld, the birthplace of the celebrated Dick Whittington, with its ancient tower and fine Norman doorway. The day is most enjoyable ; we rested under a willow, as we have said, where the beck meets the river, the banks are fringed with meadows and flowers, old lanes, by-paths, and hedgerows ; a pair of moorhens flutter from under the bank, evidently aware of our presence. Deep down in the brown pool at our feet can be seen the speckled fish, enough to make the heart of an angler leap with joy. The eye for a brief space was unconscious of the living glories around, for the ear was ravished by gushing strains, as with delicious ripple of fairy music the river glided over its shingly bed, giving forth such melodious gurglings, as if sin and death were not of this world. Yet even as we meditate, sheltered from observation by the willow, a heron, with outstretched wings, flaps slowly down the vale and alights, wades into the river, and silently watches for prey—so even on the Eden there is pillage and death. As we wander up the stream and along the by-lanes, other sights and sounds of nature greet us. A flock of rooks are holding solemn conclave, and a few lapwings and starlings join in the chatter. The cause of this strange assembly and council we find arises from the heron having dared to invade their privacy. As we proceed large trout and other fish glide from the side into the deeper

Old Farmyard, Langwathby. e. 1000.

water without any apparent effort. A few rabbits rise on their haunches, peer at us with large startled eyes, and then dart away to their burrows. How beautiful is the contrast—the brown river and green glades against the fields of ripening grain. Now on the breeze comes the sound of the harvester, the creaking of carts and waggons, and the merry peals of rippling laughter.

A mile or so below Langwathby bridge the Eamont and Eden meet. 'Tis a beautiful scene to sit and watch the silvery Eamont come flowing to meet the larger river. It was one of those beautiful moonlight nights, and at that hour when all animated nature had sunk to slumber—there was no sound save that of the bubble and flow of meeting waters. As we sat and looked through the branches of large trees overhanging the bank, it seemed verily to our musing to be typical of Thomas Moore's "Vale of Avoca," or his "Bendeemer's Stream."

> " There's a bower of roses by Bendeemer's stream,
> And the nightingale sings round it all the day long.
> In the time of my childhood 'twas like a sweet dream,
> To sit in the roses and hear the bird's song."

Yet as we sat and looked on the silver river reflecting the trees and the sky in its bosom, four large herons, with melancholy shriek, glide, ominous with noiseless wing, from the water, disturbing the harmony of the night. As I wandered back by the river through the meadows a startled otter plunged into the stream, and the rabbits sped into the brushwood. Soft-eyed kine cropping the dewy grass loomed into our vision like ghosts of night, and the moon silvered the earth in pensive beauty.

There is a substantial bridge over the Eden at Langwathby, and the river is here of great width. A picturesque cottage adorns the bank at the foot on one side. The house is overshadowed by a large elm tree; hollyhocks and other large plants are thriving abundantly, and old railings twist and twine by the water.

A Bend of the Eamont.   LOVEJOY.

We leave the road and cross the meadows to Edenhall village, less than a mile away, one of the sweetest spots, sacred in pastoral charm and peaceful seclusion, with cottages sheltered by massive trees, the home of birds; sweet garden plots, where asters, sunflowers, dahlias, peonies, scarlet, white, and yellow flowers mingle; old porches and gables, where ivy and trailing plant love to cling, and lichen and moss clothe the old roofs in sweetness. The vicarage forms a very interesting picture, with quaint gables (date about 1650). Through the park we reach the church, which is dedicated to St. Cuthbert. This is one of the spots where the monks, bearing the body of the saint, rested awhile during their long and weary pilgrimage. The present structure dates from the Norman period, but has been much mutilated during alterations. Some of the windows are of great interest, containing fragments of ancient glass — one represents King Ceowlyn and the Saint. The chancel arch is plaster, a poor imitation of Norman work. Within the chancel rails is a most interesting slab with brasses of a knight in armour and a lady, and there are several shields and crests to the Musgraves and their alliances The font is Early Norman.

The Giant's Caves are a few hundred yards from the church, on the banks of the Eamont. These recesses, three in number, are hewn out of the sandstone cliff, and have probably been used as hiding-places in the time of the Scottish raids. This is the spot where the supposed adventure of Sir Lancelot took place with the mighty
Tarquin, a knight who had never been worsted in battle ; yet Sir Lancelot, the peerless warrior, slew him, and liberated three-score knights and four. The largest caves were formerly protected with iron gates. There are several traditions respecting these caves, one of which connects them with Ewan Cesario, whose singular grave-stones are to be seen in Penrith churchyard.

The park is of considerable extent and beauty, where a herd of fallow deer browse, across which we wander to the hall, which, strictly speaking, has no architectural adornment, but is simply an ordinary English gentleman's man-sion. It is the seat of the Musgraves, whose ancestors came over in that great train of adventurers to win an inheritance in Britain. They were first settled at
Musgrave by the Eden, and afterwards at Hartley Castle, which stood so delightfully overlooking the vale of the above river at Kirkby Stephen ; from hence they removed to Eden Hall, resting so luxuriant in that angle of pasture-land, formed by the meeting of the Eamont and the Eden. To the west of the Hall are two enormous cedars, and in the gardens at the foot of the terrace steps is the Fairies' Well, which is also known as St. Cuthbert's Well. It is choicely embosomed by boxwood bushes. A tumbler is placed by the well, so that pilgrims may be refreshed. We drank to the memory of the fairies who once, and may still, sport in revelry in this sequestered and hallowed spot. But the most interesting relic of old which is interwoven by such winsome legendary is an antique drinking glass, known far and wide as the "Luck of Eden Hall." It is a rare specimen of antique art in glass,

swelling in graceful curves upwards to the rim, enamelled and ornamented on the outside with a variety of designs in crimson, blue, and yellow. Legend relates how the Musgraves became possessed of this ancient relic as follows :—Once on a time the fairies, whose rendezvous was in the park, were holding, one evening, high revel at the well already mentioned. An attendant from the Hall, having reason to go there, surprised the festive party in the midst of their gambols ; espying the curious glass near the well he adroitly seized it. The fairies, not wishing to lose their talisman, a struggle took place for its possession, in which the elvesfolk were worsted, and took to flight, crying out as they vanished—

> " If that glass should break or fall,
> Farewell the luck of Edenhall."

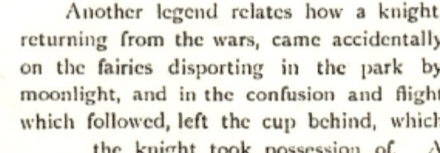

Another legend relates how a knight, returning from the wars, came accidentally on the fairies disporting in the park by moonlight, and in the confusion and flight which followed, left the cup behind, which the knight took possession of. A story in ballad tells of a foot-page fleeing in the night-time to Penrith to seek the leech to the aid of his mistress, the Ladye Isabel, who lay in a deadly swoon. On the way he was met by a weird woman, "wi glamour in her 'ee." The page-boy seeing this, told his story, and he was advised that if the efforts of the leech should prove of no avail, he must seek the fairies' well by moonlight.

> The leech he rode to Edenhall,
> The while uprose the moon ;
> But his craft is vain, and his simples naught,
> To loose the deadly swoon.

The page-boy, who dearly loved the fair ladye for her many kindnesses, &c., remembered the words of the wise woman.

> " So softly crept he down the stair,
>   And out by the secret door ;
> And he was aware of a strange music
>   He never had heard before.
>
> And slowly paced he o'er the mead,
>   And heard the self-same sound ;
> And there he saw a companye
>   A-dancing round and round.

> So beautiful their faces shone,
>   So bright their silken sheen ;
> He could but dread to look thereon,
>   And yet he looked I ween.
>
> Oh, merrily did they laugh and dance,
>   Still tripping round and round ;
> But not a blade of grass did bend,
>   No flowers sunk upon the ground.

Anon they pause, and a crystal cup
Is dipped in the bubbling spring,
And gliding goes from lip to lip,
All round the fairy ring.

And ever it dips and fills again,
And while the revellers drink,
The brimming water falls like pearls
Down from the sparkling brink.

But the fairy that bears that cup around
No mortal eye may see ;
Oh, could my lady drain that cup,
Thought the little foot-page on knee.

Scarce had he thought than to him glides
The cup from the bubbling spring ;
Him paused before, yet who it bore,
Did naught of shadow fling.

He trembled sore, but he took the cup,
For the sake of his dear ladye,
And fast the drops fell down like pearls,
As he rose up from knee.

And at his feet upon the grass,
A written scroll was thrown :
Then all at once the music ceased,
And the fairy folk were gone.

He took the scroll and he took the cup,
Them to the hall he bore ;
The Lady Isabel did drink,
And her deadly swoon was o'er.

And the little foot-page [lord ;
He brought the scroll and showed it to his
Sir Ralph he looked thereon and read
In olden style the words—

    ' If that cuppe
      Should break or falle,
    Farewell the Lucke
      Of Edenhalle.'

Sir Ralph de Musgrave made a feast,
For joy over his ladye ;
And the little foot-page he stood by her chair,
And blithest of all was he.

    Sir Ralph de Musgrave built a church
    In sweet Saint Cuthbert's prayse,
    That men might know when came the lucke,
    And think thereon alwayes."

The cup has had some very narrow escapes. Once the gay revelling Duke of Wharton let it slip from his hands, but it was saved by the dexterity of the butler, who caught it in his napkin. In reference to this incident, the same duke says, in his ballad known as the "Drinking Match of Edenhall,"

    "God prosper long from being broke,
      The Luck of Edenhall :
    A doeful drinking bout and song,
      There lately did befall."

Amongst several other ballads, one of the best perhaps is by Ludwig Uhland, which has been translated by Longfellow.

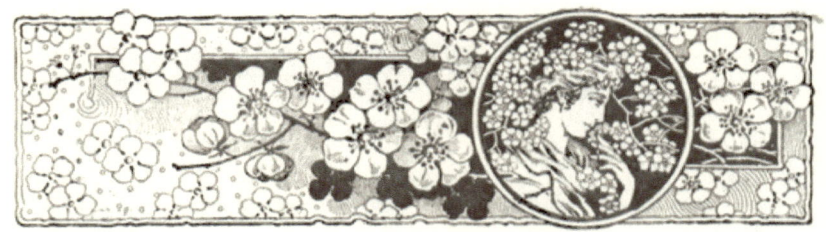

CHAPTER VI.

AN OLD-WORLD BORDER.

TRETCHING from the centre of the Tees valley a few miles below Rokeby on the east ; to Appleby, and Brougham on the west, runs an ancient Border Kingdom of England and Scotland, and in pre-Conquest days a battle-ground between the old British Anglo-Dane and the Pict and Scot. As a proof of this, we find stretched over this old border line ruins of those mighty strong-holds reared, in the first instance, to guard and protect the newly gained frontier which was never fairly won by the Anglo-Norman until the beginning of the Twelfth Century, or until after Rufus had reared that mighty castle of Carlisle, and the New-Castle on the Tyne, after which Upper Teesdale, the great table-land of Stain Moor, the Eden valley and Lakeland became part of the English nation. The dyke and rampart, stretching south from Tees valley at Gainford, is also a border-line of even earlier centuries.

Coming to Anglo-Norman times, we find the ruins of frontier defence, such as Mortham Tower, a typical border peel. Raby Castle, the home of the Nevilles, standing there so stately, like a Windsor of the north. Barnard Castle projecting defiantly over the Tees, the home of the Barnards and Baliols. A few miles higher up the Tees valley is the solitary remnant of Cotherston Castle, the home of the Fitzhughs, and Bowes Castle on the east foot of Stain-Moor.

Other fortresses also stood on the moor, and there the rude cross, set up in the first instance to mark the boundary of the two kingdoms, still remains. Whilst the imposing castle at Brough commanded the western part of the entrance across the Penine Range ; Hartley Castle and Pendragon, grim and solitary, blocked the narrow pass into the Eden valley from the south, and Appleby, Brougham, and Kirkoswald Castles kept watch and ward over the broad vale country between the Penine Range and the Lake Hills.

The most easy route from the Eden valley to the vale of the Tees, whither we are bound, would probably be by way of Brough and Stainmoor ; but as our object is to return that way in our tramp back to Lakeland, we shall take the more difficult path by way of Upper Teesdale. So retracing our steps to the bridge of Langwathby, we pass down the east bank of the Eden, and over by way of Culgaith and Milburn Forest to the upper reaches of the Tees, a distance of some ten miles across—a district wild, desolate, and savage, and over weird and inhospitable wastes, where none but the strong of limb should venture. The surroundings of Culgaith are very charming.

Old lanes with grassy waysides and brambles, hedgerows redolent with wild rose and honeysuckle, and sweet meadow paths, the land gently undulating and rising gradually from hence to the highest point of Crossfell, five miles distant. There is a neat church, rebuilt about the middle of last century. A tablet on the north wall records :—

" Daniel Dover gave to the Township of Culgaith £60, with an order that the interest arising from it shall be distributed weekly, for ever, amongst such of the poor of the said Township as shall frequent Divine Service."

This D. Dover died 1787, aged 87, and the bread is still distributed every Sunday.

Skirwith, on the Common, is a mile or so to the north-east. Here are the remains of an abbey. Blencarn, a joint township with Kirkland, is also in this district. Just to the south of Blencarn, Middletongue Beck and Mill Rigg Beck join ; the latter stream, rising on Knock Fell, and Dufton Pike is to the south. The beck enters the Eden a mile or so to the north of Temple Sowerby. In stormy weather the water fairly howls down these glens, and when the helm wind comes sweeping with resistless force down the ravines of the Crossfell range of mountains, the battling of contrary currents, and the tempest of the wind and water is something terrible ; trees are uprooted, houses unroofed, vehicles overturned, and farm produce is often carried to a great distance. We shall not soon forget our experience in one of those helm winds, when we were buffetted about like a thing of straw.

Skirting the north side of Milburn Forest, if this waste can be so called, for it is nearly devoid of trees, a high, swampy, peaty moor, with deep intermediate gullies, where a dozen rivulets have their birth, and flow north to the Tees, which rises in the south side of Crossfell, the highest point of the Penine Range, 2,892 feet above sea level.

THE TEES.

Born amidst stillness and solitude, except the sounds of nature, the wild tempest and foaming cataract, in a region where the foot of traveller seldom penetrates, the Tees rushes forward in mad career as if chafing to escape from its mountain birth. How desolate yet majestic and sublime is the scene at the Snout, and as we stand on the wooden bridge of single plank and look down on the roaring flood of water, howling, leaping, and hissing in endless confusion and whirl, a strange sensation of awe and almost fear takes possession of us. Above the Snout the Tees expands into a small lake known as the Wheel, thence leaping over cliffs 200 feet in height, forms a series of rapids wildly grand and magnificent, and passing over rugged beds of lime-

A Pack-horse Track.

stone rocks, scoured and worn into endless shapes by the storms and floods of centuries, rushes onward a mighty torrent through barren moorland to High Force, and over the jagged rocks with relentless force, it is impelled with a fearsome roar into the boiling, hissing cauldron below.

Beautiful, wild, and impressive in character is this portion of the Tees Valley, free as the wind which howls and shrieks around its mountain birth, child of the moorland and heather, in the dark glades, patches of the eternal snow, is to be seen during the hot days of summer. The dark blue pine woods which adorn the north bank for some distance below the Force afford wonderful variety and contrast. Through a bower or branch can be obtained an enchanting peep of the Force, with the Penine Range towering in magnificence, and far-reaching range of moors, rising ridge over ridge to Mickle Fell, some 2,600 feet. After rest and refreshment at the Inn adjoining the Falls, we drop down the vale; the Tees still swirling over remarkable beds of jagged rock, forced on to upright and slanting positions.

Wynch Bridge, formed of long rods or links, supports a plank footpath, and the original one is said to have been the first of this description erected in Europe. It spans the river, where it rushes madly through a narrow gorge in the rock; the water, on our visit, flashed colours of the rarest gems, beautiful hues exceeding description. Passing the village of Bowlees and Newbiggin, Middleton, the capital of Upper Teesdale, is reached. This place and its surroundings offer many attractions and special features of interest, situated on the rising ground north of the Tees, and at the foot of a beautiful glen, down which tumbles Hudeshope Beck, a charming spot for those who love nature.

The church is comparatively modern, and has a detached bell tower. Several relics of an earlier structure remain, and part of the original churchyard wall. The interior contains bits of Norman zigzag moulding, an ancient panel inserted in the north wall, and the top of a slab with floriated cross and sword, and other symbols.

At the junction of roads, near by, is an ancient sun-dial on pillar. On market and fair days the scene in the street is very animated and picturesque, the place, for the time being, being in possession of the characteristic hill-men.

Immediately below Middleton the Tees is joined by the Lune; the railway viaduct of five arches has a most imposing appearance. On the left bank of the Lune is Laithkirk, and just beyond is a singular mound, the Craigcairn, the supposed burial-place of a British warrior prince. Mickleton, a scattered village of grey stone houses, inhabited chiefly by miners, is on the opposite side of the same. Further down the Tees is Eagle-stone Bridge. Country purely pastoral and park-like in char-acter, distant peeps of purple and grey moors, dotted here and there with white-walled cottages; cloud, shadow, and sunshine, as if in play, alternately dancing over the scene, and the high

sloping banks by the river clothed in deep woods. No part of the Tees is more beautiful and attractive than that at Eaglestone; charming views, magnificent trees, pastoral stretches, woodland dells, miniature brooks, and the broad river shimmering through the woods, past sandy margins. From the higher ground, Eaglestone Church and Hall show out to fine advantage amongst the trees.

Over the meadows we stray to Romaldskirk, whose ancient tower, grey and venerable, rises so sweetly among the branches. The church is a large and imposing edifice, clothed with moss and lichen. Placed out of sight, behind the organ, is an effigy of one of the Fitzhughs, and as we stood gazing on this martial figure, visions of old border strife, and wild foray, rise to our imagination. Opposite to the church is a large green, and beneath a giant willow, now shorn to some extent of its former proportions, stands the village pump. Few places are more picturesque than this typical English village.

Still over pastoral glades to Cotherstone, on the green knoll, which rises above the confluence of the Balder with the Tees, stand the remnants of Cotherstone Castle, in bygone days the home of the gallant Fitzhughs. How charming the site, and how

Arms of the Fitzhughs.

beautiful is the diversified landscape ; the sweet little Balder dancing merrily through a charming dale, musical with the rumbling sound of water mills. Time, the great leveller, and the havoc of war, have scarcely left a vestige of this once strong border peel. There is a story connected with this castle which well illustrates the tragic deeds attendant on border strife.

Tradition tells of many sad tragedies and of honourable deeds which redound to the everlasting honour of the family, all of which give interest and significance to the spot.

Between the Fitzhughs and the Kerrs, whose castle stood so beautifully above the limpid Jed in Roxburghshire, was a long and deadly feud. The origin of this hatred, which existed between the two houses, began on the battlefields of France during the early part of the fifteenth century. Many Scotch knights of renown fought on the side of the French, and their bones were often left to bleach on foreign soil, and amongst others were the Kerrs of Cessford and Ferniehurst, already mentioned in this work. One of the latter was successful in capturing a Fitzhugh in battle, and either from some slight received by the prisoner from his captor, or from other causes not known, seems to have been the beginning of the long and deadly feud which raged between the two houses ; for after this campaign a great foray was made over the Borders by the Wardens of the English Borders, in which the Fitzhughs took an active part ; but the animosity of the latter seems to have been directed against the house of the Kerrs—the garrison was surprised and put to the sword, and even the lady of the house was slain. The Kerr was from home during this raid, and with him was his son. He had only another child—a girl—said to have been the only human being saved from that sack and ruin, and she was carried away by the enemy. Years passed, and no tidings of the lost child reached the ears of the anxious parent, who, however, seems to have entertained a hope that his daughter still lived. Meanwhile, in the castle of his enemy Mabel Kerr grew beautiful and accomplished. Naturally she was of sweet and gentle disposition, and the most charming and interesting flower in that lovely valley ; yet with all the high spirit and romance suited to the manner of the times. As years glided on she became yet more beloved by all with whom she came in contact ; her kind influence was felt equally alike by rich and poor. Up to this period she had been kept in entire ignorance of her country and parentage, having understood that she was an orphan ; her father, a companion - in - arms of the Fitzhugh, hav-ing she thought, been slain in battle, had entrusted his mother-less child to the care of his friend. The heir of the Fitzhughs had long been passion-ately in love with her, which feeling was ardently returned, and ere long Mabel promised to become his wife. It was at this period that she

Old Mill on the Balder.

became acquainted with her true history, and of the sad tragedy which had occurred when she was made captive ; for the young man, like a true knight of old, would not accept her hand whilst the dark secret remained hidden from her. On recounting, as gently as possible, the enmity between the two houses, and the tragic circumstances connected with it, Mabel's grief was inconsolable ; but the Fitzhugh had been like a parent, and more than kind to her, and as soon as the first paroxysm was over, it was arranged that the marriage should at once take place, after which the two young people should journey into Scotland, to the home of her father, and seek forgiveness and reconciliation between the two houses. Alas ! this was never to be realized, for only a few nights previous to the arranged marriage, their old enemy, the Kerrs, breathing vengeance, were stealing down Teesdale to attack the Castle of Cotherstone under cover of darkness. That night was probably one of the happiest of the young man's life, for on that day he had proved the undying love of Mabel, even in the bitterness of her sorrow ; but even as he paced the battlements and dreamt of the happiness in store for him, there came a sudden crashing and crackling and noise as of armed men in the woods beyond, and the tramp of a large force was heard coming in the direction of the castle, many of whom were observed bearing bundles of faggots, which proved to those watching from the battlements that, should the castle withstand the assault, it was to be reduced by fire. The garrison was quickly aroused, armour buckled on, and men placed in different positions to withstand the first onslaught ; huge stones and other missiles were placed ready to hurl on to the heads of the advancing foe, and the castle resounded with bustle and confusion, the clang of armour, the alarm of war. Suddenly the Scots flung themselves with fury on the weakest points of the castle, yelling out, in the still night air, the war cry of the Kerrs. Again and again the castle was assaulted, and each time the besiegers were driven back, being unable to make any impression on the strong doors, which were thickly studded with immense bolts and girded with iron bands. Yet, though repulsed, they were more determined than ever to effect an ingress. Huge faggots of wood were now brought and piled up high against the doors, and pitch and other inflammable combustibles were thrown on the fuel and fired. Soon the flames arose, lighting up the grim darkness of the night. Unfortunately, the wind carried the smoke and fire right into the faces of the defenders, and almost rendered their efforts powerless. Soon the flames weakened the entrance, and a large tree, to use as a battering ram, was brought to bear on it and an entrance forced. Fitzhugh, at the head of his retainers, had now gathered in the courtyard, ready to repel this onslaught of the enemy, and, as the gate fell, rushed into the breach, and for some time kept them at bay. In the *melee* he was struck down, mortally wounded, the defenders lost heart, the foe rushed in, and then was enacted all the horrors and butchery attendant on the deadly enmity of feud and Border war. Tradition says that young Fitzhugh was cut down by the hand of the chieftain, Kerr, and Mabel, who, with the women attendants, had been placed on horseback ready for instant flight, had the sortie been successful, in a paroxysm of love and agony threw herself on the body of the young knight to shield him from further danger, and in this position also received a mortal wound ; and the shrieks and yells of the dying chieftain, trying in vain to make known to the Kerr his relationship to Mabel, were taken by the victors as only appeals for mercy. Thus vengeance was amply satisfied—few escaped the fire and slaughter of that night. The dawn of the morning light found the young heir of Cotherstone still breathing, and gathering together his energies in one last expiring effort, he feebly enquired for the Scottish leader ; and as his bitter antagonist, the father of his Mabel, stood over him in that last hour, he told him, in plaintive words, the story of his lost child, now lying before them in the coldness of death, and of his, the dying man's, love for her, and the arrangements which had been made for their marriage and the reconciliation between the two houses, all of which had been frustrated by the last night's attack. Who can picture the agony of that father's mind when Fitzhugh pointed to the body of his daughter, struck down and slain in the beauty and prime of womanhood by the

Barnard Castle. *From an Engraving by J. M. W. TURNER, R.A.*

hands of his own men ? And with hand clasped in that of the dying man's, whose life was gradually ebbing away, he learnt from his lips how beloved, and almost adored, his daughter had been, not only by the chieftain of the castle and the retainers, but by all the peasantry of the surrounding district. The returning light of that day told the climax of that deadly feud and revenge ; and with heavy heart the stricken chieftain returned over the hills to the valley of the beautiful Jed. Victory had been theirs, yet returned they not as victors, but downcast, melancholy, and sad, bearing along with

G

them the bodies of Mabel and her lover, and with gentle hands they were laid to rest side by side in the family vault of the bereaved one. How beautiful is this story treasured, telling of feud, foray and noble deed ; and the spirit of Mabel still loves to linger in that beautiful vale, where she wandered in the flesh, and where her life was given to shield the one she so dearly loved.

On the opposite side of the Tees is a stupendous rock, called Percymyre Castle. It was over this rock that one of the Lords of Cotherstone fell and lost his life, when returning in the dusk from a grand hunt which had taken place in the chase of Marwood. It appears he disregarded the warning of one of his aged retainers, who, on account of a strange dream which foreshadowed some calamity, tried to dissuade her lord from joining the chase.

" Two faithful hounds, who'd followed well
    Their master all the way,
Now bounded on, in hot pursuit,
    As though 'twere break of day.

But night had fallen, and near by
    Yawn'd a chasm dark and dread—
'Twas to the top of Percy myre,
    The deer so swiftly sped.

But now the dogs stopped suddenly,
    A flash, as though of fire,
Revealed unto the luckless youth
    The brink of Percymyre.

And far below, in that dark dell,
    Crept the river on its way,
Like some huge serpent coiling round
    Its quivering, ghastly prey.
*   *   *   *   *   *   *
He check'd his steed, but 'twas too late—
    The tired beast reel'd and fell,
Roll'd on its rider, and both together
    Were plunged in that awful dell.

And then, amid the dark, dim night,
    Arose a fearful scream,
And horse and rider mangled lay :
    Fulfill'd was Elspeth's dream."

Cotherstone is a large, picturesque village, renowned for its cheeses. There is an interesting old inn, and a notice, giving friendly advice to travellers, hangs upon its walls. Now onward, past Lartington and its ancient hall and beautiful Deep-dale, with its twining slender rills, pretty cascades, and waterfalls, we approach the town of Barnard Castle, its old ruins impending so stately over the steep bank of the river,

" Where Tees full many a fathom low,
    Wears with its rage, no common foe
For pebbly banks ; nor sandbed here,
    Nor clay mound checks his fierce career,
Condemned to mine a chanelled way
    O'er solid sheets of marble grey."

CHAPTER VII.

～ BARNARD CASTLE. ～

FITZ-BARNARD, or Bernard, is the first of this name we read of. He was probably an ancestor of Barnard Baliol, who built the castle early in the 12th century. The latter was father to John Baliol, who married Devoragilla, daughter of Allan Earl of Galloway, and grandfather to John, who inherited, in the right of his mother, the crown of Scotland, and who was crowned King in 1292, and did homage to Edward for his crown.

From the Baliols it passed for a time into the vast possessions of Anthony Bek, Bishop of Durham, but was afterwards seized and granted to Guy Beauchamp, Earl of Warwick, and for five descents the Beauchamps and their successors, the Nevilles, kept possession of Barnard Castle, from whence it came into the hands of Richard III., by his marriage with Anne, daughter of the great Earl of Warwick, the king-maker. Anne was the first of our Queens who bore the title of Princess of Wales. By some she is supposed to have been carried off by poison. Miss Strickland says she died of a decline, the result of a broken heart. "No memorial marks the spot where the hapless Anne of Warwick found rest from as much sorrow as could have been crowded into the brief space of thirty-one years." Previous to obtaining the throne, Richard resided for some time at Barnard Castle, and was appointed Guardian of the Northern Marches. During the rising of the North, the castle was garrisoned and defended by Sir George Bowes, the insurgents being in possession of Raby, a few miles east.

"Then Sir George Bowes he straightway rose
After them ; some spayle to make,
The noble erles turned back againe,
And aye they vowed that knight to take,

That baron he to his castle fled—
To Barnard Castle then fled hee—
The uttermost walls were eathe to win,
The erles have wonne them presentlie."

After a siege of eleven days, Sir George surrendered for want of provisions, on honourable terms. James I. bestowed the castle and manor on his favourite, Robert Carr, Earl of Somerset, on whose disgrace it again reverted to the crown, and afterwards came into the possession of the Vanes, in whose family it still remains.

The ruins are approached through the King's Head yard, and are still of vast magnitude, covering an area of nearly seven acres. Here in one of the rooms, in the fifties,

a hermit took up his residence. He was one of those persons who seemed to have quarrelled with the world ; and here he remained for some time, afterwards removing to Egglestone Abbey. "I heard," says Walter White, "that he had been crossed in love, and that notwithstanding his lonely solitude, he would go out at times and find a friend, and make a night of it." The views from the windows of the castle are magnificent indeed, the river flowing deep down below, over a bed of limestone and marble ; and the walks by the river are most beautiful, the ruins impending over the precipice, and the water swirling onwards, awakening reveries dulcet and charming.

Gallowaygate, the road leading to the station, and another spot close by, known in ancient records as "Hangslave," and the name bespeaks its own story. In the street running south from the market-place, known as Throughgate, are one or two very ancient houses ; one with three stories of square bays is the most picturesque. Formerly it was an inn, and it was in this house that Oliver Cromwell slept in October, 1648. In this street was situate an Augustine Convent. The King's Head is the principal hotel, and here, formerly, Charles Dickens took up his abode when travelling in these parts, collecting notes for his "Nicholas Nickleby." We can sit in the same bow window, and look on nearly the same scenes as the famous writer did. Across the street was Humphrey the clock-maker's sign, and his name stood out so conspicuously that at length he was impressed with the original idea of "Master Humphrey's Clock." "Mr. Newman Noggs" writes, in his P.S. to the young gentlemen of Dotheboys Hall: "If you should be near Barnard Castle, there is good ale at the King's Head. Say you know me, and I am sure they will not charge you for it. You may say *Mr.* Noggs there, for I was a gentleman then; I was, *indeed.*"

The Parish Church, dedicated to St. Mary, was built by Barnard Baliol early in the 12th century, but has been restored and altered until little of the ancient structure remains, except the Norman font and one doorway. In the churchyard, on our visit, were several very old mural slabs, which are certainly worthy of better attention from the clergy and churchwardens.

Tomb of Ralph Neville and his two Wives.   EDMUND BOGG.

Proceeding east from Barnard Castle, we leave the banks of the Tees and follow the road to Staindrop, passing Streatleam Castle, the seat of the Bowes family. The castle stands in rather a low situation, but is beautifully wooded, and was formerly surrounded by a deep moat. A pretty little stream flows through the park, and thence winds through meadow and arable land. Like Tennyson's brook, it curves and twists under willow and hedgerow, and is a sweet contrast to the scenes we have left in Upper Teesdale.

Now we are approaching Staindrop, a village with many picturesque features, possessing a large green. The lower end is enclosed by large trees, through the branches of which the smoke slowly ascended on this summer's eve. How charmingly the sunlight glints on the old tiled roofs, and how cheery are the shouts of children at play. A striking feature is the grey old weather-beaten tower of the ancient church, where the renowned Nevilles sleep; what startling scenes and incidents in the historic life of this family appear before the mind of the onlooker—scenes pregnant with disaster and ruin, the rise and fall of the rival Roses; the great drama which for years deluged England with the blood of her best and bravest sons, when that great and ambitious house of Neville, with the giant form of the king-maker towering high above all other, were in their ascendancy.

To the left, on entering the church, is the beautiful alabaster tomb of Ralph Neville and his two wives. The figure of the knight is girded in plated armour, with a lion at his feet. The effigy of his wives rest one on either side—Margaret, daughter of the Earl of Stafford, and Joan, his second wife, daughter of John of Gaunt. Two little dogs, symbols of fidelity, peep from the robes of the ladies, and at the feet are monks kneeling. Other tombs, with crocketed canopies, formerly contained figures, and at the north-west part of the church is the wooden tomb of Henry, the fifth Earl of Westmoreland, and three of his wives, two of whom are represented by effigy. Around the tomb, in niches, are the figures of his children, and beneath is an inscription : "All you that come to the church to praye say pater noster and a crede for to have mercy of us and all our progeny." In the centre of the chancel and out of keeping, we should say, with the sacred character of the place, is a large, imposing monument,

hewn out of white marble, representing the Duke of Cleveland, who died in 1842. There are other monumental busts and figures, and the foundation of the church is said to date from the reign of King Canute, who presented the manor of Staindrop to St. Cuthbert. The building probably dates from the transition period.

Just beyond the church, to the north, is the magnificent mediæval castle of Raby, justly described as the finest fortress in all the north country. As we stand ruminating before this immense pile, still retaining all its ancient features, appearing like a scroll of history before us, its walls emblazoned with the armorial badges of the Nevilles, and the one who, in their glory, stood the greatest and the last of the old Norman chivalry, more kingly in pride, in state, in possession and renown, than the King himself—Richard Neville, Earl of Salisbury and Warwick.*

And those who have looked on the immense castles of Middleham, Brancepeth, and Raby ; in the days of the king-maker a vast camp bristling with armed men, the

---

* " This princely personage, in the full vigour of his age, possessed all the attributes that endear the noble to the commoner. His valour in the field was accompanied with a generosity rare in the captains of the time. He valued himself in sharing the perils and the hardships of his meanest soldiers. His haughtiness to the great was not incompatible with frank affability to the lowly. His wealth was enormous, but it was equalled by his magnificence, and rendered popular by his lavish hospitality. No less than thirty thousand persons are said to have feasted daily at the open tables, with which he allured to his countless castles the strong hands and grateful hearts of a martial and unsettled population   More haughty than ambitious, he was feared because he avenged all affronts, and yet not envied, because he seemed above all favour."

first a huge pile of ruins, and the others still standing so stately and magnificently will easily understand what the power of the Nevilles has been in the old days. The very sound of the name of Raby conveys memories of remarkable men and women, and memorable deeds, and the glory of that house and of all the illustrious alliances formed by the Nevilles. The name of that battle—Neville's Cross—sheds a further lustre, and is a memorial to their name. Ever since the days of Richard Cœur de Lion, when Aymer de Neville performed such wondrous feats of arms on the battlefields of Palestine, had there been brave and doughty knights in the Neville family. It was Robert Neville, the peacock of the north, who slew the Bishop's Seneschal in open day on Elvet Bridge at Durham. The final downfall of the

Raby Castle.

family was caused by the active share they took in the ill-fated rising of the North, fatal to the fortunes of many a noble house. Their banner, on which was displayed the five wounds of Christ, was carried by old Richard Norton, Esquire, an honourable gentleman of ancient lineage.

" Now was the North in arms : they shine
In warlike trim from Tweed to Tyne,
At Percy's voice : and Neville sees
His followers gathering in from Tees,
From Wear, and all the little rills
Concealed among the forked hills,—

Seven hundred knights, retainers all
Of Neville, at their master's call,
Had sate together in Raby Hall !
Such strength that earldom held of yore ;
Nor wanted at this time rich store
Of well-appointed chivalry."

" Thee, Norton, wi' thine eight good sonnes.
    They doomed to dye, alas for ruth,
Thy reverend lockes thee could not save,
    Nor them their faire and blooming youth.

Wi' them full many a gallant wight,
    They cruellye bereav'd of life ;
And many a child made fatherlesse,
    And widowed many a tender wife."

Through Langley dale, near the castle, flows a delightful stream. A beautiful ballad, written by Surtees, called " Langley Dale," is said to allude to the rising of the North :—

LANGLEY DALE.

" As I down Raby Park did pass,
    I heard a fair maid weep and wail ;
The chiefest of her song it was,
    Farewell the sweets of Langley Dale.

The bonny mavis cheers his love,
    The throstlecock sings in the glen ;
But I must never hope to rove
    Within sweet Langley Dale again.

The wild rose blushes in the brae,
    The primrose shows its blossom pale ;
But I must bid adieu for aye,
    To all the joys of Langley Dale.

The days of mirth and peace are fled,
    Youth's golden locks to silver turn ;
Each northern flow'ret droops its head
    By Marwood Chase and Langley Burn.

False Southrons crop each lovely flower,
    And throw their blossoms in the gale ;
Our foes have spoilt the sweetest bower—
    Alas ! for bonny Langley Dale.

Reverting to the river again, and on to Winston-on-Tees, a most charming spot overlooking the winding river, with its steep wooded cliffs.

The church, dedicated to Saint Andrew, dates from the Norman period, but has undergone restoration. Westholme Hall, a fine old manor-house, dates from 1606, and is alluded to by Sir Walter Scott in his " Rokeby" :—

" The cottage, once his sire's, he sees
    Embowered upon the bank of Tees ;
He views sweet Winston's woodland scenes,
    And shares the dance on Gainford Green."

Here a bridge of single arch crosses the Tees, with a span of 111 ft., and was built by the Robinsons in 1764. It was one of the few structures that withstood the fury of the great flood in 1771. Two miles further down the river we reach Gainford. Few villages possess more interest to the antiquarian than this.

Perhaps the most interesting vestiges of antiquity is a rampart of earth and dyke running south from the centre of Yorkshire into Scotland, marking an ancient border. A defensive line separating two hostile people ; the invaders who came east from over the sea having driven before them the original inhabitants into the hilly country west—thus along this old-world border a long and bitter warfare for final supremacy has been waged.

The church, which has been judiciously restored, dates from the Norman period, and replaced a Saxon structure built by Egfred, Bishop of Lindisfarne. Many remains of early Norman work, in the shape of slabs, sculptured crosses, with swords and other symbols, are to be seen in the old porch, and by the beautiful elm trees is the stone slab or base in which the ancient cross was formerly embedded.

At the west side of the village, and nearly opposite to the church, is an old manor-house, and near to it is a columbary, or pigeon-cote ; and on the opposite side of the river, near the ruins of Saint Lawrence's Chapel, is another dove-cote, or columbary, both having the appearance of a disused windmill minus the sails. The entrance is through a low doorway, and around the interior walls is fitted up with small niches where the pigeons nested in mediæval times. A columbary was a necessary appendage to every castle or manor-house. The Romans had similar places built, with niches to receive the urns containing the ashes of the dead.

The village has a delightful rural aspect, and is built around a large green adjoining the river, from whose banks the village, with its rustic property by the Tees, intermingled in branch, and the more pretentious dwellings in the background, form a charming village picture. Crossing to the Yorkshire side of the Tees, we note the delightful windings of the stream, and then turn our faces westward on the return journey to the vale of the Eden and the Lake country. On the high banks above the river stands, solitary and neglected, the ruined chapel of St. Lawrence. High above the valley near to is the site of the old Richmond, a strong Roman station built to guard the ford over the river at that place. Out of the ruins of the Roman station the Anglo-Normans built the town of Bereford—Robert-de-Bereford won renown under the banner of Richard I., in Palestine. Another of the Berefords gave twenty-five acres of land at this place for the maintenance of a priest to sing in the chapel here on Sundays, Wednesdays, and Fridays in each week, for the health of the knight's soul, and also those of his ancestors. A few scattered farms are the only remnants of the village of Barford. As we wander around the chapel ruins and grass-grown mounds, and note the Celtic dike and memorials of ancient Rome, and the skeleton of an old world around, and the complete silence and almost desolation which now reigns, we are struck by the exquisite beauty and romantic appearance of the landscape—Gainford village nestling below, with hoary church and manor-house, the columbary on either side of the river, relics of feudal days ; sweet lowland glades and charming ravines, where the spring flowers bloom, and near is the river, which here flows in such delightful windings, and a little further on are the old farm-houses, relics of Tudor and Stuart days. Away to the north the eye ranges to the higher ridges stretching away into the county of Durham. Two miles west is the village of Ovington, the Ulfston of the Doomsday survey, then in possession of one Ulf, ancestor of the Ulmington family. The village has a charming appearance, and there is a pretty green and a May-pole some sixty feet high. Further west the moors of North Yorkshire come into vision, and yonder is the moorland village of Barningham, where formerly the sexton

was paid a yearly sum for whipping cats out of the churchyard.   Down the old lane to
the right is Wycliffe, the cliff by the water, the birth-place and early home of John
Wycliffe, situate by the Tees in a retired spot some distance from the public highway, and is to-day almost as rural as it was in the days of the great Apostle of
the Reformation.   It was eventide on our visit, and the sun had for some length of
time disappeared below the western hills, yet the spiritual mystery of the gloaming
added a further charm to the richly wooded slopes and green meadows where the farms
nestle, and the church, embosomed in ivy, the ancient mill and the picturesque rectory.
There is an air of perfect sympathy about this spot, only at flood times the thunder
and wail of the river sounds like the agony of souls in torment rent, but when at peace

Wycliffe Church

the waters sweetly murmur a lullaby as if to soothe to rest the numberless dead laid
beside the brink.   Though nearly dark, the beauty of the spot appealed like some sweet
poem to our imagination.   The aged rector kindly led us the way to the church by
the aid of a lantern.   No words, however eloquent, can give a more impressive object
lesson on the mutability of all things on earth, than we received whilst meditating in
this quaint and venerable edifice with its flat roof, mouldering sun-dial, and other
crumbling memorials in the rude yet venerable interior.   There is a rare old font
which was lately rescued from the sacrilegious use as a water trough, and in the
chancel are brasses to the memory of the Wycliffes, and sculptured fragments of
ancient mural slabs, apparently belonging to an earlier church, inserted in the outside

walls. Within the rectory hangs a portrait of John Wycliffe, copied by Sir Antonio
Moore from an original one of the Reformer. It was presented as a heirloom by
Dr. Thomas Zouch, rector of Wycliffe towards the close of the last century.
Wycliffe is indeed a beautiful spot, resting by river, meadow, and wood, the old mill
race and the overhanging willows, the music of the water and the hum and clack of
the mill wheel. There is a sacred and venerable aspect about the village, all breathing
of perfect peace and repose, and from being the birth-place and early home of Wycliffe,
the place is doubly interesting, and although there are rival claims to that honour, we
do not hesitate to claim Wycliffe as his birth-place ; nor can we understand why
anyone should seek to claim her noblest son, for here he received his education, and
knelt in prayer at the altar amongst the generation of men who now lie peacefully
sleeping by the sweetly-sounding Tees. Where do the ashes of the great Reformer
rest ? Not here, in the silent churchyard, but scattered broadcast over the great
ocean. He died in the rectory-house at Lutterworth, in December, 1384. Forty
years after his death a decree was issued that the coffin and body of Wycliffe should
be disinterred and burnt. Crowds assembled to see the work. The grave was opened,
the coffin raised and carried down to the bridge ; there a fire was kindled by the
crowd, and the mouldering fragments of humanity consigned on to it, and Wycliffe's
ashes became charred in the fire, after which the remains were thrown into the river
Swift. " The Swift conveyed them into the Avon, the Avon into the Severn, the Severn
into the narrow seas, and so on to the main ocean, and thus the ashes of Wycliffe are
the emblem of his doctrine, which now is dis-
persed all the world over."

The walk to Rokeby, either by the bridle
way or by road, is very charming. Noble trees
of vast growth not only afford shelter to the
tired traveller, but also lend attraction to the
beauty of the surrounding country. To fully
appreciate the ideal and historic charm of this
district we must linger over the pages of legendary
lore and records of the past. Sir Walter Scott,
with the pen of a magician, has bewitched our
fancy and rendered this spot classic for all time
with story and romance, depicted in flowing prose
and verse, traditions, incident, and character—
imaginative pictures yet appealing to our minds

Arms of the Rokebys

more startling than reality. Now we have reached the winsome Greta, which comes
wandering so sweetly from Stain Moor to greet us—hence the Greta. Over the

bridge we pass and take up our quarters for the night at the Morrit Arms, an old coaching-house, renowned far and wide for its generous hospitality. From the bedroom window we could look into the woods of Rokeby, where a colony of rooks were nesting, and the sound of their croaking intermingled in our dream, and in the early morning we were aroused by all the inhabitants of the rookery giving out their hoarse cries of gladsome pleasure.

In the garden of the inn is an ancient font, of square form, set on a moulded base, and is in a fair state of preservation. It may have been brought from the old church, which was demolished about a century ago, and stood near to where the Greta meets the Tees. In the meadows immediately behind the inn is a well-defined Roman camp. Brignall Banks is further up the Greta.

"O Brignal Banks are fresh and fair,
  And Greta woods are green,
And you may gather garlands three,
  Would grace a summer queen."

Near to is the cave where Guy Denziel and his band of robbers had their rendezvous.

"Of old the cavern, straight and rude,
In slaty rock the cavern hew'd ;
And Brignal's woods and Scargill's wave
E'en now o'er many a sister cave,
Where far within the darksome rift
The wedge and lever ply their thrift.
The war had silenced rural trade,
And the deserted mine was made
The banquet hall and fortress too
Of Denzil and his desperate crew."

Mortham's Tomb, Greta Woods.   s. 8000.

At the east foot of the Greta bridge is a large and yellow-walled building, a famous posting-house in coaching days, and known as "The George." Let us follow the course of the Greta, now wandering through the woods of Rokeby, singing, in romantic strains, the fascinating legends of by-gone days. Scott, writing in 1809, says : "It is one of the most delightful places I have ever seen, as it unites the richness and luxuriance of English vegetation with the romantic variety of glen, torrent, and copse which dignifies our northern scenery." Thus wandering through the woods, which rise high above the sparkling stream, winding, like a silver thread, through scenes of wildering beauty, we arrive at Mortham's tomb, formed of immense blocks of Tees marble, richly emblazoned with crests and armorial bearings, and rendered more venerable by its coating of green and silver moss. The tomb stands in the woodland glade, under a natural arch, composed by the branches of two ancient elms. This was our first visit, but we regret to state that on our next, some two years later; one of the elms had succumbed to the fury of a tremendous storm.

> " South of the gate. an arrow flight,
> Two mighty elms their limbs unite,
> As if a canopy to spread
> O'er the lone dwelling of the dead ;
> For their huge boughs in arches bent
> Above a massive monument,
> Carved o'er in ancient Gothic wise
> With many a 'scutcheon and device."

This is supposed to be the tomb of Sir Ralph Bowes, and was brought hither from Eggleston Abbey.

A hundred paces from the tomb is Mortham's Tower, an old Border peel. The site is most advantageous, being situate on the brow of a small hill. Connected with this old tower is a legend, grim and hoary. Once on a time a certain Lord of Rokeby, in a fit of jealousy, murdered his wife in the glen below, and the blood-stains, yet to be seen on the tower stairs, and which, story says, cannot be effaced, were the blood droppings from his dagger as he mounted the stair, after committing the fearful deed ; and for years after the spirit of the murdered woman haunted the tower and vale of the Greta adjoining. At length the spectral visitor appeared so often that the services of the parson were called into request, and he, with book in hand, read the spirit down, and confined her under the bridge. During the great flood of 1771 the structure was swept away, and with it the spirit, so at least it is thought, for it has not been seen or heard since that time.

> " The 'lated peasant shunned the dell,
> For superstition wont to tell
> Of many a ghostly sound and sight,
> Scaring its path at dead of night "

On the banks of the stream, nearly opposite to the Tower, is " Bertram's Cave," which Scott often visited when at Rokeby.

Now we are at Dairy Bridge, which crosses the Greta at the foot of the woods near its junction with the Tees. How lovely is the scene at the meeting of the waters, with the environments of hill and meadow, clothed with noble trees. To stand and view the sight in the glory of a summer sunset is alone worth the journey ; or at other times to listen to the wild music of the leaping and gurgling waters, battling and charging against the huge rocks, in that mad rush for freedom. The monster boulders are hewn into fantastic shape by the washing of centuries and piled in grotesque confusion during the raging of mighty floods. Beyond the bridge branches interweave and form a beautiful canopy, contrasting finely with the grey bridge. Moss, fern, trailing plant, and wild flowers festoon the bank, and the varied shades of the water, from the dark brown pools to the more creamy current, is enough to gladden the heart of a stoic.

An army of poets and artists, at whose head are Scott and Turner, have rendered this spot classic. Scott says :—

   "The cliffs that rear their haughty head
   High o'er the river's darksome bed,
   Were now all naked, wild and grey,
   Now waving all with greenwood spray;

   Here trees to every crevice clung,
   And o'er the dell their branches hung,
   And there all splintered and uneven,
   And shiver'd rocks ascend to heaven."

And again he says :—

   "'Twas a fair scene. The sunbeam lay
   On battled tower and portal grey,
   And from the grassy slope he sees
   The Greta flow to meet the Tees ;
   Where, issuing from her darksome bed,
   She caught the morning's eastern red,

   And through the softening vale below,
   Roll'd her bright waves, in rosy glow,
   All blushing, to her bridal bed,
   Like some shy maiden cottage-bred,
   While linnet, lark, and blackbird gay,
   Sing forth her nuptial roundelay."

Just by the meeting of the Greta and Tees are the remaining vestiges of an ancient church, demolished a little over one hundred years ago. A few mouldering

Dairy Bridge and Mortham's Tower.

tombstones still show out above the green sward, to point out the sacrilegious act, the defilement of holy ground, where for centuries the children of the hamlet had been baptized, and generations of men had knelt in prayer and been laid to rest under the green turf in this peaceful and secluded spot, where the music of waters lulled them to rest, in the hope of a glorious resurrection. The base of an ancient cross and the old font still remain, sole vestiges of all that was.

We cannot leave Rokeby without mentioning that curious satirical ballad known as "The Felon Sow of Rokeby," written, it is supposed, by a Craven man, to illustrate the greed and rapacity of the monks of Richmond. It appears that Ralph de Rokeby, who lived in the time of Henry VII., had in his woods a very fierce and untameable sow, whose lair was by the Greta's side. The ballad says :—

> " Her walk was end-long Greta side,
> Ther was no bren that durst her bide,
>   That was froe heaven or hell.
> Nor never man that had that might
> That ever durst come in her sight,
>   Her force it was so fell."

This diabolical and grisly brute was given by Sir Ralph de Rokeby, in a spirit of mischief, to the Friars of Richmond, on condition they should themselves come and remove her, and so for this purpose Friar Middleton set out one day, accompanied by two brethren, one of which, the ballad says, was Peter Dale. At the end of their twelve miles' journey from Richmond to Rokeby, they found the wicked sow

> " Liggan under a tree,
>   Rugg and rusty was her haire,
>   She raise up with a felon fare,
> To fight against the three."

After a terrible struggle she was forced into a kiln hole, where they at last succeeded in placing a halter round her neck, at which she raved and roared so furiously that the monks became frightened.

> " The sow was in the kiln hole down,
>   As they were on the balke aboon,
>   For hurting of their feet ;
>   They were so saulted with this sow
>   That among them was a stalworth stew
>   The kiln began to reeke.

> She gave such brades at the band
> That Peter Dale had in his hand,
>   He might not hold his feet ;
> She chafed them to and fro,
> The wight men was never soe woe,
>   Their measure was not so meete."

Then Peter Dale, with crosse and crede, took the Book of the Gospels and endeavoured to read the furious beast down, but the sow would have none of it, and only charged the monks more fiercely, and dragged the rope from their hands.

> " The sow she would not Latin heare,
> But rudely rushed at the frear,
>   That blinked all his blee ;
> And when she would have taken her hold,
> The fryer leaped as Jesus wold,
>   And healed him with a tree.

> He say'd : ' Alas that I was frear !
> And I shall be rugged in sunder here,
>   Hard is my destinie ;
> Wist my brethren in this houre
> That I was set in such a stoure,
>   They would pray for me.' "

In the end the monks were completely vanquished, and fled away up Watling Street, for the ballad says they had no succour but their own feet. Curious enough, the sow seems to have been quite tame and gentle in the presence of Margery, the mistress of Rokeby, for we are told that after the affray the sow came unto her,

> " Scho gave her meete'upon the flower.
> Scho made a bed beneath a bower,
>   With moss and broom besprent,
> The sewe was gentle as mote be,
> Ne rage, ne ire, flashed fra her e'e,
>   Scho seemed wele content."

When the discomfited monks arrived home and told the story how, in the terrible fight, they had fought a fiend in the likeness of a sow, Friar Theobald, the warden, was more determined than ever to capture her, so he engaged two of the boldest men that ever was born ; one was Gilbert, Griffith's son, and the other was a bastard son of Spain, and many a Saracen had he slain. On meeting the sow a terrible fight occurred, in which the Spaniard nearly lost his life

> " Then Gilbert grieved was sea sare,
> That he rave off both hide and haire,
> The flesh cam' fro' the bone ;
> And with all force he felled her there,
> An waun her worthily in werre,
> And band her him alone."

> " And lift her on a horse sea hee,
> Into two paniers well made of a tre,
> And to Richmond they did hay ;
> When they saw her come,
> They sang merrily Te Deum,
> The fryers on that day."

And so they brought her to Richmond, and there was a general rejoicing in the city, and thanksgiving to God and St. Francis for that noble victory.

Proceeding, we hasten by the river side to Eggleston Abbey. Beautiful and bewitching are the peeps and vistas of the sunlit stream, flowing beneath overhanging woods and over its bed of marble, for the river has carved out a course through beds of blue marble. What duration of time has elapsed since it began that process of polishing the huge rock smooth, we know not, for time, in this instance, cannot be counted by centuries. Thousands of years before the abbey and castle were even thought of, whose grey ruins adorn its high bank yonder, had the river channelled a course through rugged rocks, swirling and leaping in its mad career onward, even as it does to-day. Time mirage change the face of its waters, but it, by the force of indomitable will, has sculptured a deep pathway in the adamantine rock, scooping and churning, in all fantastic shapes, in its herculean grasp, the marble foundations. From the abbey bridge, with its magnificent span, can be obtained a scene of enchanting beauty, long reaches of wood and stream, the river, singing so sweetly, linking the music of the past with the beauty of the present ; the relics of a summer vegetation with the first flush of nature awakening to another glory.

Yonder on the steep bank are the crumbling walls of a ruined abbey, and away in the background rise the roofs, spires, pinnacles and battlements, historic towers, relics of mediæval ages ; beneath us the woods wave in all their beauty ; united with the varied and refreshing green of spring, and the river, coursing onward at its own sweet will, mirrors the imagery of nature—the sky and clouds in its bosom, spring in her freshest charm is seen all around, river, dale, woodland, and meadow, and the song of birds, all combine to touch the inmost chords of our being into the spirit of harmony and praise for the beauties of nature—the works of the good and bountiful Creator.

Now we have reached Egglestone Abbey, which stands on a high green knoll on the Yorkshire side of the Tees, a mile or so east of Barnard Castle. It was built in the early years of the thirteenth century, and marks the pointed Gothic period. The abbey is now a total wreck, parts of the nave and chancel, which are roofless, being all that remain. Adjoining, in a sad state of dilapidation, are the later monastic buildings. Here it was that the hermit from Barnard Castle took up his abode after removing from the latter place. Within the precincts of the ruins are several rare mural slabs, of Tees marble ; one bears the inscription, in large characters,

THOMAS ROKEBY, Bastarde. Iesu, for passion's sake,
Have mercy on my sinful heart !

and others, on which are finely carved the cross and swords, from which the brasses have been removed. Unlike most abbeys, Egglestone does not rest in the bosom of the vale, but stands, most commanding, on the highest eminence, and looks down into the valleys Thorsgill and the Tees. Fairy Thorsgill has a sweet fascination for me. Beautiful and dreamlike did the little vale appear in the waning sunset. It lies at

The Old Bridge, Fairy Thorsgill.

right angle to the Tees, whilst the venerable ruins are seen to fine advantage above. As we stand by the quaint little bridge which spans the stream, winding its way so stealthily amongst the pebbles, twining here and there, like a gleam of light, the softly sloping hill sides rising gently towards the skies, whilst the beautiful brook, as it passes, swaying the grass and wild flowers that grow on its margin, whispers a refrain of old-world days, soothing our minds into a delicious reverie, and we seem to catch an echo from the past !—in procession before us passes Thor, the Viking, and his grim followers ; the more cultured Norman, in clanking mail and pomp of heraldry ; list to the noise and clang attendant on building the abbey ! the chanting of the choristers.   Fancy depicts the picture of the abbey's dedication ; bishops and priors, with their attendants, came from distant places ; barons and their retainers mingle with the holy brethren in that first worship at Egglestone.   The service choral.   The pathetic strains of the opening " Kyrie Eleison," when all heads bow, after which all would rise in body, heart, and soul, with music of the " Gloria in Excelsis," that filled the groined roof and streamed through the new-born aisles, still more thrilling and blood-inflaming, when the deep and sonorous roll of the bass, from the mighty lungs of monk and friar, proclaimed the " Credo."   Then in humble prayer, as the " Agnus Dei " was chanted, still lower would they bow, and smite their breasts, saying " Mea Culpa" ; after the solemn stillness, The Benediction.   The interval between the sacrificial rite of the Mass and the chanting of the Vespers they feasted on venison, and from

The Greta.   EDMUND BOGG.

the flagons and goblets would drink the choicest wines.   Now we see the passing forth of powerful bishops and barons, with their attendant knights and squires, attired in all the glory and pride of chivalry. Pageantry, in all its barbaric splendour of ages gone, spread before us, with banners waving, the richly emblazoned shields of the Nevilles, the Percys, the Fitz-Hughs, the Bowes, and the Rokebys, &c., their armour flashing brilliantly in the sunlight.   Thus the stream babbles its story and lulls us into reveries of the past, when resting by the quaint old bridge in the glowing sunset.   This was a favourite sketching ground of Thomas Creswick, R.A., and later of Keely, Halliswell, and other eminent artists.

The Monk's Mill, a fine relic of the past, still rests by the Tees, and the old wheel still casts up the dripping water and adds its pleasant rumbling to the music of the surrounding.

From the brow of the next hill the eye follows the graceful curvings of the Tees, whose banks are finely fringed with trees, and the town of Barnard Castle, shimmering in the sunlit mist, and the Bowes Museum in the foreground, standing so stately and noble, like some princely palace of old.   Then we turn across to, and enter into a branch of the great north road, the Watling, or Waitling, street of the Roman, over which the legions have marched with stately tramp, led by emperors from the imperial city, nigh two thousand years ago, and over which, in pre-railway days, several coaches rattled to and fro daily, in their journey between London, Carlisle, Edinburgh and Glasgow. Now the road winds over a high tableland of dreary moor, gradually rising higher and higher and growing more savage and desolate beyond the village of Bowes. To the south yonder we catch sweet glimpses of the Greta river, and ahead of us the ruins of that ancient stronghold, whose life, written and unwritten, stretches from the dawn of civilization, and now looms dark and dreary over the village, typical and significant of that great struggle which for centuries waged along this old border line.

We have now reached the foot of this moorland village. On the right, at the entrance, is a plantation, where the rooks are busy nesting, and deep warm tints of sunlight swathe the trees in golden hue.

Bowes consists of one long straggling street of grey stone houses, crooked, cracked, twisted, and cold, with door frames and windows awry and shivered, and a grass-grown cobbled causeway on either side. On the right is the church, now almost despoiled of its Norman architecture, but still shewing many interesting features. Near to is the ruin of the strong Norman castle before alluded to, and a meadow length further is Dotheboys Hall, the house made famous for all time by Charles Dickens, in his "Nicholas Nickleby," and the last in the village, if we except one or two half-ruined shanties just to the left; and further is the long dreary range of Stainmoor, over which the winds of winter shriek and howl, and phantom sprites wail a mournful dirge, enough to make the heart of mortal tremble and shiver with fear. Nearly at the entrance to Bowes, on the east, stands the Unicorn Inn, one of the largest hostelries between York and Carlisle, called into requisition during coaching days. It was in the yard of this inn that the miserable youths for Dotheboys Hall were set down, although to disguise the exact position of the school Dickens describes it as the inn at Greta bridge. "The Unicorn" is a large curious old building, in shape a quadrangle, with its capacious inn yard open to the street. The entrance to the house is under a portico from the yard. It is a most wonderful old inn, with its maze of rooms, winding passages, dark lobbies and cellars, low beams, and ancient oak panelling, thick walls, recessed windows, half hidden cupboards, and deep window seats, and antique holes and corners, here and there, the former use of which is now forgotten. On the west side of the house is a large kitchen, now the chief room of the family, with mullion windows, formed of diamond squares of glass, looking into an ancient garden, with its neglected boxwood borders, shrivelled into patches. Adjoining the yard is the large tap-room, fitted up with long-settle running into the huge and deeply-recessed fire-place, the latter showing many interesting nooks, only to be found in such houses. It is a perfect treat to find oneself benighted, say on a Saturday, at "The Unicorn," and to sit for an hour or two in this old room, and listen to the gossip of the natives and so become acquainted with the items of interest, manners and customs of the people, which appears like reading a page written at least sixty years ago.   Behind this room, and arranged so as not to disturb the rest of the house, is a smaller one, fitted up with a bedstead of seventeenth century appearance.   There some trusted servant, in old coaching days, always stayed overnight, ready should a customer require to be served with necessary refreshments, benighted travellers, stablemen, or hangers-on, &c., at such establishments.   In the centre of the small window looking into the inn yard, was a hinged pane of glass, just large enough to admit the passing of refreshments to those outside ; and

Scene in Coaching Days—(" The Unicorn," Bowes'.

the writer was informed by an elderly person, whose parents kept this inn sixty or seventy years ago, that usually a thriving trade was done through this little lattice window after the inmates of the house had retired to slumber.   Some of the furniture of this room certainly dates back over two centuries.   Martha Railton, the heroine of the " Bowes' tragedy of true love," performed the duty of attendant in this room, at least oral tradition records this story.   Widow Railton was the mistress of this inn, in those days known as "The George."   It was Martha who died of a broken heart on hearing the passing bell toll, announcing the death of her lover, and a stone at the west end of the church records her never-dying love.   "The Unicorn " is now far too large for the present traffic on this road and the declining trade of Bowes.

The little snug at the front of the house was the room occupied by Dickens during his stay here. The large dining-room, immediately facing the street, like most of the others, now wears a melancholy air of desertion, and ghosts of a bygone generation seem to flit before the visitor. There is that musty smell and flavour of age peculiar to old buildings and unoccupied places. Even my dreams during those nights I slept at "The Unicorn," were shaped with forms of a bygone people, such as would be witnessed in the coaching days. Sudden gusts of wind moaned dismally round the gables, angles, and passages, and whistled ominously within the numerous crevices of the ancient roof. The old signboard creaked and moaned dismally as it was swayed to and fro by the wind ; such sounds produced dreams and phantoms of the past ; scenes from " Nicholas Nickleby," " Dotheboys Hall," or anon the merry jokes and cracking of whips, the rattling of coaches, the shrill flourish of the driver's horn, the unloading of baggage, and the alighting of passengers attired in old-world costumes, the hurry and scurry to and fro of postboys and guards in livery. Such are the associations and memories of this wonderful old road-side house, with its savour of past generations clinging around it. The long range of stables, offices, and outhouses, &c., built on two sides of the quadrangle yard prove the importance by which it was held as a hostelry of vast accommodation to the ancient roadster. In the centre of the yard is a large pump that has witnessed very many phases of human experiences.

Pembroke College is indissolubly associated in my memory with Bowes, the reason of this is as follows : A grammar school was founded at Bowes by one William Hutchinson in 1699, when a certain sum of money was left in trust for a scholarship at Pembroke College, for the poor youths of the village. Unfortunately, this fund has been allowed to remain in abeyance for a number of years, the reason for which is not far to seek, the money not being sufficient for the full maintenance of the student, and the poor people of the successful boys not being able to add to the fund out of their scanty earnings, were unable to help their children to avail themselves of the advantages the money was originally intended for ; and the Master of Pembroke College having had possession without any use being made of it for such a number of years, wished to retain at least half of it for other purposes than the original trust, and on the Saturday evening during our last visit a parish meeting had been called, to investigate this action of the Pembroke College authorities. The curate (formerly a poor Bowes lad), who had reaped the advantages of the trust and knew the benefit of a college career, occupied the chair. All the village—perhaps I should say town, for there are still to be seen the remains of the market-cross—were assembled together at that important meeting, and as I sat, completely deserted, in the large room of the inn, for my companions had become interested and had gone with the rest to the meeting, there was not the faintest sound of a voice in the house or a footstep in the street, until it seemed verily like a place of the dead. At length I grew weary of the silence and solitude reigning around the rambling old inn, and so wended my way up the dark street, lit with one or two flickering oil lamps making the darkness more dense, to the meeting of the parishioners.   The debate was carried on in fine argumentative style, worthy of the object and a great city. At the dispersion there was quite an inrush of thirsty orators to "The Unicorn," where the discussion was still carried on, and a son of Vulcan waxed quite eloquent on the injustice of certain people ; and the night had waned into the small hours of the morning ere the landlord, who was an enthusiast on the subject, and my companions

South Doorway.

on the tramp had fully discussed the pros and cons of the ancient trust, with the Pembroke College scheme. Thus being in unison with their local topic, they expressed themselves freely, and we became acquainted and interested in the manners and customs of this historic and characteristic old town.

Higher up and on the south side of the village is Bowes Church, still retaining several features of late Norman work, and contains two piscinas, also two fonts, one of the Tudor period and another strangely suggestive of Saxon work.   The south transept has mural slabs, a sarcophagus, and relics of Roman and Saxon occupation.   Before the restoration of the church all the high-backed family pews bore the names and addresses of the owners, as for instance : John Bousfield (a well-known local name), Christopher Craddock, Archdeacon Headland, Thomas Walker Lowfield, James Langstaff, John Bourne, James Sawyer, all names suggesting memories of families dwelling in those parts less than a century ago.   There was formerly a clock-tower to the church, now only a small turret, containing two bells.   The south doorway is very interesting, over which is a carved stone, thirteenth century work, illustrating the Crucifixion.   Immediately under the west end is a headstone, to the memory of the lovers, Edwin and Emma, erected by

Dr. Dinsdale, in 1848. The traditional story of these two young people is very pathetic, and we give the story as told in ballad. Our readers will remember that Emma's mother (Widow Railton) was landlady of " The Unicorn." The inscription on the headstone reads :—

Roger Wrightson, junr., and Martha Railton.
both of Bowes,
Buried in one grave.
He died in a fever,
and, upon tolling his passing-bell, she cry'd out—
" My heart is broke,"
and in a few hours expir'd purely thro' Love.
March 15, 1714-15.

Such is the brief and touching record
contained in the parish register of burials.
It has been handed down
by unvarying tradition that the grave
was at the west end of the church,
directly beneath the bells *

A few paces westward from the church are the remains of a strong Norman fortress, around which has been waged many a sturdy fight. It was built by Alan of Brittany, made Earl of Richmond by the Conqueror. The walls of the ruin are of immense thickness, and stand on a commanding eminence nigh a thousand feet above sea level. Just to the south of the fortress is the site of the Roman station of Lavatrae, with the remains of an aqueduct and baths, still to be traced. The Romans were in possession for over three hundred years. Between the Roman time, say the middle of the fifth century, to the coming of the Normans, nigh six hundred years, the history of this place is a blank, although we know this moorland country was held for centuries sturdily by the old Britons, but who firmly, and step by step, were deposed of their lands and driven to the mountains and defiles of the west. Below the Roman station is a picturesque mill and a deep ravine, through which the Greta merrily wanders and sings.

BOWES
Crest.

* " BOWES TRAGEDY ; OR, A PATTERN OF TRUE LOVE.—Roger Wrightson, at the sign of the King's Head, in Bowes, in the N. R. of Yorkshire, courted widow Railton's daughter, at the sign of the George, in the same town, and has done more than a year. On Shrove Tuesday, 1715, he fell sick, and languished till Sunday next but one following, and after saying three times, ' Martha, Martha, come away,' then died. Poor Martha Railton, though privately, took heavily on all that time, and only had declared to her sister and mother

Now we are at Dotheboys Hall again—the place is much the same as described by Dickens. A descendant of Squeers' still dwells there. It is a cold, grey, stark-looking house, its front windows looking on to the ruined castle and the yard, outbuildings, school and dormitories at the back, and the old pump is still there.

Dotheboys Hall.   F. DEAN.

At the doors of this yard Mr. Squeers met Nicholas Nickleby. The wind was howling over the moor. "Come in!" says he. "The wind blows in the door fit to

that if he died she could not live. An honest friend is unworthily blamed for doing what I would have done myself had I known it; for Martha Railton begged of him to go and see young Roger, and tell him she would gladly come and see him, if he thought fit (knowing all his father's family was against her). Roger answered, 'Nay, nay, T—my, our folks will be mad; but tell her I hope I shall recover.' Well, the poor lass, almost dead in sorrow, first sent an orange, but Roger's mother sent it back; yet about three days before his death Martha went. His mother was so civil as to leave her by his bedside, and ordered her daughter Hannah to come away, but she would not. Poor Martha wanted only to speak three words to him, and (although she stayed two hours), yet Hannah would not let her have an opportunity, and so, in a sorrowful manner, she left him. Her book was her constant work Friday, Saturday, and Sunday; and she would oft say to herself, 'Oh! you Hannah! if he dyes my heart will burst.' So on the same Sunday se'night, at five o'clock in the afternoon, the bell was tolled for him, and upon the first toll, Martha lay by her book, got her mother in her arms, with, 'Oh! dear mother, he's dead, I cannot live.' About three minutes after Thomas Petty went in and desired her to be more easy. Her answer was, 'Nay, now my heart is burst!' And so, in mournful cries and prayers, was fainter and fainter, for about three hours, and seemed to breathe her last; but her mother and another girl of the town shrieked aloud, and so called her back again, and stayed her spirit ten or twelve hours longer, and then she died. At last things was brought to this issue, to be buried both in one grave, and the corpse met at the church gate, but Hannah objected against their being buried together, as also she did at her being laid first in the grave; but was answered that a bride has to go first to bed. She, being asked why she should be so proud and inhumane, answered, that she said, 'Martha might have taken fairer on, or have been hanged.' But oh, the loud mourning of friends on both sides at the corpse meeting, and more at the grave; wherein first she was decently laid and then he."

knock a man off his legs." " A true remark ; but the breezes of Stainmoor are invigor-ating."* It is only fifteen miles across the moor to Kirkby Stephen or Brough. Let the tired city-men, by way of change, take our advice, and he will find how much refreshed he is for the stroll and the inhaling of the moorland breeze. As we stepped out for our long tramp over Stainmoor the wind was blowing a hurricane, and an old native remarked to us that the outlook was " raither raffy." Stainmoor is a vast expanse of stunted grass and heather, dreary enough when the storm-clouds of winter sweep dark and scowling, and the winds screech and moan like evil spirits ; but when the heather is in bloom, and the sky above is blue and light, fleecy clouds trail their shadows across the sunlight and the larks sing sweetly in the heavens, and the becks, tinged with their moorland birth, weep in sinuous course onwards. The scene is extremely beautiful.

The great military road of the Roman and the Northmen of a later period ran, as it does to-day, over Stainmoor. Near the centre of this high tableland is the division of the counties of Westmoreland and York, and up to the twelfth century was the dividing line between England and Scotland, and in old days was the resort of savage and lawless men, and, even down to the eighteenth century, the rendezvous of highwaymen and robbers.

God's Bridge, a natural rock which spans the Greta, is a few hundred yards to the south of the road. On the eastern entrance to the moor there are several houses standing by the roadside, and others are fast falling to ruin, whilst here and there a heap of *débris* marks the site of former dwellings. Very ruinous are the buildings which mark the site of the old toll-bar. At Spittal-on-the-Moor there was formerly an inn, a place where the stage-coach changed horses, and passengers alighted for refreshments, and the scene early in the present century of a strange attempt at robbery ; besides conveyance of merchandise was chiefly by the means of pack-horses, strings of 50 or even more crossed and re-crossed Stainmoor from Lancaster and Kendal, *en route* for Darlington, &c., and made this a halting place. This hostel, of coaching and pack-horse days, was no doubt built on the site of an ancient house of entertainment, for even in the Norman period there would be a need of a house of this kind, and in monkish times would be presided over by some holy man, probably a Knight Templar, who, apart from attending to the wants of the inner man, could give spiritual advice and perform other religious duties.

---

* We are under the impression that Dickens, in his description of Dotheboys Hall, must have been consider-ably misinformed as to the manner in which that now notorious place was then conducted, for we have it on the authority of an old pupil there, Mr. Lloyd, that the place was well conducted and the house kept extremely clean. The food was excellent, and the boys had as much as they could eat. There was no such thing as a Smike to be seen there, and there was less punishment than in any other school. We are informed also that Mr. Shaw was a very kind master, and wonderfully attentive to any pupil who was ill. There were schools in the district which would better resemble Dickens' description than the one presided over by Mr. Shaw.

Situated on the highest range of this table-land is the Roi, or Rere Cross, as it is commonly called. It was here, after centuries of bitter warfare, that the kings of England and Scotland met to decide the boundary of the two kingdoms, and so raised this, the "Cross of Kings," on either side of which were engraven the images of the two monarchs; and here it still stands amidst the wild waste of encircling hills and the howling storms and hurricanes of eight hundred years, which have long since erased the images of the founders; a relic of the old world, though shorn of its former size, it still marks an historic deed, and as we stand meditating before it we almost catch an echo of the old border warfare.

We are now on the back-bone of the great Pennine range; from hence the scenes viewed are of the most varied and magnificent description. Away to the west spreads the beautiful vale of the Eden, with the mountains of Lakeland rising boldly forth in the background; to the south-west we look across the nine standards, high seat, Mallerstang, and beyond looms, savage and dark, Wild Boar's Fell, and to the east are the moors of North York, stretching far away between the vales of the Tees and the Swale. The natives still fearfully tell you of strange sights and strange sounds, as of men in tumult, and eerie forms of ghost and warlock, or peradventure a headless

Stainmoor—Rere or Roi Cross.

horsewoman gallops swiftly across the moor, concerning the latter is the following tradition: Once on a time, long centuries ago, when the wolf, wild boar and red deer roamed over this moor, and at about the period the Norman adventurer began to build those immense strongholds in the Eden and Tees valleys, a Saxon chieftain dwelt in a rude fortress on the edge of Stainmoor acknowledging no king as his master, and between him and Fitz-Barnard, the Norman—whose stronghold was by the rushing Tees, near to where the immense castle, whose ruins we now can see, was reared in after years—was a bitter hatred and deadly feud; perhaps from the natural antipathy the two races had to each other, or it may have been over the right of chase over the wide moor, which both claimed as their own. Be this as it may, the two parties had more than once come to blows whilst hunting, and in one encounter several retainers and the daughter of Fitz-Barnard, a beautiful young lady of some twenty summers, were taken prisoners. The object of the chieftain was to make her his wife, and she was treated with all the courtesy and kindness possible in that rude age. All his attempts to win her love were, however, fruitless, and after remaining a prisoner for some time, she was rescued by stratagem, and was being borne triumphantly across the moor, when the Saxon appeared on the scene with a number of retainers and charged madly into the group of rescuers, who were unable to withstand the onslaught, and the chieftain, furious at the thought of losing his fair captive, with one savage stroke severed the head of the young lady from her body; hence the reason of the headless horsewoman often seen galloping over the dreary moor at midnight.

We now pass the source of the Greta, and a little further on the edge of the moor, guarding the pass on the west, is another Roman camp, for these conquerors of the old world held the key of Stainmoor east and west, the two camps being about twelve miles apart; for this was an ancient trackway of the British centuries before the legions of Rome appeared on the scene, in fact it was the main connecting link between the east and west from pre-historic time, and, as such, has been sternly guarded alike by Briton, Roman, Saxon and Norman, for the duration of two thousand years.

Near to the camp above mentioned the road bifurcates, one leading to Brough, the other to Kirkby-Stephen. We follow the latter as far as the "Slip Inn," into which we slip and partake of a good square meal, rest awhile, and listen to the gossip of the landlord about the wild scenery of Upper Swaledale, and then bend away to the right, pass the haunted mansion, which, when tenantless, and as late in the century as the matter-of-fact days of 1896, became suddenly illuminated in the night, as if by electricity, and the interior shone with unwonted brilliancy, the country people flocking from near and far to view the strange phenomena. Soft and subdued sounds from the vale below commingle with the music of the church bells from the towers of Brough, Kirkby Stephen, Musgrave and Warcop.

CHAPTER VIII.

BROUGH AND KIRKBY STEPHEN DISTRICT.

 E now have reached Brough, the hoary ruins of the
castle, a relic of old, holding sentinel and guard over
the town resting under the western edge of Stainmoor. The position, the effect of the *tout ensemble*
seen as you enter Brough from the Kirkby Stephen
road, is both extensive and remarkable. In the foreground are paddocks, hedgerows, old walls, sweet
old lanes, and a few cottages on the right, help the
composition of the picture. Beyond is a belt of trees through which filters the
evening light and where the rooks have established a thriving colony, and the place
resounds with their uncouth melody. Through the branches is seen the battlemented
walls of the church, with its substantial Norman-Gothic tower, and further still,
crowning the next eminence, is the ancient castle keep, rearing its ragged outline
against the sky, as if proud of its heritage, the third fortress which has crowned
this position, and marking three epochs of our history, and the primitive town of
grey and whitewashed houses slumbers peacefully in the vale, and around rises into
the clouds the amphitheatre of hills and mountains, ever changing in hue as the sunlight plays upon them, and feathery mist circles in phantom-like form, lending mystery
and effect to the scene, all forming a picture of great natural beauty.

Brough is the site of the Roman station of " Veterae," and its position can still
be traced in the castle grounds. The church is a large building, and has been recently
restored. The floor of the church is not level, but slopes upwards, following the

course of a bed of limestone. During the Restoration a most interesting slab was discovered, which proved to be in Greek characters, to the memory of one Hermes (Mercury), of Commagene, a Syrian youth, who appears to have lost his life during an expedition against the Kymry, the original inhabitants of Cumberland. The south door is a fine example of decorative Norman work, and the old roof, covered with moss, has a most antique appearance, and seems almost as if robed in a velvet mantle. The stone pedestal of the sun-dial is richly tinted with moss and lichen, as if to produce perfect harmony with the grave knolls around, both small and great, silent monitors on which the daffodils were blooming on our visit.

Brough is noted for its great autumn fair, a mart for the sale of horses and mountain ponies and cattle, to which vast crowds of dealers and others interested

A Mountain Stream.

annually resort. Bull and badger-baiting was a most popular pastime at Brough up to the present century, and the stone into which was affixed the ring to which the bulls were fastened still remains. The Westmoreland men, like the Cumberland men, are famous wrestlers. The landlord of the inn (Steadman's) at which we took up our quarters, has quite a large collection of trophies won in the skilful art of wrestling. His son has also won renown in the ring. Both the food, attendance, and sleeping accommodation at this inn were all that could be desired.

A droll and singular character we fell in with at Brough—Tommy Wilkinson, a sweep by " profession," a tall, lanky old man, who had seen over seventy summers, and his appearance, attired in a battered hat, frock coat, with the sweep's brush and barrow, but the comical expression of features, is not to be easily forgotten.   His remarks were smart and witty, and he was well versed in local information.   Nature had evidently meant him for a gentleman, and he possessed a keen insight into character.   For some contravention of the local bye-laws he had been summoned before the magistrates just previous to our visit, and, in his defence, said : " Gentlemen, I stand before you aged three score years and twelve, and ev lived in Brough all me life, and not yan o' ye that can say Black's me neame ! "   To the question we put to him regarding the weather, he replied : " Duck eggs 'ell be ever sea mich longer in the mornin's.   Indeed, why !   For gobbing up sneaks (worms)."

Now proceeding past Brough, Sowerby, and over the Belah vale, where gentle little purling brooks rippled over pebbly beds, transparent in the sunlight, the rich

Street View, Kirkby Stephen.

green of hedgerow and meadow, the twittering of birds, and the perfume of spring all round.   The labourers toiling in the fields, one of which is employed with hopper strapped in front, scattering the seed broadcast, brings to memory the parable of "The husbandman who went forth to sow," followed by others, with teams of horses harrowing the seed in the earth, formed a series of sweet rural pictures in our walk to Winton, where we observe its curious manorhouse, date 1726.   There are several old houses at this place, with mullioned windows and inscribed slabs over the door lintels. The village of Winton is much more suitable for the residence of the Vicar of Stainmoor, owing chiefly to its position, number of inhabitants, and contiguity to Kirkby Stephen, and possesses features of great interest to the archæologist.   As we passed out of the village we heard the dull sound of the thrasher's primitive flail beating the corn out on the barn floor, calling back memories of another village, and our childhood days.

The mind may have been more easily susceptible to impressions on that beautiful spring morning as we passed through the little village and vale of Hartley, a perfect type of a happy valley, peaceful, rural, secluded ; all unknown to the great busy world it slumbers, just hidden from the vale of the Eden by the land rising slightly higher than the roofs, and on the east by ravine and mountain, stretching far-away south, the village ends under the eminence where once the imposing castle of the Hartleys (known in ancient days as the castle of the Harcla's, *i.e., hard clay*) stood, and Mallerstang and Wild Boar Fell uprear majestically in the background. The sweet little stream wends its course in easy and graceful curves under quaint and rustic bridges down the centre of the street, if street it can be named. On either side the footpath rises and falls in easy undulations by the side of the stream, and the walls and roofs twist in sinuous manner in all that picturesque and fanciful irregularity of outline, and a soft delicious sweetness of colour and secluded rural charm, which are requisite to form an ideal village.

On the prominent hill overlooking the vale of Hartley and Kirkby Stephen, in the vale of the Eden, formerly stood the castle of the Musgraves, and later the De Harclas. A few shrivelled stones still remain to testify of this old stronghold of Sir Andrew de Harcla, warden of the western marches, and whose death, in the reign of Edward II., by the hands of the executioner, he being hung, drawn, and quartered by the order of the king, form a tragic ending to a brilliant career, which marks a dark page in the history of our country. There are many strange legends still recounted of this ancient family, and the people of Westmoreland still believe that Sir Andrew was innocent of the charge for which he suffered death.

From Hartley, a few hundred paces, brings us to Kirkby Stephen, a small market town near the head of the Eden valley, still containing many antique and interesting features. It is composed of one long street with a few side alleys or lanes, with a market place and square in the centre, and here, on market days, the scene is of the most primitive and rural description. Old-time carriers' carts, carrying two or three passengers, probably farmers' wives and daughters, with baskets laden with butter and eggs, the product of the farm for the week, and farmers, with their wives and daughters, in their rickety and unwashed traps, rumbling through the town, or, perchance, a sporting character, mounted on a highly-mettled and raw-boned steed. The confused medley and grouping of various types and characters, and the noise of chaffing and bargaining, adds a picture to the ancient town. The church, with its noble Gothic tower, is an imposing structure, and has of late years been most judiciously restored. The south entrance to the churchyard is beneath a classic porch. A tablet in the wall gives the names of the churchwardens in 1763, and another list of names in 1721. There is a fine peal of eight bells, rung from the ground under the tower. The west end of the nave contains the shaft of a runic cross, with a figure carved on. The interior consists of tower, nave, aisles, and chancel, with side chapels. The ancient custom of ringing the curfew bell was still in existence on our visit. The church contains several mural tablets, but the monuments and effigies to the memories of the Musgrave and Wharton families are indeed of great interest.   Under a canopy in the wall of the south chapel is an ancient altar tomb, bearing the Musgrave shield, and another in the centre of the chapel holds an

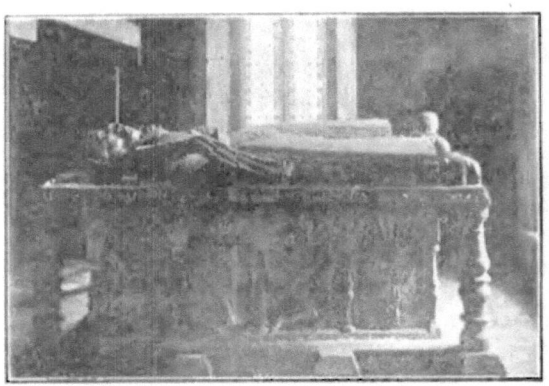

effigy, representing a member of the house of the Musgraves, attired in mail-armour.   At his feet is a lion *couchant*.   In the north chapel, resting on a beautiful alabaster sarcophagus, are the effigies of Thomas Lord Wharton and his two wives.   It was long supposed that the said Lord Wharton and his two wives were interred here, but as we have previously mentioned in our work on "Wharfedale," an exact counterpart of this monument,

Effigies of Lord Wharton and his two Wives.   *f. 1060.*

on which repose the effigies of Lord Wharton and his two wives, rests under the immense chancel arch of Helaugh church, in the Ainsty of York.   Part of the elaborate inscription reads : " My family gave me my name, but my victorious right arm gave me my honour."   In the year 1783 the arch of the vault at Helaugh, having become ruinous, fell in and exposed to view three skeletons, which were supposed to be those of Thomas Lord of Wharton and his two wives, one skeleton being raised above the other on a kind of platform ; so it appears quite evident that he and his wives rest at Helaugh and not at Kirkby Stephen.   The south chapel also contains fragments of runic work : Norman capitals and vestiges of an earlier church ; and the chancel a perfect sedelia and piscina.

The residence of the poet Close, the Westmoreland bard, was in the upper part of the town, and a large sign-board still points to the exact spot.   For sixty years he wrote verses and prose, and annually, for a number of years, issued a Christmas book, which had a large circulation.   He was granted an annuity from the Queen's civil list, which was afterwards suspended ; but a gratuity of a hundred pounds was substituted.

Near the station are the rocks of Stenkrith, where the Eden winds through the deep gorge of freestone rock, into which the waters have worn deep fissures and singular crevices and caldrons, and a walk of some miles up the valley of Mallerstang, with the Eden winding at our feet and High Seat on the east, and Wild Boar Fell towering into the clouds on the south-west. Here the last wild boar, tradition says, was slain by a chieftain of the Musgrave family. Up among the hills to the right is the old home of the Whartons.

Pendragon Castle is one of the smaller Norman keeps, evidently standing amidst the earthworks and vestiges of an earlier structure of defence, which is supposed to have been one of the fortified residences of Uther Pendragon, father of King Arthur, and legend says that deep below the foundations a great treasure has remained hidden ever since the days of Merlin the Arthurian bard.

It was Uther who led the Cymric, and fought so bravely against the Saxons both in the West and North Country. His death was caused by drinking water from a poisoned well, and young Arthur, the peerless knight, succeeded to the royal dignity.

It was evening, and a wild one, on our visit to the old keep. On two previous occasions we had been dis-appointed in not reaching Mallerstang ; this time we were determined, and so passed down the valley during a hurricane of wind and rain, when the howling of the tempest sounded like evil spirits battling in the mountains. It was nearly dark on our arrival, and as we sheltered among the ruins and mused on the mouldering relics, bleached and battered by a thousand winters, bringing to memory stories of the

A Bit of Old Kirkby   EDMUND BOGG.

old border days, the wind howled and shrieked through the crevices of the ruins, ghosts seemed to ride on the skirts of the storm ; voices weird and dismal, echoes of other days. Such a change from what we passed through, where beauty vied with beauty, grandeur with grandeur ; now wood and stone, and wind and water, are moulded into wild and thrilling forms ; we hear the shriek of the weird sisters, and dimly descry Macbeth, blown forth to know his destiny. Hush ! 'tis the spirits of men slain in battle, whilst defending this narrow pass, that sounds dis-mally, and of men who once languished in the dreary dungeon beneath our feet :

I

it is only the wind moaning down the glen. Yet hark to the bugle call and clash of arms! Pull up the drawbridge and down with portcullis! the Picts and Scots and wild men of Galloway are burning and plundering down the valley. Now we see the battle raging, and the curtain rises and falls on scenes of siege, victory, death, and glory, and thus the wind wails and shrieks out its story, and the rain beats piteously on the old walls, but peace has come to the land; no need now for castle, foss, or moat, only those shrivelled bones are left, linking our minds to a mystic past, to tell us of strange battle, adventure, high-born knights, and ladies fair.

Crossby Garrett is three miles from Kirkby Stephen, and stands in the valley, at the foot of Crossby Fell. The church occupies a steep eminence, just to the north of the village. On this hill the early missionary raised the cross, symbol of Christianity, and the village rose in the valley, hence Crossby, the village by the cross. The church is a very interesting structure, and is a conspicuous object for miles around. Legend says that the building was commenced in the valley, and the material for its construction was accordingly brought hither, but in the night-time it was removed by some unseen agency and placed on the summit of the hill, where the edifice was at length reared.

A Village Picture.   1. 8060.

Starting again from Brough we follow the Roman road to Appleby. Hillbeck Hall, with its background of woods and mountain, is on the right, and further is the village of Warcop, beautifully secluded, the land around rich and fertile. The name is said to be derived from an ancient castle which formerly stood near the village, the walls of which were of great strength. The church is a most interesting structure, and, from appearances, has evidently been surrounded by a moat. Here we are reminded of the old story of Dr. Fell's dog. "As clever as Dr. Fell's dog" is still a saying amongst the people. The story is as follows :—Some villagers meeting Dr. Fell in his walk, they mutually commended each other's dog, when the Doctor asked one of them what his dog could do, the villager replied, "Oh, he could do ought ; he would fetch and carry, and lurry any beast or sheep off the moor, and would drive them through any gap he liked. Will your dog do all that, Dr. Fell ?" "Eh !" said the Doctor, "that's nought ; my dog will do all that ; and I will tell you what else he will do, and that is, after he's ta'en the beasts home he'll go back and *stop up the gap !*" Hence the proverb : "As clever as the Vicar of Warcop's dog."

Still onward ! As we pass through the beautiful vale country we are reminded of that magnificent sunset which we witnessed between Warcop and Appleby, the wonderful fascinating and mystical effect of which impressed us greatly. The sun had just drooped below a bank of dark blue truculent clouds of ragged outline, and a delicious yet solemn hush and purple haze of night spreads over the earth. Stretching away from our feet is a flat expanse of wavy green cornland ; on one side of the picture was a clump of dark firs, partly screening the sombre roofs of a farmhouse. Solitary and lonely it appeared in the deepening hues of night. Across the middle distance ran a long straggling row of serried trees, every twig and branch etched out distinctly against the evening light. Further to the right, as if to give contrast, is a dense mass of dark woods, now quiet and restful—a deep peace holds this stilly hour, an inner sense of repose and delight steals in upon the heart, while the air is filled with the perfume from a thousand flowers.

Away westward the peaks and ragged outline of the lake hills are pencilled in sharp outline, and fringed with a delectable glimmer ; and still beyond is a scene of such celestial splendour, surpassing in ethereal loveliness the dream of some fabled shore. Domes, pinnacles, and purple ridges are resplendent with burnished gold, and in the foreground is one huge cumulus cloud, shaped like a lion couched majestic, as if guarding the entrance to some classic sea ; and away over the tops of mountains, and stretching far away into the realms of space, bathed with all the soft luminous hues of gold, crimson, purple, vermilion, and pale cadmium, vessels of stately form and wondrous sail were floating amongst amber isles on a storied sea, and the far-away horizon line tinged with the glory of heaven and the calm of eternity. Such a scene—the outward robe of the thoughts of the divine—never to be transferred on canvas by the hand of man.

CHAPTER IX.

⚬⚬ APPLEBY. ⚬⚬

NOW we have reached the old town of Appleby, standing so stately and restful in the bosom of the vale, the most ancient part, lying to the west of the river, composed chiefly of two streets, running east and west and north and south. The appearance of the town from the high land east of the river is pleasing, and the stretches of water are most charming. Just across the river rises the battlemented walls and tower of Saint Lawrence's Church, and the vicarage, embowered in trees. From the church to the castle gates is a wide thoroughfare, called Boroughgate, still retaining its middle-row, with interesting bits of ancient architecture. Here is the Moot Hall, where the burgesses assembled, a relic of the Mote Hill of ancient times. There are two crosses or pillars. Near to the one at the bottom of the street is the Bull Ring, where the bulls were baited, and a ring let into a stone still testifies to that rude sport. Higher up the street is a quadrangular square of almshouses. This is the Hospital of St. Anne, founded by the Countess of Pembroke (for thirteen widows), and in the walls are to be seen shields and armorial bearings of the families into which the Cliffords have intermarried.

Appleby is the capital of Westmoreland (Westmuirland), or the land of the western meres, and the smallest county town in England, and is a place of great antiquity. Numerous relics of a pre-historic race of people, which inhabited this district long anterior to the Roman period, are to be seen scattered within a few miles of Appleby. The great Roman road, over which we had been travelling, from Rokeby, Bowes, Stainmoor, and Brough, and then north-west to Carlisle, ran within half-a-mile of Appleby, but the nearest station, Redlands, was fully three miles away. After the withdrawal of the Romans, Appleby became a place of strategic importance to the ancient British, and later to the Anglo-Dane. Castle Hill (naturally a strong position), is half circled, and rises in precipitous position above the river. On the west side of the castle is a narrow vale down which filters a small stream called "Doomgate Syke," which empties into the river just to the north of the town.

In pre-Norman times this was a swampy piece of ground, always more or less covered with water; thus, the water cutting off connection from Castle Hill on every side but the south, on which side the fort is protected by immense earthworks and double moats of great depth, the inner one being forty feet deep and eighty feet from crest to crest; in fact the defensive lines of earthworks excite wonder, and almost amazement, in the mind of the spectator, and shows the long struggle which has been waged before the old British have been ousted by the invading Angle or Dane. A long list of Danish village names bearing the terminal "by," go far to prove that

Cæsar's Tower, Appleby Castle.

after the sack of Carlisle in the ninth century the wave of Danish conquest swept down the fruitful Eden valley, and at that period probably ousting and capturing the entrenched position of the old British, for we know the latter were in possession of the lake country two centuries later. After this raid and conquest came the gradual settling of an alien race. Thus we have a dozen or more villages whose origin can be traced to this influx of the Scandinavian, as, for instance, Scotby, Lazonby, Gilmonby, Somerby, Crossby, Melmerby, Kirkby, Sowerby, Langwathby, Appleby, Wailby, Watelyby, &c. In the reign of Edward the Confessor it must have been of some importance, both as regards population and strength, for on the division of Northumberland (North-Humber-land) it gave its name to a shire, "Appelbi-Schir," and to this period, say after the ninth or tenth centuries, must be ascribed the building of the two churches, St. Michael's and St. Lawrence's. Twice, at the least, was the castle and town destroyed by the Scots, first in 1173 and again in 1388, by a furious raid, made by the Douglases, after which, for the space of one hundred and fifty years, it lay in ruins; indeed, the place never rose again to its former size and prosperity. Nine parts of it still remain in ruins, and instead of twenty marks a year it only paid two marks.

The foundations of buildings and even streets have been laid bare, thus proving the devastation and havoc wrought by these inroads of the Scots.

Annie Clifford, the celebrated Countess of Pembroke, fortified and garrisoned the castle in the cause of King Charles, 1641, and gave the command of it to Philip Musgrave. However, in 1648 it capitulated to Cromwell's forces, when the whole wreck of the royal army, which had just previously blockaded Cockermouth, gave themselves up prisoners of war, all but the undaunted Countess, who seems to have been left alone, and she was right loyal, "hip and thigh," and would not yield until the old castle of her ancestors became shattered and rent by the guns of the enemy. When the proscription of Charles II. was issued by Cromwell, not a man in the little capital would raise his voice to proclaim it, "so the soldiers had recourse to a fellow in the market, an unclean bird, hatched at Kirkby Stephen (the nest of all traitors), who proclaimed it aloud, while the people stopped their ears and hearts and had nothing open but their eyes, which were filled with tears; and when the Protector, to punish them for their obstinacy, issued a restrictive charter, they stuck to their old one, and could not be induced to yield it up." At the Restoration the mayor would not handle the staff of authority nor suffer the oath to be administered to him until he had taken Cromwell's charter and, in the presence of all the court, cut it in pieces with his own hand (a daring deed, but he was too wise a man to do it in Oliver's lifetime). Then looking about he espied some tailors, and, casting it to them, with the remark "that it should never be a measure to them." "Bravo, little Mayor of Appleby!" says one writer, "he knew that grim Oliver and many of his stern old Ironsides were then in their graves, and so the little dog played with the once-dreaded paws of the dead lion." The Restoration, we are told, was celebrated at Appleby with as many bonfires as there were houses in the town. "After service was done at the church the Countess of Pembroke, with the aldermen and gentry of the county, with the sound of trumpets and an imperial crown carried before them, ascended the stately scaffolds at each end of the town, hung with cloth and arras of gold, when they proclaimed, prayed for, and drank the health of the king on their knees. The aged countess seemed young again to grace the solemnity.

What an imposing spectacle this scene would form for a nineteenth century person to gaze upon! Yet in spite of all this loyalty to the House of Stuart, James II.

demanded all the old charters of Appleby to be delivered up. This is in keeping with the unstableness of his whole conduct, and was a most exacting and arbitrary proceeding. The charters have never since been heard of The countess was a woman of remarkably strong and indomitable will power, and to none would she yield an inch of her rights." There is a story which will illustrate her firmness. In her old age the court tried to force a person into one of her boroughs who was most objectionable to her. This proceeding her high spirit would not tolerate, hence the following outburst, in a letter to the prime minister :—" I have been bullied by an usurper ; I have been neglected by a court ; but I will not be dictated to by a subject ; your man shall not stand ! " After the death of her second husband she spent her time and money in deeds of charity and the building and repairing of numerous castles and churches, besides the keep of Appleby, the castles of Skipton, Brougham, Pendragon, Brough, and Barden Tower, the churches of Skipton, Ninekirks, Brougham, Mallerstang, and Appleby were either rebuilt or restored.

The church of Saint Lawrence, at the latter place, dates from the twelfth century ; for, in 1173, the town, as we have said, was sacked and burned by the Scots, whilst in charge of Gospatric, son of Orm, who had a fine of five hundred marks imposed on him and smaller sums upon the other head men for allowing the castle to be surprised and stormed and the town burnt. The church was destroyed in the general ruin attendant on this raid, and two years later, in 1176, it was rebuilt by the orders of the king, and a strong tower added, to act as a place of refuge and defence in the time of war, and thus it remained without much alteration for nigh 500 years, until the good Countess of Pembroke restored it at a cost of 700 pounds, and in her own words, she says : " I caused a vault to be made in the north-east corner of the church for myself to be buried in," and there, in the north side of the chancel, in the chantry chapel, is the vault of the Cliffords, on which rests an effigy of Lady Annie Clifford, of glorious memory, and on her tomb are the armorial bearings of her

Arms of the Cliffords.

ancestors, dating back to the days of the early Norman kings. Another recumbent figure within the altar rails is to the memory of Eleanor, Countess of Cumberland, mother of Lady Annie. The church is spacious, yet lacking the interest we might expect to find here. For magnificence and splendour of armorial bearings, richness and delicacy of workmanship, the tombs of Lady Annie and her mother at Appleby do not at all vie with the tombs of the Cliffords at Skipton, and here, as one of the most worthy members of the great Clifford family, she ought to have rested adorned, but it was the filial love for her mother which prompted her to be buried at Appleby.

At the top of the street, near the entrance-gate to the castle grounds, stands the Countess Pillar, on which are inscribed the following lines :—

> "Retain your loyalty,
> Preserve your rights."

Passing the entrance-gate we reach the seat of the Earl of Hotam. The present structure has been built upon the site and partly into the wall of the old castle. The

Knights Templars.

venerable and majestic keep, known as Cæsar's tower, stands at the west end of the quadrangular green, testifying to the strength and importance of this stronghold in past centuries, and the remains of other earthworks also tell of an earlier structure of defence. The hall, amongst many interesting pictures and ancient furniture, contains the the magnificent suit of armour worn by George Clifford in the tilt-yard, as champion to his royal mistress, Queen Elizabeth. It is richly gilt and embossed in gold, and ornamented with *fleurs-de-lis*, and his horse-armour is of equal splendour. This is said to be the finest suit of armour extant. George, the third Earl of Cumberland, was one of the most noted men of his time, and one of the forty peers who tried the unfortunate Mary, Queen of Scots, and was also one of the four charged to carry out the execution.

The views from the battlements of Cæsar's tower are both extensive and beautiful, the vale of the Eden winding, dreamlike, beneath.

The names Battlebarrow, Doomgate, Bondgate, Gallows Hill, Douglas Ing, and Weind Row are strangely suggestive of the past.

Crossing the bridge again we follow the Great North Road to Crackenthorpe. At the ancient Manor House dwell the Machells, who claim descent from Malus Colutus, a Roman centurion. Apart from any legendary claim, there is certain evidence of their possession of the estate here for upwards of 800 years.

The village of Long Marton and its church is very interesting. Kirkbythore, two miles away, is the site of a Roman station or camp. This district has yielded many antiquities, and during the rebuilding of the bridge over Troutbeck in 1838, an immense quantity of coins and ancient jewellery were discovered embedded in the old foundations. Two miles further is the village of Sowerby, granted in the reign of the second Henry to the Knights Templars,* hence its present name Temple Sowerby. It is a beautiful village, and the scenes along the river Eden, which here slightly bends to the north-east, are very charming. Formerly it was a custom at this village for the men to assemble on the green on the first of May, to compete for several prizes, three of which were reserved for the singular contest in the noble art of lying, the inhabitants to be the judges. The first prize was a grindstone, a useful article for a villager ; the second was a hone or wetstone, useful in sharpening knives, razors, or small tools ; the third prize was a wetstone of an inferior description. The candidate who contests for the prize begins a story—the most absurd and improbable— the more marvellous and romantic the better. After a considerable part of the day is spent in foolish-like pastimes and games at wrestling, the day often ended in a free fight or two. The Bishop of Carlisle was once passing through the village when this festival was in full swing. He inquired the reason of the assembly of the villagers, and on being made aware of the facts, he lectured the people rather severely on the sin and foolishness of such a diversion. " For my part," the Bishop said, " I never told a lie in my life ; " upon hearing this the judge immediately awarded the hone to his Lordship, and when he refused to accept it he threw it into his carriage after him, telling him that in the future it would be useful to sharpen *wits* with.

---

* The Knights Templars, an order of monkish warriors, which was formed soon after the capture of Jerusalem from the Saracens, by the Crusaders, under Godfrey de Bouillon, 1099. They resided near the Temple in the Holy City, hence the name of Templar, or Knights of the Temple. They observed many of the monastic rules, and made a vow to defend the Holy Sepulchre from the infidel, and also to entertain pilgrims who went to Jerusalem for devotion, and to guard them in safety when visiting the scenes of our Saviour's wanderings in the Holy Land. Their dress was white, with a red cross on their breasts. They were composed of men from all nations in Christendom, and were possessed of great riches ; in this country they held many a rich castle and manor. When the Crusaders were on the march, the Knights Templars led the van, and the Knights of St. John brought up the rear. St. Bernard says of these Knights : " They detest cards and dice, and abominate all shows, songs, and discourse of a loose nature. When they enter into a battle, they arm themselves with faith within, and steel without ; having no ornament either upon themselves or their horses. Their arms are their only finery, and they make use of them with courage, not being daunted either at the number or force of the barbarians." For such a cause was formed this great chivalrous order of Knights Templars. In after time, as they acquired more wealth, they also grew remiss in the practice of their former virtues, until at length their order was finally suppressed. At Temple Sowerby there was also an hospital entirely supported and attended to by these Knights Templars for the benefit of pilgrims and warfarers.

CHAPTER X.

VALE OF THE LOWTHER.

GAIN diverging some twelve miles west from the Eden country, we renew our wanderings in the Vale of the Lowther, which flows for several miles along the eastern fringe of Lakeland. The Lowther river rises and has its numerous feeders in High Street, Hater Fell, Blea Water, Kidsty Pike, whilst to the east other streams rise in Harrop Pike and Shap Fells, flow through Mossdale and Swindale and unite at Bampton, and thence through the beautiful Vale of the Lowther, past Lowther Park and Askham Village, passing Brougham Hall, and entering the Eamont near the ruins of Brougham Castle. The ruins of the Abbey of Shap lie embosomed in a deep and lovely vale, on the west side of the river, a spot well adapted for religious seclusion, hid, as it were, from the world, and surrounded on every side by bleak moorland.

Hawes Water is a very small lake, being less than three miles in length, and not much more than a quarter in breadth in its widest part. The situation of the water amongst the mountains is most wildly picturesque. On the south-east side is a steep wood, called Naddle Forest, which casts a deep solemn shadow across half the lake. At the upper end, Kidsty Pike on one hand, Silside Pike and Hater Fell in the immediate background, towers high above all.

The grey shades of a Sabbath evening in October were fast drawing a silent mantle over hill, dale, and water, as we wandered across the Bampton Moors, until we reached the highest point, and looked down on the lake for the first time ; the silence amongst the hills was most profound, neither the sky above, or the earth beneath being disturbed by any force. The lake, far below, lay deep, placid, and sombre, the only contrast being when the gentle breeze faintly rippled the surface of the water, and on one side the dark hues of Naddle Forest were reflected in darker form beneath. A fringe of land juts out into the lake, so as almost to form two sheets of water.

THE SUN WORSHIPPERS

From our position we could see the grey mountain road turning and twining round the foot of the serried hill, and along the edge of the lake, where some half dozen houses and farms can be discerned resting under the hills, which rise in billowy form, tier above tier, half hidden in by the deepening shadow of night.

The silver grey and green of moss and rock, rendered more harmonious in tone by gorse and bracken, now assuming the deep yellow tinge of Autumn. Yet even here, as we rest, musing, undisturbed amidst scenes formed by the convulsions of

Nature ages ago, and far away from the innovation of man, we can see a thin curling line of smoke, and hear the sound of the locomotive speeding on its way to some busy hive of industry ; soon the smoke disappears and the train passes out of hearing. The gloaming silently steals apace ; all is hushed in Nature's temple ; the veil of night, with its dark shadows, brings forth from the mist of ages visions of the old British warriors, who fought, worshipped, and were buried in the solitude of the moors around, as the numerous stone circles, monoliths, and other pre-historic monuments and cairn in the district of Shap, Bampton, Heltondale, and at Moor Divock still testify.

Turning our steps across the hills, past tarn and morass, awesome and lonely in the evening light ; then over the waste of moorland, across which sweetly sounded the pealing bells of Bampton Church, typical of the religion of the Christian Church of the present, and a striking contrast to those rude circles and monoliths, telling of dark superstition of the past ages. Mistaking our course, we went stumbling along for some time evidently lost, and it was now dusk—luckily we were guided to a moorland farm by the sound of children's voices, who, courteously, at our request guided us over the moor. An old water mill, with its wheel and sound of falling water, is certainly a pleasing feature, and marks a lovely spot just before passing into the Bampton road ; from whence could be heard the bellowing of stags in Lowther Park, some three or four miles away, sounding in the stillness of night like roaring lions thirsting for prey. Now forward through Helton, with its echoes of the past, and clinging to the hillside on the west bank of the Lowther we reach Askham, our destination for the night.

Reverting for a moment, before proceeding, to briefly mention the paths from the south to Hawes Water, are by way of Kentmere and High Street, 2,700 feet, along whose ridge ran a Roman road, said to be the highest in England, hence High Street. Mardale Green is near the head of the lake. Here is an inn, the Dun Bull, where the traveller can obtain needful refreshment. Another route from Windermere is by the vale of Troutbeck, and over by Scot's Rake and Thornthwaite Crag. From Patterdale the path leads by way of Low Hartsope, along the side of a wild torrent, past the east side of Hayes Water to the head of the stream, thence to the left over the summit of the mountain and forward to Mardale. The only danger of mishap to the tourist in the above mentioned routes, is that of being caught in a storm of mist and rain ; at such time there is real danger, yet the effect of the light and shadow, gloom and grandeur, showers sweeping the hill tops, huge clouds of mist—like some awful dream shrouding the mountains in darkness, then as suddenly dissolving into patches, and gliding mysteriously away like some ariel shreds of a lost world, is truly wonderful in panoramic effect and beauty. The writer and a friend one morning left Ambleside intending to dine at Mardale, but after wandering among the mountains all the day, instead of reaching the above place, arrived at Howtown, Ulleswater, at eleven in the evening. A light shower or two of rain swept over the hills as we toiled up the twining road to the White House—the Kirkstone Pass Inn. Here, bending to the right, we left the road and every sign of track, and turned into the hills, where for several hours we wandered in silence, except for the sound of our own voices and footsteps, and the noise of unruly torrents leaping from the hills. The extreme wildness and majesty, and the wonderful effects of mist and cloud, accompanied by all the marvellous transforming hues and grades of sunlight and shadow—sometimes we were wreathed in a mist cloud, which, like a curtain of night, enveloped mountain and vale in its embrace. Again the sky was blue overhead, whilst beneath was the cloud shutting the world beneath from gaze. Then as if angered, sullenly rolling away under the effect of some strong unseen agency revealing to our astonished gaze a deep ravine, along whose brink, all unknown, we had been walking. One most charming atmospheric effect which we can never forget, was obtained from the heights of Stony Cove, some two thousand five hundred feet. We looked down the vale of Troutbeck,

winding and twining so mysteriously through mountains and clouds to Lake Windermere, which could be discerned resting as it were, in the clouds, for the water, wreathed in a golden network of mist, shone with the brilliancy of molten silver, appearing to be framed or suspended in the clouds, for neither hill or any other object were visible. Instead of crossing High Street and passing eastward to Blea Tarn, we bore too much to the north, and thus after toiling for hours in the mountains, through drizzling showers and grey vapour, with the accompaniment of a stray gleam of sunshine and shadow, we arrived at Low Hartsope at five in the afternoon, the first house we had seen during our eight hours' wandering. Here we were provided with a good tea, and, thoroughly refreshed, we resumed our journey, determined to sleep at Mardale. We were unable to obtain definite instructions as to the route, we inquired particularly if we should pass Hayes Water before bearing to the left, but were told by the farmer, who had only been at Mardale once, to turn to the left before reaching the Tarn; trouble was in store for us on that night, for after struggling up the mountains, through rain and mist-cloud, and the deepening shadows, we again lost our bearings on Briggendale, and after wading through several noisy torrents and round the north base of Kidsty Pike—the mountains looming out like huge giants, silent and majestic in their loneliness. On the slopes of the Pike, we sighted a herd of red deer; owing to the wreathing of the mist we had approached them unseen, and their graceful movements, as they timidly peered down at us, and then sped into darkness, gave interest to a scene that was otherwise becoming wearisome. Now we struck a large stream, which we followed for two or three miles, thinking meanwhile, by following it, we must sooner or later arrive at Hawes Water. Passing into a rough trackway, evident signs of civilization, we reached a farm, but the occupants had retired to rest, and evidently to sleep, for only after repeated knocking, a head was thrust forth, and a voice exclaimed, "Wha's there?" "How far are we from the Dun Bull Inn, Mardale?" "In ta teens a miles; ye'll nivver get there te neet," and sure enough to our surprise, we discovered that for the last hour or more, we had been traversing Martindale, for a bend in the road disclosed to our view the modest church of Martindale, a spot well known to us. We found lodgings for the night at Howtown, where the good people soon had a roaring fire, and after we

A Mountain Road, Kirkstone.

retired to rest, spread our attire to dry. Next morning we were up betimes and took a stroll on Swarth Fell, paid a hurried visit to a few old scenes, and then took boat up Ulleswater, and the coach from Patterdale Hotel to Windermere, over Kirkston Pass, etc., a most enjoyable drive although thoroughly fatigued with the previous day's wild tramp.

The sublimity and majesty of the effect of mist and rain-cloud witnessed, amply repays, for once in a while, the aching bones and the discomfort of a thorough drenching. Yet it is not given to everyone to fully appreciate and enjoy these sublime phases of nature; for instance, a friend of the writer, and a great enthusiast on lake and mountain scenery, took two of his neighbours for a day or two to the lakes, he having previously given them glowing accounts of the scenery. The first day was spent in climbing Helvellyn, etc. Unfortunately for the comfort of his friends, the day was rather misty, yet giving forth wonderful effects and vistas on lake and mountain. For a long time his companions trudged on in silence ; at last one of them spoke out as follows : " Ah say, Jack, if this is what tha calls thee lake scenery, ah think nout ta it. Ah don't naw wheer tha puts thee een. I'm shure its God help thaa, for tha'll niver be able to help thee self."

Askham is a most picturesque and rural village on the west bank of the Lowther river, some five miles from Penrith. The situation is both romantic and charming. The houses are irregularly scattered on the borders, and high sloping banks of a large green, being more attractive by the number of large trees, and the beautiful park and woods of Lowther on one hand, and Fell on the other. It is used as a rendezvous for all kinds of disabled implements of husbandry, stick heaps, etc., where children and flocks of geese, ducks, and fowls disport at pleasure. It was against the wish of one man at least that we should not do likewise during our stay at Askham. The cottage, our abode during our visit, was near the centre of the green. One night, after retiring to rest, we were disturbed by the angry voice of an over-officious game watcher. This person had, an hour or so earlier, eyed us over, as I thought, rather suspiciously at the village inn near by. Whether he had taken a wee drop too much, and, under such conditions, had mistaken us for dangerous poachers, we knew not ; anyhow, at closing time, and just after we had retired for the evening, a loud knock sounded on the door, and on our host opening it, the game-keeper, a big, burly, sour-looking fellow, enquired if two men—strangers to the village—were staying at his house. On our host answering in the affirmative, he questioned him regarding our antecedents, business, and object in staying at Askham. On being told that we were in bed, and it would be best for him to call and interview us in the morning, he declined to do so, and threatened to fetch the village constable, and have us arrested as suspicious characters. Our bed-room window being immediately over the doorway, and the evening being warm, it was wide open, and thus we heard everything which passed. At first we were indignant, but soon the outrageous demands of the keeper caused us to become inwardly convulsed with laughter. Our host expostulated with him, and told him to be careful before proceeding to such extremities, acquainting him with the fact that we had obtained an interview with the Countess of Lonsdale, and had written per-mission to sketch or wander on any portion of the estate. This the keeper said was false, and still persisted in his original charge, the scene being only terminated by closing and bolting the door in his face, and we could hear the fellow pass over the green growling vengeance on our heads. We give this fact to show that there still remains in certain districts that high-handedness and overbearing officiousness, more akin to the sixteenth century than the closing part of the nineteenth. Had we apprised the Countess of the fact, no doubt the insolent and ill-bred fellow would have been summarily dismissed.

The stream is crossed at the foot of the village by a very rustic old bridge, and near to, on the west bank of the river, stands Askham Hall, now the Rectory, belonging to Lowther Church. "Thomas Sandford, Esquire, for this paid meat and hyre, the year of our Savioure, XV hundredd and seventy foure." It stands between the village and the river, which is here contracted into a narrow gorge. The house is really a massive peel tower, sheltered on two sides by dense woodland, and beautified by ever-changing foliage. The front is protected by a deep hollow or moat, in former days being filled with water, and now forms a very beautiful garden.

There is a very ancient and curious gateway to the courtyard, decorated with rope moulding. Askham Church, on the opposite side of the road, is situated on the first plateau above the sounding river, and its grey walls stand out in fine relief against a background of deep green woods. From the church we cross over to Lowther Castle, situated in a beautiful timbered park, comprising several hundred acres, where a herd of red deer roam, and in the rutting season the stags make the place resound with their bellowing. The castle, a magnificent Windsor of the north, stands in palatial splendour, with its numerous towers, terraces, and battlements, impressing the beholder with the dignity and importance of the Lowther Family.

Lowther Church (half circled by the river, which here winds deep below, ever singing a requiem to the dead as it passes the graveyard) consists of nave, chancel, aisles, and two chapels, filled with memorials of the family. In one reposes the effigy of Sir Richard, who died early in the 17th century. The south aisle also contains several memorials of the Lonsdales. Four semi-circular arches divide the nave from the aisle, and date from the late Norman period. The church has been thoroughly renovated, and was most beautiful on our visit, being adorned with fruits of the woods and fields for harvest thanksgiving. The Lowthers are said to have been settled in Westmoreland generations before the Conquest. The name is supposed to be Danish, and derived from the words "Loth" and "er," signifying fortune and honour. However this may be, ever since the 12th century, the period when the Westmorelands became annexed to the English Crown, has there been a Lowther of Lowther; the present castle is probably the fourth structure which has stood on or near this spot. The one standing in the 16th century was in the shape of the letter H, a central building, joined on to two tower-like wings. The Lowthers have ever been notable men in the cause of the country, and although rarely have they increased their estates by marriage, yet their wealth and possessions have been accumulating through the centuries until they have become equal to princes in a social position, frequently entertaining monarchs as their guests.

Vale of the Lowther, Lowther Park.   FROM A PHOTO BY E. BOGG.

A Sir Hugh de Lowther, a notable soldier, took part in the Wars of France and fought under Henry the Fifth at Agincourt. In the reign of Queen Bess, Sir Richard Lowther, as Lord Warden of the Western Marches, met Queen Mary when she landed on English soil, after the disastrous battle of Langside, and it was whilst she was in the custody of the nobleman that she was visited by the Duke of Norfolk, for which Sir Richard incurred the severe displeasure of Elizabeth. A Sir John Lowther greatly distinguished himself in the cause of William and Mary, by seizing a vessel laden with arms and ammunition, laying in Workington Harbour (for the use of the garrison at Carlisle), then in the service of King James.

K

This was done before the landing of the Prince of Orange, and if the latter had failed in his expedition, it would have been a sorry day for Sir John.

De Quincey says of Sir James Lowther,* the first Lord Lonsdale :—" He was a true feudal chieftain, and in the very approaches to his mansion, in the style of his equipage, or whatever else was likely to meet the public eye, he delighted to express his disdain of modern refinement by the haughty carelessness of his magnificence. The coach in which he used to visit Penrith was old and neglected ; his horses fine and untrimmed, and such was the impression diffused about him by his gloomy temper and his habits of oppression, that, according to the declaration of a Penrith contemporary of the old despot, the streets were silent as he traversed them, and an awe sat upon many faces. In his park you saw some of the most magnificent timber in the kingdom—trees that were coeval with the feuds of York and Lancaster, yews that perhaps had furnished bows to Cœur de Lion, and oak that might have built a navy. All was savage

Clifton Peel Tower.

grandeur about these native forests ; their sweeping lawns and glades had been unapproached for centuries, it might be, by the hand of art ; and amongst them roamed, not the timid fallow deer, but thundering droves of wild horses ! Superstition made his 'ghost' more terrible and notorious after his death than the veritable 'despot' had been during his life." Mr. Sullivan says :—" He was with difficulty buried, and whilst the clergyman was praying over him, he very nearly knocked the reverend gentleman from his desk ! When placed in the grave, the power of creating alarm was not interred with his bones. There were disturbances in the hall, noises

* There is a story of how the eccentric Sir James Lowther fell desperately in love with a young woman of no connection, whom he casually met. He induced her to live with him, hired a handsome residence in Hampshire, kept her a large establishment, and was passionately fond of her society. It is doubtful whether his love was returned, or the lady was very happy in the midst of her splendour. She was, however, taken seriously ill and died, and so great was the grief of the earl, that none of his servants durst mention the subject in his presence. The body remained unburied for a considerable period, until the servants, who, unlike their master, had not lost their sense of smell, found it impossible to continue in the house, and so steps were taken to have the corpse removed. His favourite valet undertook to speak to his lord, but no sooner had he mentioned the subject than he was driven from the room, and ordered never to speak to his master again. At length, however, the body was deposited in a tomb at Paddington, which he had ordered to be prepared for its reception ; and a detachment of the Cumberland Militia sent to London to mount guard night and day until the tomb was finished ; but he himself was for a long time overwhelmed with grief, and continued to wear deep mourning for her whom he had loved so well and so soon lost. Such are the strange stories still told of this nobleman.

in the stables; neither men nor animals were suffered to rest. At length, after many an effort, a priest laid him under a large rock called Wallow Crag, and laid him for ever. The mind and character of his successor, the second earl, was very different."

Two miles east from Lowther is Clifton, the scene of the battle of Clifton Moor, fought between Prince Charles the Pretender and the Duke of Cumberland. Both parties claimed the victory. However, after the engagement the highlanders retreated in the direction of Carlisle, whilst the Duke and his men slept for the night on the scene of the engagement.

The village of Clifton possesses an interesting and very ancient church, also a massive peel tower of the fifteenth century. The church is dedicated to St. Cuthbert, and is one of the spots where the monks, bearing the body of the Saint, rested awhile during their long and weary pilgrimages. The church stands on a slight eminence overlooking the roadway. The structure wears a most venerable and antique appearance. The porch is beautifully decorated with ivy. A sun-dial is mounted on the shaft of an ancient churchyard cross. Clifton belongs to the Wyberghs, and has done since the days of Edward the Third. A tablet in the church has the following inscription:—

CREST OF THE WYBERGHS
CLIFTON HALL.

Wm. de Wpbergh

married Eleanor, ye only daughter and sole Heiress of Gilbert de Eugam of Clifton, in ye County of Westmorld in ye 38 of R. Edwd. ye 3rd. By such Eleanor came ye manor of Clifton to ye Wyberghs.*

The strong peel tower, with its stout walls and battlements, in close contiguity to the church, now stands peacefully enough in the midst of a farm-yard, and surrounded by corn ricks. Its days of warfare are passed, yet its appearance appeals strongly to the imagination, and to the times when might was right. It is now used for a combination of domestic and farmyard purposes.

Proceeding a mile or so from Clifton, we bear to the right, skirting Brougham Park, where the Hall, the seat of the Brougham family, stands so charmingly situated on the bank of the Lowther river. It is a most interesting place. Near by is a fine old church dedicated to St. Wilfred. The Hall was the residence of the illustrious

---

* The Wayberghs, or Wyberghs, are a very ancient family; they gave their name to a small parish in western lakeland, namely, Waberthwaite, on the south shore of the Esk.

Lord Brougham, Lord Chancellor of England. A mile further east, and some two miles from Penrith, on the south bank of the Eamont, just immediately below where that river joins with the river Lowther, stand the ruins of Brougham Castle.

The surroundings are most picturesque, and is the site of the Roman Camp of Brovacum. The place is well chosen, and would be almost impregnable in the old days. The ruins of the castle are extensive, and from them we learn the former magnificence of the place, and the power and glory of the Clifford family. From an artistic point of view, not geographical or architectural, the element of beauty and impressiveness, combined with sentiment, colour and technique, is most absorbing to a true student of nature. The castle stands grim and ragged, like the mighty wreck of some stranded ship. It was not always thus—the mute memorials tell us of belted

Brougham Castle.

knight, the tramp of armies, and the noise of war. To-day the scene is peaceable enough, crows caw and croak as they flit in and around the ruin, the sun throws warm rays on the old sand-stone walls, light-ing it with an almost luminous brilliancy, the other part sombre in deep shadow ; grass and rank vegetation thrive

in the walls and courtyard, and the Eamont flows sweetly past, sparkling into beautiful wavelets, singing its lullaby song as of yore.

A deep moat and other defensive work are still visible. The castle came into the possession of the Cliffords, by the marriage of Roger de Clifford with an heiress of the Vetteriponts, Barons of Westmoreland, an important family who have left their impress on the scroll of fame. It was a member of this house, who at Senlac, rescued and remounted William Mallett, whose horse had been killed, and the knight placed in the greatest jeopardy.

During the possession of the Vetteriponts the place was known as the House of Brougham. It was strengthened and castellated by Roger de Clifford, who, over the inner gateway, caused to be carved the inscription : " This made Roger," alluding no doubt to the rise in his fortunes by his marriage with an heiress. An ancestor of this Roger, Walter de Clifford, was father of "Fayre Rosamund," Mistress of Henry the Second, and mother, by the King, of the gallant William Longspere, or Longspear, Earl of Salisbury.

In the time of the first Robert de Clifford, Edward Baliol, King of Scotland, stayed some time with him at Brougham, and other places. During his visit they coursed a stag, with a single hound, out of Whinfell Forest to Red Kirke in Scotland, and back again to the same place. Being both spent, the stag leaped over the pales, and died there ; but the dog, attempting to leap, fell, and died on the opposite side. As a memorial of this incident, the stag's horns were nailed upon a tree close by, and the dog being named Hercules, this couplet obtained currency amongst the people :

> "Hercules kill'd Hart-a-grease,
> And Hart-a-grease killed Hercules."

> * * * *

> " Then went they down into a laund,
> These noble archers three ;
> Eche of them slew a hart of grease,
> The best that they could see."
> — *Song of Adam Bell.*

In course of time, it is stated, the horns became grafted, as it were, upon the tree, by reason of the bark growing over their root, and there they remained more than three centuries, till, in the year 1648, one of the branches was broken off, and ten years afterwards the remainder was secretly taken down. " So now," says Lady Ann Clifford, in her Diary, " there is no part thereof remaining, the tree itself being so decayed, and the bark of it so peeled off that it cannot last long ; whereby we may see that time brings to forgetfulness many memorable things in this world—be they ever so carefully preserved—for this tree with the hart's horn in it, was a thing of much note in these parts."

" Here stood an oak, that long had borne, affixed
　To his huge trunk, or, with more subtle art,
Among its withering topmost branches mixed,
　The palmy antlers of a hunted Hart,
Whom the dog, Hercules, pursued—his part
Each desperately sustaining, till at last
Both sank and died, the life-veins of the chased
And chaser bursting here with one dire smart.

Mutual the victory, mutual the defeat !
High was the trophy hung with pitiless pride,
Say, rather, with that generous sympathy
That wants not, even in rudest breasts, a seat ;
　And for this feeling's sake, let no one chide
Verse that would guard thy memory.
　　　　—*Hart's-Horn Tree."*

Saint Ninian, a British bishop, said to have been a native of Galloway, preached and baptized the people in the Eamont, at Brougham, and a church was soon afterwards erected, some two miles lower down the river; and in memory of the bishop's visit was dedicated to St. Ninian, hence the appellation Nine Churches (nino—nine).

Half-a-mile north from Brougham Castle we reach Penrith, pleasantly situated and sheltered from the north by the land rising considerably up to the beacon, from whence magnificent and far-reaching views can be obtained. Southward the town

Street Scene, Penrith.   FROM A PHOTO. BY E. BOGG.

looks over the lovely pastures and wooded vales of the Eden, the Eamont, and the Lowther, on the verge of which, tower in amphitheatrical form, hills and crags, the most wild and grand in England. In the east, Cross Fell, Stainmore, and the great Penine Range. South, is Wild Boar's Fell, and High Seat. West, the peaks above Ulleswater and Hawes Water crown the scene with wildness and beauty, with the grand crest of Helvellyn and Skiddaw showing out bold and majestic. The name of the town is said to be derived from Pen—a Hill, Rith—or Rhudd, the red hill.

It is a place of great antiquity, and is supposed to have been inhabited with a large population for those early times. Such names as Penruddock, Pendragon, Blencowe, Blencathara, and the relics around —for instance, the Round Table, Maybrough, the Giant's Grave, the numerous stone circles, etc., all suggest to us memorials of an ancient British kingdom, with Penrith as its capital.

It was totally destroyed by the influx of Caledonians, on the withdrawal of the Romans, about the end of the fifth century, and the present town was then established in the centre of the great forest of Inglewood. From the ninth to the twelfth century it was in the possession of the Scots, and on three occasions, between the above dates and the fourteenth century, the town suffered considerably at their hands. During the reign of Edward the Third, thirty thousand warriors burst on the town like an avalanche, burnt it, and carried off the inhabitants, and sold them like cattle to the highest bidders. In 1715, and again in 1745, the Pretender's forces passed through Penrith ; no opposition of any serious nature was offered them, except on their return, during the last insurrection, when the skirmish took place on Clifton Moor, already

THE GIANTS GRAVE. PENRITH.

GIANTS Thumb

mentioned. The approach to Penrith from the south is very wide and imposing. Anciently it was considered the greatest thoroughfare in the North of England.

There are also several narrow side streets containing curious bits of ancient property. The chief objects of interest are the rude-shaped monuments in the churchyard, the church tower, and the ruins of the castle. The two most remarkable stone pillars, standing on the north side of the church, are venerable objects of antiquity. Tradition reports they were placed over the grave of a mighty warrior and prince, who dwelt in those parts during the old British occupation. His name was Ewen Cæsarius, and his strength and stature were so great that no man in those days was his equal. He was also celebrated as a hunter, and woe be the wild boar which came within measurable distance of his spear or felt the full effect of his club.

The pillars which mark the resting-place of this chief are in the shape of ancient spears, over ten feet in height and fifteen feet apart, standing east and west, parallel with the church, and between, as if to protect the sides of the grave, are four stones, about two feet high, of hog back shape. Before the alteration of the church in the eighteenth century, these stones stood exactly opposite to the north, or devil's door. Whatever object the stones may have been raised to commemorate, they are most remarkable evidence of the antiquity of Penrith, and we seem almost to catch a vista into the past, whilst ruminating before them. A few yards distant is another upright stone with two perforations at the top, as if meant for a cross—this stone is about five feet in height, and is undoubtedly Saxon. We are told that Sir Walter Scott never failed to visit these remains of antiquity, when passing through Penrith.

The church, dedicated to St. Andrew, is, apart from the tower, a plain Corinthian structure, with a flat panelled ceiling, with side galleries, reminding one of a city

Window in which are the Portraits of Richard Plantagenet and Cicely Neville.

tabernacle of the eighteenth century. On the east window over the altar table are two very fine allegorical subjects, representing scenes in the life of our Saviour. There are also rare portraits in stained glass, in a south window, of Richard Plantagenet and his wife, Cicely Neville.

The ancient churchwarden's chest, with its four massive locks, is specially interesting. The modern structure is tacked on to an early Norman tower, the walls of which are of great strength, and has outlived three churches.

The castle ruins, like a giant skeleton, command the town from the west, but are by no means picturesque. Penrith is a good centre from which to visit the many beautiful and historic spots in the district.

Renewing our pilgrimage we pass on to Eamont Bridge. The village is very quaint and interesting, many of the houses dating from the seventeenth century, there is a substantial old bridge, with fluted arches. Opposite the Crown Hotel, and at the junction of the Pooley and North road is King Arthur's Round Table. It consists of a circular area or platform, surrounded by a fosse. The outer embankment seems as if formed for spectators, and the central plateau for the combatants to perform their feats of arms, such as, for instance, Sir Walter mentions in his " Bridal of Triermain."

> " He passed Red Penrith's Table Round,
> For feats of chivalry renowned ;
> Left Mayborough's mound and stones of power,
> By Druids raised in magic hour,
> And traced the Eamont's winding way,
> Till Ulfo's lake beneath him lay."

On the opposite side of the Pooley Bridge road to the Round Table is the Druid's grove, or Mayborough. It is a circular area of some three hundred feet in diameter, surrounded by a mound of pebble stones twelve feet high. The entrance is from the east, and is twelve yards wide within the arc. This district is wonderfully rich in monuments of pre-historic times, and formerly they were much more numerous. This is the region where the most celebrated of King Arthur's knights roamed in search of adventure. It was near Brougham, on the banks of the Eamont, that Sir Lancelot, the noblest knight of the world, slew the mighty giant Tarquin, and liberated three-score knights; and there are many similar feats recorded of these knights.

Barton Church.

It was here, also, in Great Inglewood, or Caledonian Forest, that Paladin Rinaldo wandered in search of fame and adventure; where, amongst "antique shady oaks, the sound of sword against sword was frequently heard."

Yanwath Hall, the one wathe or ford, is situate, as its name implies, by the Eamont, and the old peel tower was built to guard the ford over the river. It is now a farm-house, but the old tower still remains. It was formerly the seat of the Threlkelds. A mile further is Barton Church, crowning a circular eminence, and dedicated to St. Michael. The tower of the church is not very high, but is of immense strength, and has evidently been used as a peel, or place of refuge in time of war. Apart from the strength of the tower, the church could easily be surrounded by water, and from appearances this has often been done in the olden days.

Near by, in the direction of Dalemain, is a good specimen of an ancient manor house, now used as a farm. Its yellow walls, antique windows, and gables form a very interesting picture of a sixteenth-century house. Crossing the Eamont by a wooden bridge, we enter the beautiful park of Dalemain, belonging to the Hasells, where is a large herd of deer which have a good range over Martindale and Place Fells.

Passing the mansion, through beautiful scenery, we reach Dacre Castle, some four miles from Penrith. The fortress is still in a fair state of preservation, and now the

An Interior View, Dacre Castle.   O. BOWEN, FROM PHOTO. BY F. BOGG.

abode of a working man. It is a strong, though plain, building, with battlemented parapets and a square turret at the four corners. Portions of a deep moat can still be traced, and one room is still known as the room of the three kings, from a conference which took place here in 933, during the reign of the good king Athelstan, who had given his sister in marriage to Sithric, King of Northumbria ; but the latter having violated all his obligations to Athelstan, was only saved from swift punishment by death. His sons, Anlaf and Guthred, fled to the court of Constantine, King of Scotland, who, with the assistance of Donal of Strathclyde, attempted to reinstate the refugees in their dominion, but were unsuccessful.

The three kings met at Dacre, and there agreed to terms dictated by Athelstan. Soon after this conference all the Northern Kingdoms were up in arms against the Saxon monarch, and his destruction seemed inevitable. In this huge confederacy were the Kings of Cumbria, Wales, Ireland, and Scotland, assisted by a large Danish fleet of 615 sail, who entered the Humber and occupied Northumbria.

This immense army, composed of many nations, was met by Athelstan on the field of Brunnanburgh, and his army fell on their foes with such terrible onslaught that few returned to their country to carry the dismal tidings of ill-omen. As the Danes, and Irish, and Scotch, fled to their ships, the west Saxons pressed hard in the footsteps of the loathed nations.

"They hewed the fugitives, behind, amain, with swords mill sharp," "while on the battle stead lay five youthful kings, and seven eke of Anlaf's earls." "Constantine, hoary warrior, he had no cause to exult in the communion of swords. Here was his kindred and friends. o'erthrown on the falkstead, in battle slain; and his son he left on the slaughter place, mangled with wounds, young in the fight, thus a terrible vengeance was enacted, but the throne of Athelstan was secured, and his northern subjects humbled. He left behind him a terrible carnage field, the sallowy kite the corse to devour, and the swarty raven with horned nib, and the dusky 'pada,' erne white tailed. the corse to enjoy, greedy war hawk. and the grey beast, wolf of the wood. Carnage greater has not been in this island ever yet, of people slain before this. by edges of swords, as books say, old writers since from the east hither, Angles and Saxons came to land. o'er the broad seas Britain sought, mighty warsmiths. the Welsh o'ercame, earls most bold, this earth obtained."

The church contains an effigy of a Lord Dacre, attired in chain mail. Near the entrance are stone figures of bears sitting on their haunches. The whole place is lovely, and breathes in eloquent language memories of days that will never come again.

Two miles further up the Eamont we reach Pooley Bridge, where the water beautifully filters from Lake Ulleswater into the river. At Pooley are two good hotels, and a bridge of many arches spans the Eamont. The scenery around is most charming, and as you ascend to the higher reaches of the lake the hills rise out of the water more precipitous and bold, forming scenes of noble grandeur the most magnificent in England. 'Tis an evening in early autumn; we are resting on the bridge at Pooley. The sound of the last coach passing to Penrith can be heard in the distance. Before us spreads a vision of rare charm and pastoral sweetness; the peace of nature overspreads lake and mountain, and nothing disturbs the harmony of the calm, soft twilight of evening, breathing a sweet verdant tone on to the herbage, massing the tall trees that overhang in sombre hue the beautiful Eamont, which glides in shallow ripples from the lake under the bridge, and murmurs around the modest islets resting in the wide bed of the stream, covered with a rank growth of tall grass and willowy shrubs, as the water intersects the narrow channel in the hue of the evening, the sweet flowings and purling of mimic waves add an unspeakable charm and beauty to the spot. The deepening hue of twilight has now softened the outlines of the grey stone dwellings adjoining the brink of the river, until they assume the appearance of nature's rock under that shadowy mystery of night.

Turning from this spot we follow the course of the river until it widens into the lake, above which the mountains loom grim and spectral ; sylph-like boats and their occupants glide in and out of the vision ; silently the shadows gather : a languorous feeling prevails, gently the full-orbed moon rises over Swarth Fell, the lake becomes illuminated with phosphorescent brilliancy, and the air odorous with the

A Rush grown Bay, Ulleswater.   EDMUND BOGG.

perfume of nature. Boats glide on the bosom of the lake without apparent effort, and the huge hills and giant peaks seem eternally at rest. We hear the sound of voices on the Fells, softened by distance into melody ; lights twinkle from ancient home-steads, resting along the sides of the hills, almost seeming like a part of them. In one of these we take up our abode for the night.

One great charm of the Fells to the spectator is the repose which pervades every object which the eye rests upon. Morning from our bedroom, we look on to the lake, which I have seen often burnished in a blaze of gold and silver, like some tropical sea, and have watched the waves sparkle and flash, pulse and throb, under the effect of the moon, emitting brilliant rays, as if from some storied sea ; or as gradually the sun retires, the western hills are bathed in purple, crimson, and scarlet, as Ruskin would say, " I cannot call it colour, it was conflagration, the curtains of God's Tabernacle." A sombre hue of grey overspreads the lake, the glens deepening to purple, whilst the hill tops are still stencilled with rays of gold.

An evening scene : we are gliding over the surface of the lake, smooth as a mill pond. The last steamer has departed to Pooley Bridge. We have engaged our boat for two days, and stocked it with provisions for that period. Our destination is a small island seven miles away, situated on the lake near the steep white rock of Stybarrow Crag. Now and again we can hear in the distance the rythmic splash of oars and the merry sounds of laughter, or, may be, a snatch of some sweet melody

comes stealing and rippling above the surface of the waters. We take up the refrain, and the rocks and crags echo and re-echo it. Now the mountains rise out of the water sheer perpendicular several hundred feet in height, and huge rocks, which have been hurled into the lake, now lay by the shores like

The Reapers, Swarth Fell. EDMUND BOGG.

stranded ships. The water in many places is so pure and transparent that we can almost, as one writer says, " imagine that our boat was suspended in an element as pure as air." Now we drift past a fairy little cove, a grassy bay in the hills ; a wood adorns one side and a sparkling little stream. glides to the lake on the other ; hanging trees and shrubs cling to the rugged projections of the rock, and broad flakes of nodding fern overhang and add to the beauty of the little dell. In this recess a party of tourists, hidden from the world, have raised their tents, and the lines of smoke from their fires are curling upwards into the hills, and shadowy forms can be discerned flittering hither and thither. A bell can be heard tinkling in the direction of Lyulph's Tower, and a light faintly glimmers from the window. A few large fowls, probably wild ducks, skim swiftly over the lake, causing that rushing sound of air by the swift motion of their wings.   Gradually the stars creep out one by one, and ere we reach our island home not a sound but that caused by our own oars disturbs the tranquility of the lake and mountains surrounding.   Mooring our boat, and removing the firewood and provisions, whilst two of us reared a rude tent the other made a blazing fire and prepared the evening meal.   About eleven we turned in, with Stybarrow Crag, like some huge monster, ready to fall and crush our small isle

Stybarrow Crag.   A. G. BOWEN.

into the lake.   We were just on the point of slumber, for we were tired with our exertion of the day's enjoyment, when sounds of voices and the splash of oars aroused our attention : our fire had been descried from the Patterdale Hotel, and a boating party sailed down to ascertain the cause, but we could not prevail upon them to land, they rowed several times round the island, singing to the music of their oars the beautiful Canadian boat song, " Faintly as tolls the evening chime."   It was nearly eleven, and the sweetness of the refrain, "Row, brothers, row," echoed among the rocks of Stybarrow.   I shall never forget the sweet cadence of the song dying away in the distance as they returned to their hotel at the head of the lake.   The moon rose above Place Fell in stately beauty, bringing into bold relief the jagged outlines of the mountains, and lit up the lake with a silvery brilliancy.   The fir trees stood out dark and silent against the pale evening light.   The chimes of a clock sounded distinctly over the waters.   Early morning the lake and the mountains were clad in a winding sheet of white, which the sun gradually dissolved as it rose in majesty over the highest part of Birk Fell, cragged, seamed and fretted by ravine and overhanging rock.   As we pass upward into Patterdale the little islets in the lake have a pleasing and refreshing effect against a background of sterile peaks, the base of which are finely clothed with woods to the water's edge, above which a heron comes lazily flapping—without which the picture would not have been complete.

From Brother's Waters a rivulet twines through a vale of magic charm, past the grey homesteads, wearing an air of artistic seclusion, from whence we obtain delightful glimpses of loveliness. A dozen giant peaks overhang it and scowl on the little valley; Helvellyn rises majestically above Grisdale, half hidden by a mist, which creeps around its ridgy crest. Far away above us, on the verge of Place Fell, we can see a shepherd, and hear him calling the sheep together. It is the Sabbath, and the tinkling sounds of bells rise from Patterdale Church. Truly this is a land of beautiful mountains, vales, lakes and streams, where dense mist, deep shadow and sunlight, alternately flit, ever forming a variety of scenic charm, the most captivating in nature.

Airey Force.

Lyulph Tower, a picturesque mansion, with walls battlemented and ivy-clad, stands a few hundred paces from the water; near the centre, and on the north side of the lake, a beautiful beck winds through a deeply-wooded ravine; trees of immense growth, mingling with wild flowers and waving fern, kissed by the spray, form exquisite scenes of loveliness. The crowning sight is Airey Force, a waterfall of some eighty feet, and thence the stream passes a wooden bridge to the lake, and from hence the scenery of Ulleswater is magnificent, approaching the sublimity of the Norwegian Fiords. It is along this shore of the lake that nature, with lavish hand, has scattered the wild flowers so abundantly, and the graceful bend of the lake, with the islands and the mountains in the middle distance and in the background, form such a beautiful picture, so exquisite in outline, colour and finish in every detail. It is this spot, where the Aira Beck joins the lake, that Wordsworth and his sister immortalised in prose and verse.   Miss Wordsworth, speaking of the daffodils, says :

"As we went along under the boughs of the trees we saw that there was a long belt of them along the shore, about the breadth of a country turnpike road. I never saw daffodils so beautiful. They grew among the mossy stones, about, and above them ; some rested their heads upon these stones, as on a pillow for weariness, and the rest tossed and reeled and danced, and seemed as if they verily laughed with the wind that blew upon them over the lake. They looked so gay, ever glancing, ever changing. This wind blew directly over the lake to them. There was here and there a little knot, and a few stragglers higher up, but there were so few as not to disturb the simplicity, unity, and life, of that one busy highway. We rested again and again. The bays were stormy, and we heard the waves at different distances, and in the middle of the water, like the sea."

THE DAFFODILS.

"I wandered, lonely as a cloud
    That floats on high o'er vales and hills,
When all at once I saw a crowd,
    A host of golden daffodils ;
Beside the lake, beneath the trees,
Fluttering and dancing in the breeze.

  *   *   *

Continuous as the stars that shine,
    And twinkle on the milky way,
They stretched in never-ending line
    Along the margin of a bay ;
Ten thousand saw I at a glance
Tossing their heads in sprightly dance.

  *   *   *

The waves beside them danced, but they
    Outdid the sparkling waves in glee,
A poet could not but be gay
    In such a jocund company !
I gazed—and gazed—but little thought
What wealth the show to me had brought.

  *   *   *

For oft when on my couch I lie
    In vacant or in pensive mood,
They flash upon that inward eye,
    Which is the bliss of solitude ;
And then my heart with pleasure fills,
And dances with the daffodils."

  *   *   *

Aira Force is the scene of a sad yet romantic legend.   In the far-off centuries there dwelt, at the tower adjoining the Force, a beautiful lady named Emma, betrothed to a famed knight (Sir Eglamore), who had long been engaged in war in Eastern lands. His long absence had affected her health, and she was wont in the night-time to wander forth in her sleep by the bank of the torrent, dreaming of her lover. It was in this situation that the knight found her on his returning unexpectedly from the east. He was so struck with her appearance that he watched her for some time plucking the twigs from the trees and casting them into the stream. Uncertain how to proceed, he at length touched her ; she suddenly awoke from her slumber, and, starting back affrighted, fell down the deep precipice into the water below. The knight leaped into the torrent to rescue her, and bore the inanimate form to the bank. There was a brief moment of consciousness ; she opened her eyes and recognised him, and expired in his arms. The heartbroken man built a cell near the Falls, where he dwelt in solitude, humbling the flesh in prayer and fasting for the repose of her soul.

List, ye who pass by Lyulph's tower
  At eve, how softly then
Doth Aira Force, that torrent hoarse,
  Speak from the woody glen.
Fit music for a solemn vale,
  And holier seems the ground
To him who catches on the gale
The spirit of a mournful tale
  Embodied in the sound.

Soul-shattered was the knight, nor knew
  If Emma's ghost it were,
Or bodying shade, or if the maid
  Her very self stood there.
He touched ; what followed who shall tell ?
The soft touch snapped the thread
Of slumber—shrieking. back she fell ;
The stream it whirled her down the dell
  Along its foaming bed.

In plunged the knight ! When on firm ground
  The rescued maiden lay.
Her eyes grew bright with blissful light,
  Confusion pas-ed away.
She heard, ere to the throne of grace
  Her faithful spirit flew,
His voice—beheld his speaking face ;
And, dying, from his own embrace,
  She felt that he was true.

Wild stream of Aira, hold thy course,
  Nor fear memorial lays,
Where clouds that spread in solemn shade
  Are edged with golden rays !
Dear art thou to the light of heaven,
  Though minister of sorrow ;
Sweet is thy voice at pensive even,
And thou, in lovers' hearts forgiven,
  Shalt take thy place with Yarrow.

Such is the story connected with the wild stream of Aira. 'Tis indeed a beautiful spot : the overhanging trees blending with the rocks, the refreshing spray falling on trailing plant and creeper ; the deep shadow of the gorge ; the sunlight in the tree tops.

From the high bank we note the rich green of the park, the deer basking in the sunshine, and the ivy-clad mansion in the background.

Onward and upward, past Dockrey and Matterdale, and its little church with ivy-mantled tower, and bend to the west, over the moor, the source of many a stream, the array of mountain peak to the south and west being beautifully grand, then we drop down past Wanthwaite into the Vale of the Glendermakin, to where Threlkeld and its whitewashed, modest house of prayer, with ivied porch, rests peaceably under Blencathra's frowning sides. Threlkeld village is comprised chiefly of whitewashed cottages, with flaggy roofs, scattered irregularly along the base of the hill. The church is a simple, unpretentious structure ; the ivied porch and bell gable are its only pleasing objects. High over all rises stern Blencathra. The interior adornment of the church is of the barest description ; no chancel and no font, only a pedestal holding a metal plate, some eight inches by two deep. At the restoration of the church in 1777, the old font was cast out and the plate described substituted. The present church was built in 1776, £260 being expended in the work, subscribed by the parishioners. The old church was roofed with thatch, and the seats, or, we might say, benches were rudely shaped from trees. In those days men and women sat on separate sides of the nave.

The place has an ancient history. The name Threlkret, or Threlkeld, is said to have come from a Viking named Thorgell, who, in the tenth century, conquered

L

the Cimbric people and settled in this fair valley.   Centuries before this time, as early as 553, St. Kentygern reared the cross at this place and preached to the inhabitants. This cross, we are told, stood for centuries near the "Priest's Acre."   The mother of St. Kentygern was a daughter of a King of Cambria, and for her refusal to marry a neighbouring chief, was expelled from home to a life of drudgery in the fields, where she was held in ambush by her former lover, and destroyed of her virtue. Her shame and sorrow being discovered, the punishment of death was pronounced, and her execution was to be carried out in the following manner : bound to a chariot,

St. Kentygern raising the Cross under Blencathra.   F. DEAN.

she was doomed to be hurled from the top of the Traprain Law, the Dun Pelder of bygone days.   By some miraculous cause she escaped her doom, so they brought her to the sea-shore and placed her in a coracle, without any oar to guide, and pushed it out to sea.   Yet, though the tide ran seawards, she again escaped death, for in the early morning she was cast on the coast of the Firth of Forth.   Here Thenew, for that was her name, gave birth to a boy.   A hermit, who lived near, had compassion, gave the mother and child shelter, and named the latter Cyentgen, or Kentygern, meaning : "Head or chief of the Lord."   For many years the boy remained with

his foster-father, gaining in knowledge and piety day by day. At length he
journeyed to Cathures, now Glasgow, where for years he was a faithful missionary,
until at length one came to the throne, a pagan, who knew not God, and, after
undergoing many persecutions during this man's reign, he journeyed southward into
Wales, by way of Carleolum (Carlisle), thence for several miles down the vale
country; but on learning that most of the people in the mountains were still pagans,
he turned west into the lakes, and preached and baptized at Thanet Well—the name
of his mother, and so called from his visit. At Threlkeld he again halted, and set up
the cross, and numbers gathered round him to hear this Gospel of Christ. Many
there would be who had never heard of the doctrine of redemption, for this was
nearly half a century before the Roman missionary landed on the coast of Kent.
St. Kentygern was not instructed of Rome, for the new light had spread south by
way of Ireland and Iona. Here was a man of Cymbria publishing the glad tidings
of the Cross in the language of the natives, and, we are told, they gathered from the
hills and vales, from the Derwent, from the Greta, from the shores of Thirlmere, from
deep mountain passes of Skiddaw and Honister, chieftains and their followers, and
the priesthood from that hoary circle still to be seen standing sentry over the Derwent
and St. John Vale. The real nature of their religion is still unknown. Nearly all
we can learn is from a close study of those silent stones, grey with the lapse of
ages. Thierry says :—

"When the shouts of the multitude, who stood in a dense circle around the spot, the
frenzied chants of the Druids, and the despairing shrieks of the dying victims, were drowned in
the sullen roar of the thunder, then must the fearful nature of their creed have stood forth in
all its horrors. Yet, with all this, there was a sort of grandeur in the seclusion and simplicity
of their worship. All was not blood ; and though they bowed down to the unknown God, in
an erring and mistaken spirit, yet must their conception of him have been fine. The God of
nature and the wilderness, the God of the tempest and the storm, was a nobler idea than the
immortalized humanities of Greek and Roman mythology. The choice of the situations for
these sacred monuments were amidst the melancholy waste, or buried deep in the recesses of
some vast forest, where the wide-spreading branches of their sacred tree (the oak) casts its deep
shadows over the consecrated spot, with no canopy save the heavens, shows the dark and gloomy
spirit of their faith. They worshipped the God of the thunder-storm, not the God of peace ;
and it was amidst the thunder-storm that their horrid rites appeared most horrid. When
illuminated by the lurid glare of the lightning, the gigantic osier figure, filled with human
beings, sank into the flames."

The sun-worshippers would doubtless be antagonistic to the apostle
and his story. What a strange assembly this would be : the Druidic priests,
chieftains, and their warriors, attired in skins of wild beasts, with shield and spear,

L2

children of the original Cymri, whose empire, like their religion and superstition, was at this period gradually being swept away. The almost superhuman efforts of Arthur and his dauntless knights had been inadequate to stem and roll back the advancing wave of invading Saxon and Northman. It was at this age of internal warfare, immortalized by brilliant feats of arms and barbaric splendour of Arthur's court, when the inhabitants of the hill country, still shackled with Pagan worship, that St. Kentygern made his advent into the vale of the Derwent, and planted the cross, symbol of Christianity. Hither also, in after years, came St. Herbert, of Derwentwater, and other good men, to preach in the rude church which arose after St. Kentygern's visit.

At the east end of the churchyard there is a granite pillar, erected to the memory of the celebrated hunters who have chased Master Reynard across Blencathra's Cliffs.

" JOHN CROZIER'S TALLY HO !

The hunt is up, the hunt is up ;
Auld Tolly's on the drag ;
Hark to him, beauties, get away,
He's gone for Skiddaw Crag.

Chorus.
Rise fra ye'r beds, ye sleepy heads,
If ye wad pleasure knaw !
Ye'r hearts 'twill cheer, if ye but hear
John Crozier's Tally Ho !

Hurrah ! hurrah ! he's stown away,
Through forest wild he's gean ;
Sweet music tell, mang t' heather dell,
What track sly Reynard's tean.
Chorus.

To Carrick Fell, to Carrick Fell,
His covert theer 'll fail ;
Unlucky day, he cannot stay
Blancathra's heights to scale.
Chorus.

Ower Lonscale Fell, by Skiddaw Man,
An' doon by Millbeck Ghyll ;
To t'Dod he's gone, his reace is run ;
Hark ! Tally Ho ! a kill ! "

Many are the stories told anent the chase. We were most forcibly reminded of this when passing the village alehouse on the night of a hunt. Sounds of revelry and hunting song were heard issuing from the deep throats of the thirsty crew. On entering, we saw the head of Reynard, killed that day, suspended from the ceiling, and as the revellers hiccoughed out the strains of John Peal each glass was hob-a-noobed against Master Reynard's nose.

The inscription on the stone in the churchyard reads :—

> A few friends have united to raise this stone in loving memory of the undernamed, who in their generation were noted veterans of the chase, and all of whom lie buried in this churchyard.
> Daniel Walker, of Threlkeld, died February 8th, 1849, aged 82.
> Henry Gill, died January 28th, 1850, aged 61.
> Ben Graves, died May 26th, 1856, aged 75.
> Wilson Nicholson, died January 15th, 1864, aged 50.
> James Bainbridge, died September 1st, 1866, aged 82.
> Mark Fisher, died December 16th, 1867, aged 81.
> Clement Akitt, died May 12th, 1868, aged 66.
> Isaac Todhunter, of Threlkeld, died November 17th, 1868, aged 59.
> Thomas Morley, died March 3rd, 1871, aged 69.
> John Cockbain, died May 5th, 1873, aged 89.
> Joshua Fearon, died June 19th, 1874, aged 86.
> John Hodgson, died September 30th, 1874, aged 91.
> Joseph Wilkinson, died December 15th, 1875, aged 87.
> Joseph Brownrigg, died April 30th, 1877, aged 67.
> Thomas Newton, died February 14th, 1879, aged 84.
> John Porter, died December 31st, 1852, aged 35.
> Also James Dixon, of Burns, died September 21st, 1870, aged 55, and was interred at Patterdale.
> Thomas Cockbain, died April 7th, 1861, aged 58.
> Thomas Hodgson, died July 8th, 1862, aged 73.
> Thomas Hutchinson, died October 22nd, 1882, aged 73.
> Edward Bainbridge, died July 23rd, 1883, aged 71.
> Thomas Cockbain, died July 13th, 1884, aged 67.
> Thomas Edmondson, died November 29th, 1883, aged 59.
> Robert Holliday, died December 24th, 1850, aged 82.
> William Greenhow, died July 9th, 1884, aged 77.
> Joseph Harper, died May 30th, 1854, aged 74.
> William Ablott, died February 17th, 1840, aged 43.
> John Bill, died December 14th, 1875, aged 98.

> Joseph Mayson, died 1871, aged 77.
> Henry Bowe, died 1880, aged 87.
> John Mumberson, died 1880, aged 83.
> Jos. Atkinson, died 1881, aged 95.
> Ben Wilson, died 1884, aged 85.

> " The forest music is to hear the hounds
> Rend the thin air, and with a lusty cry
> Awake the drowsy echo, and confound
> Their perfect language in a mingled voice."—GAY.

There are several houses in the village dated the seventeenth century, and half-a-mile east, and a meadow's length from the Glendermaken, is a farmhouse called Threlkeld Hall. This cannot be the old hall of the Threlkelds, as from appearances no part of it seems earlier than the eighteenth century. There are evidences of an earlier structure on the opposite bank of the rivulet, which may have been their home.

The site is both well chosen and the outlook pleasing. The Glendermaken winds beautifully past the base of the mound ; Blencathra uprears in grand form ; cattle grazing in the meadows fill in the foreground ; Threlkeld's whitewashed walls blend with the green in the middle distance. The hill sides about Latrigg are beautifully wooded, whilst the background is filled in by the dark ridges and peaks of mountains around Derwentwater—a picture which combines both grace and majesty.

> " Across yon meadowy bottom, look
>   Where close fogs hide the parent brook,
> And see beyond that hamlet small
>   The ruined towers of Threlkeld Hall.
>
> There at Blencathra's rugged feet
>   Sir Lancelot found a safe retreat
> Among the million of hills,
>   Crags, woodlands, waterfalls, and rills."

It was at Threlkeld that the good Lord Clifford (the Shepherd Lord) spent sixteen years of his life hiding from the house of York, his anxious mother being fearful lest he should fall into the hands of the revengeful Edward, and his life

The Shepherd Lord and Anne St. John.

sacrificed as an atonement for the cruelties committed by his father, the bloody Clifford. And here he remained hid until the accession of Richmond as Henry VII, who united the rival houses of Lancaster and York, when he was restored to his rank and estates. Towards the end of this period, or when he was about thirty-two years of age, Sir John St. John, of Bletsoe, in Bedfordshire, came on a visit to Threlkeld, and with him came his daughter Anne, a fair girl in the bloom of youth and beauty. The Shepherd Lord, who oft met her riding amongst the hills, fell in love with her, and she, probably learning the secret of his birth, reciprocated his affection, and so, after being restored to his estates and honours, he married Anne St. John, and dwelt amidst the woods and moors of Barden, the tower of which he considerably enlarged.

" Love had he seen in huts where poor men lie ; Glad were the vales, and every cottage hearth,
   His daily teacher had been woods and hills,   The Shepherd Lord was honoured more and more,
The silence that is in the starry skies, And ages after he was laid in earth
   The sleep that is among the lonely hills ;   The good Lord Clifford was the name he bore."

Further to the east is Scales ; near to, attached on the walls of a farmhouse, is the following legend :—

I. W
This building's age
These letters show,
MDCCXIX.
Though many gaze
Yet few will know.

About half-a-century ago this house was the Sun Inn, a favourite call-house on the road between Keswick and Penrith, and kept by Isaac and Betty Hutchinson for nigh three score years. It was an old-world house, with its open fire-grate and huge chimney, and its landlord was a typical Cumbrian. When Burton ale first came into public favour, Isaac was asked for his custom by a traveller who was accompanied by

a landlord from Thirlspot ; rubbing his hands, Isaac said, " I git aw my yal fra Alfred Eemison, o't Burns, and its allus varra good ; but I divvent want to be unneighbourly, what ye mun send me a hofe quarter [4½ gallons]."

Motherby is a long, straggling village, near to Penruddock station. Greystoke is an old-fashioned village of well-built houses and trim gardens—there is a cross and green ; the castle is modern. A little to the east stands Blencow Hall, for five centuries the residence of the family of Blencow ; the ivy-clad tower, evidently built for stern resistance, is a relic of Border feud.

From the summit of Blencathra wonderful and astonishing views are to be obtained on clear days. Scriffel, over the Solway, can be descried, and Derwentwater, like a mirror, with its beautiful refreshing isles, appears most charming. Many and astonishing are the tales told by travellers of the danger attending an ascent of this mountain, all of which will cause a smile of contempt on the face of a climber. The morning of our ascent was rather dull, yet when far up the mountain we turned and were surprised at the wonderful views to the south, beautiful Thirlmere and the green vale of St. John, to the west Derwentwater, the fairest of the lakes. The windings of the Greta, the Glendermaken, and the Glenderaterra, silver streaks amidst the green, and golden tinge of autumn, above all rise in the background ; Mell Fell Place and Swarth Fell, Kidstay Pike and High Street, Helvellyn and Kirkstone Dodd, Great Dodd, Naddle Fell, Raven's Crag, Bleaberry Fell, and the Pikes towering into the clouds. Near the summit we were suddenly enveloped in the folds of a fleecy grey mist, which gradually floated downwards and obscured the valleys beneath ; every object was now hidden, except the stunted herbage around our feet, broken by patches of stunted moss-mottled rock, behind which rose, wall-like, the dense curtain of mist, which now and again would open and disclose bewildering peeps of the country below. The solemnity of a mountain summit, shrouded in its mantle of grey mist, must be witnessed to be fully realised. From afar we hear the bark of the house dog, the bleating of the mountain sheep, the low of the distant herd, and the neigh of horses ; from the vale the village school bell summoning the children to school. Yet, meanwhile, we are alone, seated on the summit, surrounded by mist, ravine, rocks, and the everlasting hills.

> " To sit on rock, to muse o'er flood and fell,
> To slowly trace the forest's shady scene,
> Where things that own not man's domain dwell,
> And mortal foot hath ne'er or rarely been.
> To climb the trackless mountain all unseen,
> With the wild flock that never need a fold,
> This is not solitude : 'tis but to hold
> Converse with nature's charms
> And view her stores untold."—BYRON.

> " With toil the king his way pursued,
> By lonely Threlkeld's waste and wood ;
> Above the solitary track
> Rose stern Blencathra's ridgy back.
>
> The monarch judged this desert wild
> With such romantic ruin piled,
> Was theatre, by nature's hand,
> For feat of high achievement planned."

> " Amid whose yawning gulfs the sun
> Cast umber'd radiance red and dun,
> Though never sunbeam could discern
> The surface of that sable tarn,
> In whose black mirror you may spy
> The stars, while noontide lights the sky."

Secluded on the east side of Blencathra, in a deep hollow, surrounded by a desolate amphitheatre of peaks, with a rocky precipice above, is Scales Tarn, alluded to by Sir Walter Scott in his " Bridal of Triermain." From the peculiarity of its position it seldom receives the warm rays and light of the sun. On our visit, just before reaching the tarn, the sun for a few minutes was shining brilliantly, and cloud shadows trailing up the mountain gave a beautiful effect of light and shade. On reaching the tarn a change came over the scene ; the dark clouds which lay on the north-east edge of the Blencathra overspread the sun, and the mountain became enveloped in a shower of hail and sleet. Such was the condition of the atmosphere when we reached the tarn, and truly the spot had a desolate and awe-inspiring appearance. The surface of the water, disturbed by the sudden gusts of wind, almost inky in colour, lay grim and dreary. The steep, grey precipice of rocks overhung, fit haunts for the ravens and foxes, which still inhabit its fastnesses. Of the fox many a story of desperate chase in this region is recorded.

An evening stroll into the Vale of St. John, returning by Thirlmere Valley, the Druidical Circle, and the Greta.

Old Lane, Millbeck. o. bowen.

The rays of the sun gleamed fiercely on the vast craggy heights above Linthwaite, as we bent our steps from Threlkeld up the vale of St. John. Wanthwaite, resting under a precipice and surrounded by a belt of immense fir trees and a carpet of cool green grass ; high above upreared the vast craggy ridge, scarred and seared by centuries, where the hoarse croak of ravens is still heard, from whence huge rocks have at some period been hurled and now lay athwart the vale. Now and again a deep gorge splits the mountain, and the waters of a gill bound through it into the quite valley far below. Wanthwaite Crag and White Pike are lit with a deep red gleam, a strong contrast to the cool, flower-decked vale of St. John, with the greenest of foliage overhanging the graceful winding of the beck, wimpling, limpid, and tuneful ; and in the vale to our right stands the lonely little chapel of St John A glamour of gold and purple softens and mellows the riven sides of Blencathra into loveliness. Thirlmere is seen encragged and encompassed by a succession of mountain peaks. At the entrance, on the right, is Raven's Crag ; on the left, above the path, Castle Rock, like some immense fortress, rises perpendicularly over the vale. Scott has thrown a halo of romance around this spot for all time. The rock may crumble away, but its name, and that of the Vale of St. John, is imperishable.

" But, midmost of the vale, a mound
Arose with airy turrets crown'd,
Buttress, and rampire's circling bound,
    And mighty keep and tower ;
Seem'd some primeval giant's hand,
The castle's massive walls had plann'd,
A ponderous bulwark to withstand
    Ambitious Nimrod's power,

Above the moated entrance slung,
The balanced drawbridge trembling hung,
    As jealous of a foe ;
Wicket of oak as iron hard,
With iron studded, clench'd and barr'd,
And prong'd portcullis, join'd to guard
    The gloomy pass below."

Evening, with all her lovely tints of pearl, gold, and purple, has overtaken us as we reached the margin of the charming lake, its bank sweetly diversified by sloping wood, rock, and bay. The heights above the Vale of Legburthwater and Wythburn were suffused with the last faint lustre of the dying orb, and the lengthening shadows of the mountain were thrown on the water. We rested where

the becks meet, a most beautiful bend of smooth, glassy water, reflecting the graceful overhanging foliage on its surface; the only sounds which broke the stillness were the ripple of the stream and the gurgling melody of a distant waterfall, and that of cattle cropping

Druidical Circle.

the herbage near by. Passing onward we reach the bridge which spans the stream. Now over all steals the solemn calm of eventide wrapped in the coverlet of a tangible repose ; no carol of birds, no wing of insect disturbs the stillness of the hallowed air ; the rustling of leaves has ceased, and the denizens in the crannies of the grey and purple rocks hold the deep hush—a silence holy. We passed Thirlmere as the mantle of night was gently stealing on the sleeping lake, blending mountain, woodland, crag, and water into peace profound, and the subdued tone of soft purple haze. A gleam of luminous brightness stole on the surface, reflecting Raven's Crag, the sky, trees, and every other object, whilst the slumbering background of hills threw in a sombre shadow, all forming an exquisite, natural, and harmonious picture, beautiful and holy. Turning our steps in the direction of Keswick, the gloaming spread on the earth, deepening grey and purple shadowed the foreground of rock and glen. The serried line of the hill tops were still flushed and burnished with gold ; white, ominous mist wreaths were mysteriously creeping, curling and gathering in the vale, like shadowy denizens of a past world. How strange is the stillness! save the almost pathetic moaning of streams and the pitiful bleating of one stray sheep on the mountains. Crossing the moor we pass the grey, solitary stones, crumbling witnesses of a creed and tragic scenes now enshrouded in solemn mystery, from which the veil will never be lifted. Now we drop into the Vale of the Greta, and forward to Threlkeld, to rest for the night under the shadow of Blencathra.

Again resuming our journey west from Threlkeld, with the Vale of St. John and Castle Rock standing out conspicuously, Wanthwaite Crag appears dimly wreathed in a mist-cloud. A warm ray of sunlight lit up the craggy side of High Rigg and the range of mountains dying away in the distance. Wescow Hamlet, antique and lonely, with grey, mottled walls and brown moss-covered roofs, beautiful in its loneliness and picturesque simplicity, is situated on high ground in the midst of the hills above the Greta valley and near the junction of several streams. A fountain bubbles from the earth to refresh man and beast, and trickles to the ravine below. It is the Sabbath, and a few farm servants are laying stretched on the side of the grassy lea enjoying that cessation from toil on the Seventh which the Commandment says is accorded to man and beast. Just beyond the hamlet and overlooking the Glenderattera and the Greta valley a sublime scene unfolds. The noble forms of mountains and peaks in the background, Keswick nestling in the vale, and Derwentwater sleeping beneath; hillsides and vale in the foreground, beautifully wooded, and the river winding through; smoke ascending from a mountain farm, and Skiddaw uprearing high over all, the ever-changing aspects of the atmosphere and "nature's melody," echoing streams falling from the mountain, the utter silence of human sound, produces a grand, solemn, and impressive picture—touching the life springs of our higher nature. The ear can drink in her melody, the eye perceive her form and colour, and the soul her poetry.

Proceeding, we pass into the Lonscale Valley, the wild, lonely ravine which separates Skiddaw and Blencathra, and down which leaps and gurgles the Glenderattera, the most beautiful mountain stream. The track crosses the water by the most primitive of bridges—a few boulders and slabs thrown roughly across—which gives access on this side of the mountain to Skiddaw House, a lone mountainous dwelling, 1,500 feet above the sea level; lower down the stream is bridged for foot passengers by an equally primitive structure.

Up the mountain path and through the woods we wander, and presently drop down from the heights of Skiddaw to the vale of Derwentwater, which opens to view like some Arcadian dream, a vast amphitheatre of mountains, rising peak above peak, and piercing the clouds, encircle a landscape of rich, cultivated fields and green meadows, interspersed with orchard, village, and town, with antique towers, stately pinnacles, and spire uprearing above the roofs ; the lake reposing like a rich jewel in a setting of magnificent hills ; the exceeding loveliness of the green wooded islands studding its surface are reflected with rocks, woods, and mountain in its glittering bosom.   Behind is Skiddaw, and in front Keswick, surrounded by delightful environments, its roofs and walls suffused with delicate rays of sunlight, seems to our wonder-

Applethwaite near Keswick.   BOWEN

ing gaze a city beautiful, where sin, sorrow, and death may never enter. 'Tis a scene ever to be remembered. To sit and drink in all the beauty and tone of colouring, the grey rocks, the limpidity of the crystal lake, the greens of the woods and pastures, the saffron, golden, and purple hues from the afternoon sun glinting the mountains, the brown of moorland, the flashing of lake, river, brooks, the Falls of Lodore, and the vista into Borrowdale— it is marvellous, 'tis impressive, 'tis enchantment, and fills the mind with awe, delight, and wonder.

Applethwaite is a poem, a dream, teeming with charming pictures ; typical Cumberland cottages rest on the edge of a brawling stream, which leaps and bubbles from old Skiddaw. Antique porches covered with creepers and woodbine, grey roofs adorned with moss and tendril, zigzag steps of undressed rock, and passages leading to nowhere in particular, a place of orchards, a perfume of blossom, and the aroma of turf-fires and larch woods which clothe the rugged hillside above Mill-beck. Situate on the banks of a ravine bearing the above name is another out-of-the-world, curious, and antique village, resting under the west fringe · of Skiddaw, grey Cumberland homesteads peep from under rock, orchard and pine wood, the white and grey walls and deep mullions covered with rose and woodbine, where the bees hum and the twittering birds fly in and out. One house, where we stayed, is deeply impressed on the memory. From the windows we could look down on Derwent-water and Bassenthwaite, and watch the everchanging aspect of lake and mountain, and the heavenly glory of the setting sun. As the fire faded down the western sky, pencilling the hill tops with a crimson halo, suffusing the valley in purple haze, the beautiful lakes reflecting the celestial lustre, slowly fades the light ; the stars creep out, and the mantle of night casts a veil over this earthly paradise.

Down the old lanes and over the rich pastureland, which divides the two lakes, we pass to Crossthwaite Church, memorable as the spot where Saint Kentygern raised

Derwentwater (Winter). ABRAHAMS, KESWICK.

the cross and preached upwards of thirteen centuries ago, to be followed by that good man, Saint Herbert, half-a-century later. As we pass through the graveyard we pause before a tomb on the north side of the tower, where sleeps all that is mortal of Robert Southey, Poet Laureate, and also of Edith his wife ; a wreath of immortelles, typical of life everlasting, was laid on the grave. It was a mild spring day, when the early flowers bloom, and we placed a snowdrop on the tomb of the sweet singer—only a simple flower, yet a tribute pure and sweet. Beautiful is the situation of this "God's-acre," surrounded as it is by the unsparing glories of nature, a spot sacred in the annals of Church history.

This structure is probably the third which has stood on this site, since the visit of St. Kentigern in the 6th century. Little of the present building dates beyond the decorated period. Southey's effigy, by Lough, rests by the chancel doorway; the face of the poet wears a sweet, saintly aspect. In the south chapel are the marble tombs, and effigies in alabaster, of the Derwentwaters, a family of Norman extraction. Their castle stood on the ridge near the village of Grange. Early in the 15th century Sir Nicholas de Ratcliffe, of Dilston, became united to Margaret,

Gossips, Millbeck.   EDMUND BOGG.

daughter and heiress of Sir John de Derwentwater, and the estates of the latter passed to the Ratcliffes. In the reign of James the First, Sir Francis Ratcliffe was created Earl of Derwentwater, on the marriage of his son Edward, the second earl, with Lady Mary Tudor, daughter of Charles the Second.

From this union with the house of the Stuarts can be traced all the calamities which fell so swiftly and tragically on the family of the Ratcliffes. James and Charles, sons of the above, and noble members of a noble race, suffered on the scaffold for their adherence to the lost cause of the Stuarts. James, the last Earl of Derwentwater, suffered in 1715, and Charles in 1745.

The brasses on the tombs are in a good state of preservation, and are to the memory of Sir John Ratcliffe, High Sheriff of Cumberland, and also to his wife Alicia. Sir John, as doughty knight as ever bore sword, is represented in a suit of plate armour, and bears a long, cross-hilted sword and dagger; his hair is parted on the forehead, and falls back in curls. His wife is attired in a flowing dress confined at the waist by a girdle fastened by a clasp of three roses. The hands of both are placed as if in prayer.

" Of your charite pray for the soule of Sir John Ratcliffe, Knyghte, and for the state of Dame Alice, his wife, which Sir John dyed the 2nd day of February, Anno Domini mdxxdii, on whose soule Jesu habe mercy."

Passing from this hallowed ground, beneath the grateful shade of yew trees, Keswick is soon reached. To the right, on entering, will be noticed the Keswick School of Industrial Art, founded by John Ruskin.

" The patient hand shall work with joy to bless the land."

The old bridge which spans the Greta at the foot of Keswick, with Ann's Banks Pencil Works, is another point of interest. The Greta, or Grieta—to greet, to cry aloud.

" Greta ! what fearful listening ! when huge stones rumble
Along thy bed block after block,
Or twirling, with reiterated shock
Combat, while darkness aggravates the groans."

Greta Hall, once the residence of Southey and Coleridge, stands on a slight eminence to the left, just above the Greta, whose murmurings can be heard, as in many semi-circles, it flows to the lake. Coleridge, writing to a friend in 1800, says : " I question if there be a room in England which commands a view of mountains and lakes, and woods and vales, superior to that in which I am now sitting." Wordsworth also speaks, when visiting Coleridge, of

The Hills above Derwentwater, from Crosthwaite.   EDMUND BOGG.

the magnificent sunsets and the net of mountains by which Greta Hall is enveloped, like great floundering bears and monsters all couchant and asleep.

Ruminating by the old bridge, on the wonderful scenes around, and of the great poets and writers who have dwelt or been guests at Greta Hall, the river, almost resonant with echoes of the past—merrily the rippling wavelets danced o'er its shimmering bed, over which the trees hung so graceful and feather-like, and old railings twist by the side of stream and meadow, clouds cleave the peaky background, the base of the mountains are clothed in a golden purple, whilst sunlight and shadow skim the higher reaches.   The name of Banks, so conspicuously displayed on the walls, reminds us of Chief Justice Bankes, a native of Keswick, whose wife, Lady Bankes, so gallantly defended Corfe Castle against the forces of the Parliament from June, 1643, to 1646, and then only yielded through the treachery of a traitor within the walls.

Keswick is composed chiefly of one long thoroughfare, with two or three side streets, and numerous alleys and ancient yards, typical of bygone generations.   The Market Hall and Museum, in the centre of the street, are objects of interest.   At Keswick congregate people from all parts of the civilized world, and of various walks in life, some in search of health and pleasure, others to wander amongst that beautiful combination of enchanting scenery, the most delightful in Great Britain.

CHAPTER XI.

✎ CLIMBS IN LAKELAND. ✎

ERHAPS no portion of Great Britain has received so much notice in prose and verse as the exquisite group of lakes, moors, and fells situated in Cumberland and Westmorland. Known as the Playground of England, or, more shortly, as the Lake District, it invites year by year a great number of visitors. Disliking or wearied of the artificial amusements which monotonously characterize our pleasure resorts, the true lover of natural scenery flies to this fairy-land, where much of the original charm of wild nature may be found in its more secluded recesses.

Although so often described in the prosaic language of the guide-book, or in the fanciful imagery of the poet and novelist, there is one feature of the Lake District which has only comparatively recently attracted attention. I refer to the development of mountaineering as a sport. Here on the steep faces of the loftier mountains are scores of opportunities for practising almost every phase of the cragsman's art. Close at hand, with splendid problems of every degree of difficulty, there is no wonder that men anxious to develop their skill, or to keep in training, resort to the well-known climbing centres of the Cumbrian Hills.

Herman Prior's "Pedestrian Guide" and Haskett-Smith's "Climbing in the British Isles, Part I.," are at present the best guides for the climber, and in addition to these a miscellaneous series of articles, which have appeared at different times in sundry papers and magazines, of which one of the best was published in "All the Year Round," in November, 1884. At Wasdale Head, too, the book devoted to climbers' notes contains much valuable information, entered at various times since its commencement in January, 1890, by men who have made first and second ascents. At first there was a tendency to chronicle too much; but happily of late records of "new work," or variations of recognised routes, have only been recorded. "Climbing Notes" has been copied more than once, and this valuable record will be the nucleus of the literature of this special kind emanating from Wasdale Head. Occasionally, some irrepressible individual sacrilegiously intrudes his little doings and ideas on its pages; but, generally speaking, it is treated with profound respect.

New roads and modern improvements will soon drive the men of the old school from their favourite haunts, and, like Zermatt or Chamonix, Wasdale Head may

Helvellyn, from the Red Tarn,   F. LEACH.

become hackneyed and commonplace. There has been for some years a tendency among climbers to practise their favourite pastime among the Scotch mountains, notably in Skye, and on the north face of Ben Nevis, and in North Wales.

In the brief space allotted to me, I cannot hope to do more than hint at a few of the principal attractions to the mountaineering fraternity. To know and appreciate the district thoroughly is the work of a lifetime. The perfect proportions of the landscape, and the ever-varying atmospheric effects, produce impressions never to be forgotten.

Easter is the time when most of the climbing men congregate at Wasdale Head and other similar centres. After a severe winter the gullies and sheltered nooks are filled with snow which has had time to get into condition. In a good season excellent practice is thus afforded in the use of the ice-axe, then many a lonely ghyll resounds with the pikes of these useful implements and the tread of nailed boots.

A brief outline of our visit in 1895 will best illustrate the joys of such a holiday, and show what can be done in a few days. Our party, a strong contingent of the

Y.R.C , arrived at Ambleside late on Thursday night. Next morning we proceeded by coach to Wythburn, whence an hour's warm going brought us to the summit of Helvellyn. We were delighted to find snow in abundance on the eastern face, and the West Hills of Cumberland streaked with white and promising good sport. From the Swirrel Edge a grand glissade shot us down close to the frozen waters of the Red Tarn, from which the amphitheatre looked almost arctic compared with the green slopes of the west side.

> " . . . . . a cove, a huge recess,
> That keeps, till June, December's snow ;
> A lofty precipice in front,
> A silent tarn below !
> Far in the bosom of Helvellyn."

Getting on to the Striding Edge we quickly traversed this gable, and then kicked our way up a steep snow cornice which fringed the eastern brow of Helvellyn. Having rested and admired the glorious panorama once more—

> " A record of commotion
> Which a thousand ridges yield ;
> Ridge, and gulf, and distant ocean
> Gleaming like a silver shield ! "

—we walked down to Thirlspot and then on to Keswick, which we entered at half-past five.

The next day's work was commenced with a pleasant innovation for mountaineers : we rowed down sunny Derwentwater, which presented the appearance of a gently undulating mirror reflecting all the foothills with beautiful clearness. The usual route

The Pillar Rock from Jordan Gap.   F. LEACH.

from Lodore to Rosthwaite and Seathwaite was followed, then over Stockley Bridge to Sty Head Tarn, between Great Gable and Great End—" The native bulwarks of the pass "—down to Wasdale Head. Below lay the tiny hamlet at the head of the desolate lake, which is sighted round the shoulder of Lingmell, and far away to the south-west the sea glistening in the sun.* At four o'clock we entered the hospitable doors of Tyson's Hotel, the " Monte Rosa " of this English

* There is just now a strong agitation for the construction of a road over this lonely pass. For my part I fail to see who will benefit by this desecration except perhaps a few innkeepers.

Zermatt of the olden time.   Life here is home-like and free and easy.   With its old frequenters I re-echo the wish "long may it remain so."   Save the early starts it is almost the same as at a Swiss mountaineering centre.

On Easter Sunday the right thing to do is to join the customary strong party who spend the day on the Pillar Rock of Ennerdale.

> " You see yon precipice ;—it wears the shape
> Of a vast building made of many crags ;
> And in the midst is one particular rock,
> That rises like a column from the vale,
> Whence by our shepherds it is called THE PILLAR."

There are many recognised ways to the summit ; but the Ennerdale face, which rises in one grand precipice on the north, is perhaps the finest rock climb in the Lake

Outline Sketch of Scafell

Country.   It was first accomplished on Monday, 27th July, 1891, by Messrs. W. P. Haskett Smith, Geoffrey Hastings, and W. Cecil Slingsby.   After a little scrambling on the ordinary ascent and the Jordan Gap by the split rock, we descended by the west and oldest route towards Gillerthwaite.   All the gullies on this side were packed with snow.

In the evening, round the long dining table, were gathered upwards of thirty men in strange costumes of rough tweed, and as they ate with wondrous appetites, their talk was of rocks, hand-holds, traverses, arêtes, and all the peculiar jargon of the mountaineers' art.   It was particularly noticeable that the greater number were for the time being water-drinkers.

In the early morning the front of the hotel was crowded with men lacing or nailing boots, coiling ropes, snatching snap-shots, and stowing away the necessities for a long day among the mountains.   Many of them were well-known frequenters of this out-of-the-way corner of England—notably, J. W. Robinson, A. Holmes, &c.

Perhaps the most enjoyable hours of the day were spent in the little snug recess of the billiard room. Here, after dinner, cherished briars were produced, and 'mid a palpitating cloud of smoke the climbs were fought o'er again, and mutual hints and advice given with friendly interest. Now and then a few untiring spirits indulged in strange hand-traverses round the billiard table, with feet in mid-air against the wall, or in other gymnastic feats.

Among these mountains there are a few on which sad accidents have occurred. Of recent years Haarbleicher's fall from the rocks between the Broad Stand and Mickledore Chimney, and Professor Marshall's from the rocks to the north of the Lord's Rake, are perhaps the most deplorable. Owen Glynn Jones, too, experienced a mishap alone in Moss Ghyll, 9th January, 1893, from the jammed stones at the Collie traverse. His rope, however, saved him, and, continuing, he pluckily finished the ascent at 5.45, in the dark.

From the Pulpit Rock on Scafell Pike a complete view of the noted climbs near the Mickledore Ridge and Lord's Rake may be obtained. After plodding up the Brown Tongue from Wasdale Head the climber may either toil up the awful screes to the Mickledore Ridge, and thence by the Broad Stand to the top of Scafell, or he may

In Piers Ghyll.   F. LEACH

have the choice of such routes as Moss Ghyll, Steep Ghyll, Deep Ghyll, and the Lord's Rake. The order fairly represents the degree of difficulty.

The Broad Stand in fine weather offers no serious hindrance to a practised climber; but when wet or glazed with ice the case is far different. Remember that a slip on these shelving rocks is fruitful of dire results. You had better use the rope, and with strict attention to the rules for the manipulation of this aid. The amateur should carefully study Claude Wilson's "Mountaineering" before essaying to pose as an Alpinist skilled in the use of the rope. Once past the Broad Stand the rest is easy with care. The issues of the various climbs can be examined and notably Scafell Pinnacle, which is readily accessible from the north-east; but which, if ascended by the ridge or the Pinnacle nose route, affords one of the finest climbs in England. This feat was first performed by Messrs. Slingsby, Hastings, E. Hopkinson, and Haskett Smith, on July 15th, 1888.

The view was grand, and, thanks to the severe winter, the crevices and hollows on all the higher elevations were thick with snow fit for glissading, step-cutting, or more often of real service on the "crack" climbs, as many a trying bit was rendered readily passable by the snowy mantle. Returning we crossed Scafell Pike to the shoulder of Lingmell, and then descended Piers Ghyll for a considerable distance.

Two days later five of our party, reluctantly compelled to leave us, departed by Burnmoor Tarn for Boot. The remaining three then went off to the base of the Scafell precipice, and after working up a snow slope to the Rake's Progress made the ascent of Moss Ghyll. This gully was first climbed on the 26th December, 1892, by Dr. J. N. Collie, G. Hastings, and J. W. Robinson. The incident is fully described

in the "Scottish Mountaineering Club Journal," January, 1894. It was a most interesting climb, and we accomplished it by precisely the same route. An axe would have been of great service in bridging the short traverse at the "hacked step" above the jammed stones, but it had been left at the foot of the climb. A knob of rock known as the "belaying pin," immediately above this step, serves as a safe support for the rope whilst traversing the long crack on the steep sloping rock on the right (east) above it. A fall might entail disastrous consequences, and, therefore, the ascent should be attempted only by experienced cragsmen. The descent was made more to the westward by a series of mossy pitches to the Lord's Rake, and along the Rake's Progress and screes to the foot of Moss Ghyll, and proved fairly easy but somewhat slippery.

Moss Ghyll, from Rake's Progress.   F. LEACH

The dining-room at Wasdale Head is adorned with photographs of climbs, some of which are on Simon's Seat in Yorkshire. Of these the most conspicuous is the Napes Needle and Ridge, on Great Gable. Among the mountains in Cumberland Great Gable is held in high estimation, perhaps ranking only second to Scafell. Its jagged and precipitous brow is full of varied and interesting work. Approached by the Green Tongue after leaving the confluence of the Kirk and Lingmell becks, its ascent induces a feeling of excessive warmth, and the struggle over the upper screes of Little Hell Gate a wealth of expletives excusable on such a vast accumulation of rotten *débris*. The cliffs on this side project in forbidding sharp ridges leading up to the shoulder. The fourth from the Sphinx's Head terminates in the Napes Needle, a singular piece of detached rock, about sixty feet high from the ledge, shaped like a violoncello, as seen from the base of the Eagle's Nest. It is essentially a problem in rock-climbing, and necessitates no little care before its head is under the foot of the climber. I heard of more than one party coming back defeated from the attack. It was first ascended by Haskett Smith in June, 1886. The upper crack on the west face is a tight jam for the left knee; but once over the small wedged stone the platform behind the neck gives one a fair and perfectly safe breathing space from which the last portion is assailed. A shoulder lifted our leading man to the tiny ledge beneath the headstone, a good step at the left lower side of which enabled him, by pressing well on the rock, to work his right hand along the sharp angle to its upper corner. Then just below the very top a knobby projection gave the left hand sufficient purchase to enable him to force himself with his chest on to the top. A few spasmodic struggles and the top was reached. During this bit it is well for the others to keep the rope just taut, so that in case of a slip the leader can be pulled

View of Napes Needle.   F. LEACH

back on to the platform. There is barely sufficient room on the head-stone for three persons, but ample for two. In descending, the last man, after lowering his companions to the platform, hitches the rope behind the rock under a convenient hump, and descends by the double rope, which is carefully played by those below. The rest from the platform is easy by the steep staircase to the south, though the rope should not be discarded.

Behind the Needle the Ridge rises almost precipitously.   It is easier than it looks, and affords magnificent practice all the way.   We stuck throughout to the comb of the ridge, and thoroughly enjoyed the climb, which is a fitting sequel to the ascent of the Napes Needle.

Here I may be excused for mentioning, as a consensus of the opinions I heard on "Climbing in the British Isles," by Haskett Smith, that most men thought the book would be infinitely more valuable if the climbs were allocated under the name of the mountain on which they are situated, with an outline map for each showing the exact position.   More is sure to be written, and let us hope some such classification will be attempted.

After a week of continuous sunshine the weather changed, and as we returned, driven back by a misty rain from an attempt on the Arrowhead Ridge, our party

decided, if there was no improvement, to recross the pass and make for Langdale by Rossett Ghyll. Next morning the dense vapour hung low o'er all the valley, and through this we regretfully left Wasdale Head by the ancient grass track on the left bank of Lingmell beck to the summit of Sty Head, and then from Sty Head Tarn to Sprinkling Tarn and Esk

Wasdale Head and Great Gable.   F. LEACH.

Hause, where lunch was taken in a thick Scotch mist.   Just then a burst of sunshine revealed a patch of bright green on the Langdale Pikes, high in the clouds.   A glimpse, and then the sullen mist enveloped us once more.   Soon another brilliant break appeared, and by the time we had passed the inky waters of Angle Tarn, at the foot of Hanging Knott, all ahead was bright in sunlight, while behind, the hills were covered with a dark canopy of heaving clouds.

From the sheepfold at the foot of the Stake Pass, the springy turf and genial warmth proved a welcome change from the rough stony track down Rossett Ghyll.

The remainder of the ramble, by frequented tourist tracks and along well-laid roads, does not come within the scope of an article of this kind, descriptive of

> "unpeopled glens
> And mountainous retirements, only trod
> By devious footsteps, regions consecrate
> To oldest time."

To many climbers the fascination of a first ascent is too strong for words, and unfortunately for them most of the best things in the Lake Country have been done ; but variations of recognised routes are constantly being made, and in numerous instances there is yet left the opportunity of obtaining distinction by making the first descents of the best climbs.

It only remains to be added that the experience gained in this manner among our English Alps is invaluable for the best work among the loftier mountains of Switzerland. A note of warning must be struck, however, for on our lowly hills accidents have happened, and will happen again, even to the most skilful climbers. Therefore, let there be no relaxation of care and attention to the work in hand. A single moment of carelessness may imperil the lives of all upon the rope, and opprobrium thus be cast upon a splendid and manly sport, that in the highest sense of the term brings out the best of our physical and mental qualities. Remember, too, that when to advance entails unjustifiable risk, the man, who really understands the work, should insist on his party turning back, and to do this requires an exhibition of courage, true moral courage, which is frequently wanting. No pastime worthy of the name is without its risks. The spice of danger and the physical fitness to overcome it are the incentives which attract and finally enthral the lovers of this truly elevating pursuit.

G. T. L., 1896.

CHAPTER XII.

KESWICK TO WINDERMERE BY COACH.

EW things will be found more pleasurable in the life of an ordinary mortal than a ride by coach from Keswick to Windermere. Several four-in-hand coaches run the journey daily (in the season); the vehicles are of the high-built pattern, light and breezy, and generally drawn by four handsome, clean-limbed, high-mettled horses, well equipped and well driven. Just before starting there is the usual bustle so dear to the hearts of coachmen and grooms; then the horn is sounded, all passengers are seated, the driver tightens the reins, and we are rattling over the stony street. A turn to the left, and again to the right, and the long climb of Castle Rigg is begun; at the top, a thousand feet above Keswick, the coachman draws in his steeds for a few moments, and, looking back, a glorious prospect spreads before us. The town, lit up by the morning sunlight, lay like a dream far below us; the hills to the west are in deep shadow; the mountains north of Borrow-dale are ablaze in golden light; Derwentwater gleams like a mirror, and over Crosthwaite Church the long blue bed of Bassenthwaite stretches away. The morning mist has not yet been dispersed from old Skiddaw and Saddleback. Now we drop down into the vale of St. John. "What a beautiful name," said a lady, "and how suggestive of loveliness"; but not a whit more lovely than it appears, with its streams and grey roofs of white-washed cottages resting under rocks and sheltered by fir woods, with the deep green of meadow land around. Yonder is the Church of St. John. Now we have reached Thirlmere, and Castle Rock, stern and grey, rises above to guard the gloomy pass below. In front is Helvellyn, rising like a mystic curtain wall, as if to bar the entrance to some unknown land. Now the road descends rapidly, the horses dash forth in fine style, the leaders are in a canter. Soon the shrill sound of the guard's horn is heard, and the driver reins in his panting steeds for a short breathing time at the King's Head Inn, Thirlspot, a low antique house, with the fell rising behind. At Dalehead a torrent, in a series of falls, leaps to the vale below. This is a place of memories ; we

are in the footsteps of Southey, Wordsworth, Coleridge, Wilson, Foster, Matthew Arnold, and Rossetti. Away over the lake is haunted Armboth Hall ; by the shore of Thirlmere is the " Rock of Names," the meeting place of the poets of Grasmere and Keswick, and here they have left a memorial by carving their initials in the rock.

Wytheburn Church

" An upright Mural block of stone,
Moist with pure water trickling down ;
Thy power, dear Rock, around thee cast
Thy monumental, shall last
For me and mine : O thought of pain
That would impair it as profane,
And fail not thou, loved Rock, to keep
Thy charge when we are laid asleep."

Near to these rocks was the Cherry Tree public-house, where Wordsworth stopped his peasant waggoner during his famous drive from Rydal, over Dunmail Raise, to Keswick.

The sound of the driver's horn is heard, a light flourish of the whip, and we are off at a swinging pace, by Thirlmere, silent and peaceful, gleaming below, and far away west, summit behind summit, and range after range, with wreaths of mist still curling round, as the soft fingers of distance smooth the stronger outlines and melt the hues of lavish richness into the setting of the bounding heavens ! onward rumbles the coach, and the blood courses through the veins quicker as we inhale the pure mountain air. Now we have reached the Nag's Head, Wytheburn. Wytheburn's house appears as lowly as the lowliest dwelling. Coleridge wrote :—

" Humble it is, and very meek, and very low.   But God himself, and he alone can know
And speaks its purpose by a single bell :   If spirey temples please him half so well."

In olden time the living was only worth £3 a year, but the parishioners lent the parson a helping hand, besides he had "a goose run" on the slopes of Helvellyn. It was formerly known as the smallest church in England, but of late years it has been slightly enlarged. Opposite to the church is the Nag's Head Inn, which we have found most comfortable on more than one occasion after a stiff day's tramp. It lies at the base of Helvellyn, and from this place is one of the shortest paths to the summit. Still the coach rattles through the hills that peer above clothed with the tints of moss

Red Tarn, Helvellyn.   W. G. FOSTER.

and lichen, past pine wood and winding brook, and now the vale opens to view like a veritable land of enchantment. Helm Crag, with open jaws, in its wraith of ghostly mist, appears as if about to fall on some unwary foe. Here is Dunmail Raise, where the last king of Cumbria was slain, and a heap of stones raised over his corpse, hence the name Raise.* Opposite the base of Helm Crag the driver drew in his steeds for a moment's rest. The foxhounds were searching for Reynard amidst the fastness

---

* It was one of these Wythburn worthies who had but two sermons, which he kept in a crevice near the pulpit. One Sunday he was compelled to announce that as some mischievous "lads" had pushed the sermons so far in as not to be got hold of, he would read them a lesson from Job instead, the first two chapters of which were great favourites with the dalespeople.

of the mountain. The black and white of the hounds contrast finely with the dark grey, slatey rock—the music of the baying hounds swells louder as they climb the Helm. They have sniffed Master Reynard, and are bounding over the sharp rock, and the breeze wafts across the vale that loud, eager music of the chase.

Now other objects claim our attention—Away to the left is Easdale Tarn.

> " Tranquil and shut out
> From all the strife that shakes a jarring world,"

partitioned off by a screen of rock from the vale of Grasmere, pierced only by a tiny brook threading in silvery line to the lake. This is Easdale Beck, and here is Emma's Dell, which Wordsworth called his own. Here he told the shepherds : " When years after we are gone and in our graves, when they have cause to speak of this wild place, may they call it the name of Emma's Dell."

Helm Crag, with its ever-changing form from lion couchant to cowled priest, or ancient woman, is left behind, the smoke rising from the grey roofs of Grasmere in front. The dewdrops glisten on the leaves of the coppice, the green and brown of the wood, and golden gorse and bracken which clothe the hillsides, sweet surprises and magic charms on every hand. Scene follows scene in one unfailing source of delight. At a steady trot we pass the " Swan " associated with the wagoner, and from whence Wordsworth, Southey, and Scott started to ascend Helvellyn together. Onward speeds the coach, past stream, homestead, and crag. What memories linger around, memories of men now sleeping peacefully beneath the shade of yew trees, in the quiet churchyard, to the music of Rothay's stream ! What romance, pleasure, and fascination ! Yonder is Allen Bank, where De Quincey and Christopher North first met. Both were brilliant among the literati of " Modern Athens." Wilson filled the chair of Moral Philosophy in the University—"a man of fine physique, leonine aspect of head and contour ; a mind so equally balanced he could ascend to the highest strain of moral excellence, or descend in his portrayal to the nether extreme "— De Quincey. There are two incidents in his chequered life that are not widely known. A German student enquired of his professor what English author to read, and was told De Quincey. The student's enthusiasm became so great after perusal—came to Edinburgh purposely to see the man who wrote these books, and, strange to say, he found him in a tavern. Sir William Hamilton, the logician, at whose house gathered the Edinburgh men of letters, resolved to have a special night with De Quincey to discuss philosophy. But he at that time, through the excess of opium eating, avoided society and sought isolation. He lived in a rural district (Loan Head) six miles south from Edinburgh. The company sallied forth, found him in a quiet lane, put him into a carriage, wheeled him off to Edinburgh, and when he was primed with the drug he became the lion of the evening. Poor De Quincey ! we might truly say of him : "The muse often gives what the gods do not guide." In Dove Cottage, Grasmere, the latter dwelt for thirty-seven years ; here he stored his thousands of volumes, many of which his friends borrowed, but never returned. It was here he made the acquaintance of the strange Malay man, and drank so deeply of his dreamful opium. Thus he describes the cottage as he first saw it, when on a visit to Wordsworth, who also dwelt here before removing to Rydal Mount : "A white cottage, with two yew trees breaking the glare of its white walls." A little semi-vestibule between two doors prefaced the entrance into the principal room of the cottage, which is 8 ft. high, 16 ft. long, and 12 ft. broad, wainscotted from floor to ceiling with dark polished oak. There was one perfect and unpretending cottage window, with little diamond panes, embowered at almost every season of the year with roses, and in summer and autumn with a profusion of jasmine and other shrubs.

Dove Cottage.

Wordsworth, in his "Farewell," wrote—

" Sunshine and shower be with you, bud and bell,
    For two months now in vain we shall be sought ;
We leave you here in solitude to dwell
    With these, our latest gifts of tender thought.

Thou, like the morning, in thy saffron coat,
    Bright gowan, and marsh marigold, farewell,
Whom from the borders of the Lake we brought,
    And placed together near our rocky well."

" Oh, happy garden ! whose seclusion deep,
    Hath been so friendly to industrious hours,
And to soft slumbers, that did gently steep
    Our spirits, carrying with them dreams of flowers,

And wild notes warbled among leafy bowers ;
    Two burning months let summer over leap,
And coming back with her who will be ours,
    Into thy bosom we again shall creep."

But here we are at Grasmere—the jewel of Lakeland, the sweetest spot ever man found, rich in associations, the haven of dreams, a spot the most sacred and peaceful. At the quaint lych-gate we part from the coach, for we feel compelled to linger. A holy calm and peace pervades the churchyard, yet the aspect of the ground is slightly changed since the poet wrote :—

" Green is the churchyard, beautiful and green,
Ridge rising gently by the side of ridge ;
A heaving surface almost wholly free
From interruption of sepulchral stones,
And mantled o'er with aboriginal turf

And everlasting flowers ; these Dalesmen trust
The lingering gleam of their departed lives
To oral record, and the silent heart ;
Depositories faithful and more kind
Than fondest epitaph."

It is not free of memorials now, for the ground is thickly covered with tombstones.

Here in St. Oswald's Churchyard, under the shade of yew trees which the poet himself planted, sleep William Wordsworth and his wife ; also his sister Dorothy, and near to is the grave of Hartley Coleridge. Few spots make a deeper impression on the soul of the pilgrim than this quiet corner in Grasmere Churchyard. The deep, almost solemn shade of the yew trees, the Rothay gliding past the holy walls and under the grey old arch, its brown waters still murmuring a song as of old, to soothe, as it were, the souls of the immortal bards. The old lych-gate, the surrounding hills—to-day in a blaze of sunlight ; the grave mounds at our feet, the antique church with its grey, square, cobbled tower and intricate lines of plaster ; the rude antiquities and severe originality of the interior, the unique double arches, with rare oak beam and rafters, and curious Norman font.

"To lie under the mound on which the shadow of that grey tower falls," says one,

Grasmere Church, and Wordsworth's Grave.

"seems scarcely like a banishment from life, only a deeper sleep, in a home quieter, but not less lovely than those which surround the margin of the lake. Voices of children come up from the village street, with the hum of rustic life. From sunny heights the lowing of cattle is heard, and the bleat of the sheep which pasture on the hillsides ; and by day and night unceasingly, the Rotha, hurrying past the churchyard wall, mingles the babble of its waters with the soft susurrus of the breeze"

Wilson says :

"There is a little churchyard on the side
Of a low hill that hangs o'er Grasmere Lake ;
Most beautiful it is, a vernal spot,
Enclos'd with wooded rocks, where a few graves
Lie shelter'd, sleeping in eternal calm.
Go thither when you will, and that sweet spot
Is bright with sunshine."

The road now passes by the shores of Grasmere. Nothing can excel the charm and beauty of this lake resting in the bosom of the mountains, which are reflected, with trees, meadow, and cattle, as in a mirror. The delicious green of its isle seems like an abode of fairies. The water fowl glide out of the reeds, leaving long streaks of silver on the waters; golden larch and huge fir trees hang their branches over limpid brooks passing to the lake under picturesque bridges; ivy-clad cots, where the honeysuckle and woodbine entwine about the rustic porch, and snow-white mullion contrast with the warm green of the meadows—exquisite pictures, a dreamland of the soul.

At the base of White Moss Moor stood the old Wishing Gate. The old moss-grown gate of Wordsworth's youthful days was demolished in his lifetime.

> " 'Tis gone—with old belief and dream
>   That round it clung."
>
> " And yet, lost Wishing Gate,
> To thee the voice of grateful memory
> Shall bid a kind farewell."

It stood on White Moss Common, on the old road from Grasmere to Rydal. Another gate still stands there, but the view is not what it used to be in the poet's lifetime.

Ambleside has two distinct aspects, and presents startling contrasts—the very old

Brathay Bridge.

and the new. Ancient lanes, streets, and archways curve and twist in every conceivable manner and position. The mill-stream and the old mill, also the bridge house, are tempting subjects to every passing artist or photographer, and cottages clinging here and there to the crooked lanes ascending the hillsides form pleasant rustic pictures. The church is a new, handsome structure, although the spire is not architecturally all that can be desired. Here, and also at Grasmere, the old custom of rush-bearing still exists, only instead of rushes to strew the mud floor, the votive offerings are in the shape of garlands made from rushes and wild flowers. These are hung on the walls of the church.* There are several handsome hotels and shops, and a market

---

* EXTRACT FROM THE NOTE BOOK OF A TOURIST WHO ARRIVED AT GRASMERE, JULY 21ST, 1827.—On entering the church, found the villagers strewing the floor with fresh rushes. Among the seasons of periodical festivity at this place was the rush-bearing, or the ceremony of conveying fresh rushes to strew the floor of the parish church. This method of covering floors was universal in *houses*, while floors were of earth, but is now confined to places of worship. The bundles of the girls were adorned with wreaths of flowers, and the evening concluded with a dance. In Westmoreland the custom has undergone a change. Billy remembered when the lasses bore the rushes in the evening procession, and strewed the floors at the same time that they decorated the church

square hall and Mechanics' Institute. Some of the streets are very precipitous, and the manner in which the drivers guide their four-in-hand steeds down, and round the sharp angles, is admirable. Ambleside is a convenient centre from which to make excursions. It is aptly named "the axle of the wheel of beauty," every spoke of which holds gems. Several rivulets join their waters near the town. Up Stock Ghyll are a series of fine waterfalls, and on the hillside, behind that mass of trees, is The Knoll, for many years the home of that charming authoress, Harriet Martineau. The sundial on the lawn still bears the inscription of her heart's desire : "Come, light, visit me!" Nearly opposite is Fox How, where the good Dr. Arnold dwelt. Further south, above the shores of Windermere, is Dove's Nest, the residence, for one summer, of Mrs. Hemans.* Added to our admiration of the beautiful magnificence and varied

---

with garlands ; now the rushes are laid in the morning by the ringer and clerk, and no rushes are introduced in the evening procession. I do not like the old customs to change ; for, like mortals, they change before they die altogether. Wordsworth is the chief supporter of these rustic ceremonies. The procession over, the party adjourned to the ballroom, a hayloft at my worthy friend Mr. Bell's, where the country lads and lasses tripped it merrily and heavily. They called the amusement dancing, but I called it thumping, for he who could make the greatest noise seemed to be esteemed the best dancer, and on the present occasion I think Mr. Pooley bore away the palm. Billy Dawson, the fiddler, boasted to me of having been the officiating minstrel at this ceremony for the last six-and-forty years. He made grievous complaints of the outlandish tunes which the "Union Band Chaps" introduce. In the procession of this evening they annoyed Bill by playing the "Hunter Chorus is Friskits." "Who," said Billy, "can keep time with such a queer thing ?" Amongst the gentlemen dancers was one Dan Burkitt ; he introduced himself to me by seizing my coat collar in a mode that would have given a Burlington Arcade lounger the hysterics, and saying, "I'm old Dan Burkitt, of Wytheburn, sixty-six years old—not a better jigger in Westmoreland." No, thought I, nor a greater toss-pot. On my relating this to an old man present, he told me not to judge of Westmoreland manners by Dan's. "For," said he, "you see, sir, he is a statesman, and has been at Lunnon, and so takes liberties." In Westmoreland, farmers residing on their own estate are called "statesmen." The dance was kept up till a quarter to twelve, when a livery-servant entered, and delivered the following verbal message to Billy : "Master's respects, and will thank you to lend him the fiddle-stick." Billy took the hint ; the Sabbath morning was at hand, and the pastor of the parish had adopted this gentle mode of apprizing the assembled revellers that they ought to cease their revelry. The servant departed with the fiddle-stick, the chandelier was removed, and when the village clock struck twelve, not an individual was to be seen out of doors in the village. No disturbance of any kind interrupted the dance. Dan Burkitt was the only person at all "how came you so?" and he was *non se ipse* before the jollity commenced. He told me he was "seldom sober," and I believed what he said. The rush-bearing is now, I believe, almost entirely confined to Westmoreland

* Mrs. Hemans thus describes Dove's Nest :—"The house was originally meant for a small villa, though it has long passed into the hands of farmers, and there is, in consequence, an air of neglect about the little demesne, which does not at all approach desolation, and yet gives it something of touching interest. You see everywhere traces of love and care beginning to be effaced—rose trees spreading into wildness—laurels darkening the windows with too luxuriant branches ; and I cannot help saying to myself, 'Perhaps some heart like my own in its feelings and sufferings has here sought refuge and repose.' The ground is laid out in rather an antiquated style, which, now that nature is beginning to claim it from art, I do not at all dislike. There is a little grassy terrace immediately under the window, descending to a small court, with a circular grass plot, on which grows one tall, white rose tree. You cannot imagine how much I delight in that fair, solitary, neglected-looking tree. I am writing to you from an old-fashioned alcove in the little garden, round which the sweet-briar and the rose tree have completely run wild ; and I look down from it upon lovely Windermere, which seems at this moment even like another sky, so truly is every summer cloud and tint of azure pictured in its transparent mirror."

N

scenery of the Lakes, is that almost holy pleasure which appeals to our higher sympathies and emotion when visiting the abodes of those children of the muse who have lived here in the past, and who, by the nobility and goodness of their writings, have made these spots sacred, and though now dead and gone, the music of their inspiration still breathes through the changing years.

It was the witching hour of sunset as we turned from the road between Ambleside and Grasmere, said to be the finest four miles of coach-road in England, and crossed to the west side of the Rothay by one of those charming bridges, half-hidden by leaves, moss, wild flowers, and grass. Under the wooded slopes of Loughrigg Fell we wander, the paths alluring us on through scenes of exquisite beauty and softness. Now we enter the deep shade of the old wood, where overhanging projections of crags cast a sombre hue. Below, through the branches of shady groves, we obtain bewitching views of distant mountains, and can see and hear the Rothay hurrying along, giving forth a dreamful song. From under the trees we emerge into the open glade, past bossy knolls and "heath-clad rocks," where the light from a cottage window gleamed through creeping woodbine and branch, which half-smothered the walls.

> " 'Turn where we may,' said I, we cannot err
> In this delicious region—clustered slopes,
> Wild tracts of forest ground and scattered groves,
> And mountains bare, or clothed with ancient woods surround us."

Such were the lovely scenes and impressions on our mind, of holy calm and pastoral sweetness, as we stood in the twilight before Rydal Mount, the home of William Wordsworth for 37 years. The spot, ever sacred, is embowered in branches, and the walls embraced with clinging ivy ; beautiful trees, in all the luxuriance of vegetation and growth, thrive ; ferns, plants, and flowers, both cultivated and wild, abound, scenting the air with a delicious aroma. Below is the lovely lake, with its tiny islands, around which immense-limbed trees fling out their arms over green, velvet margins and grassy, moss lawns, the most lovely. As one has said, nature is a vast Temple, down whose glorious aisles floats the breath of the Divine ! The modest church, peeping from the branches, and over and above all loom the circling crests of the everlasting hills. Here lies all that harmony and repose in nature, and that delightful grouping of wood, meadow, river, lake, and mountain impregnated with the glamour of poetry and the charm of literary association. Ruminating beneath the branches of an aged tree, we marvelled on the beauty of the spot ; sweetly on the ear came that bubble and even flow of water, and the distant melody of cascades.

> " No sound is uttered, but a deep
> And solemn harmony pervades
> The hollow vale from steep to steep,
> And penetrates the glades."

The surrounding ranges of hills were sparkling with a lustre almost heavenly; here and there could be seen the twinkling lights of cottages, nested, as it were, in leafy bowers. A veil of mist gradually crept over the lake, from whence the splash of oars and the music of voices floated; the blackbird had ceased his warbling, and the cushats had fallen to slumber in the pine trees, bats whirled hither and thither as if in aimless flight; a buzz clock droned past, causing that peculiar, slumberous, dreamful sound. Thus musing, as the clock in the church tower chimed the hour of ten, we turned away with loftier feelings by this communion with nature around Rydal Mount.

"O vale and lake, within your mountain urn,
  Smiling so tranquilly, and set so deep!
Oft doth your dreamy loveliness return,
  Colouring the tender shadows of my sleep
With light Elysian; for the hues that steep
  Your shores in melting lustre, seem to float
On golden clouds from spirit lands remote,
  Isles of the blest and in our memory keep,
Their place with holiest harmonies. Fair scene,
Most loved by evening and her dewy star,
O, ne'er may man, with touch unhallowed, jar
The perfect music of the charm serene!
Still, still unchanged, may one sweet region wear
Smiles that subdue the soul to love, and tears and
      prayer."   MRS. HEMANS.

Another poetess says :—

" Thee, too, I found within thy sylvan dell,
  Whose music thrilled my heart, when life was new,
  Wordsworth! 'mid cliff, and stream, and cultured rose,
  In love with Nature's self, and she with thee.
Thy ready hand, that from the landscape cull'd
  Its long familiar charms, rock, tree, and spire;
With kindness half paternal, leading on
My stranger footsteps through the garden walk,
'Mid shrubs and flowers that from thy planting grew;

The group of dear ones gathering round thy board,
She, the first friend, still as in youth beloved;
  The daughter—sweet companion—sons mature,
And favourite grandchild, with its treasured phrase,
The evening lamp, that o'er thy silver locks
And ample brow fell fitfully, and touch'd
Thy lifted eye with earnestness of thought,
Are with me as a picture, ne'er to fade,
Till death shall darken all material things."

                          MRS. SIGOURNEY.

CHAPTER XII.

THROUGH THE LANGDALES, UP ROSSETT GHYLL, AND OVER ESK HAUSE TO BORROWDALE.

EFORE leaving the Vale of Rothay, we climb the steep ascent of Red Bank, and rest on a soft, green knoll beside a crystal brook, embosomed in woods, and feast our eyes on, perhaps we might be allowed to say, the gem scene in Lakeland. Far below lies the whole vale of Grasmere, with a startling beauty baffling our wildest dreams. The foreground of the picture is broken by delightful copse, with the intermingling branch of oak, larch, silver birch, and Scotch fir; and meadows green as emerald, dotted with cattle, slope down to the edge of the lake, with its numerous small bays and inlets, and one little island. On the opposite shore is Grasmere, its grey roofs and church tower reposing so exquisitely amid the trees. In the bosom of the vale we obtain silvery glimpses of the Rothay, and the shattered head of Helm Crag, on the left of the picture, has a fine effect, with twining road passing over Dunmail Raise* to Keswick—the background of mountains rising ridge over ridge, like huge billows, to four distinct ranges. Nothing glaring or unsightly disturbs the perfect repose of the picture. Wordsworth, in his "Excursion," says :—

---

* Dunmail Raise perpetuates the name of the last King of Cumberland. Joining his forces with Leolin, king of the Welsh, he was met, defeated, and slain by Edmund, the Saxon monarch, who, we are told, barbarously put out the eyes of the two sons of the dead king, raised a heap of stones over the corpse to mark the spot, and gave his kingdom to Malcolm of Scotland, who held it in fee of Edmund, A.D. 944.

" Upon a rising ground a grey church tower,
  Whose battlements were screen'd by tufted trees,
  And towards a crystal mere, that lay beyond,
  Among steep hills, and woods embosom'd, flow'd
  A copious stream, with boldly winding course,
  Here traceable, there hidden—there again

To sight restored, and glittering in the sun :
On the stream's banks, and everywhere, appear'd
Fair dwellings, single or in social knots ;
Some scatter'd o'er the level, others perch'd
On the hillsides—a cheerful, quiet scene."

To the west, over Red Bank, is the hamlet of Elterwater, perfect in its rural seclusion, quaint cottages, and overhanging porches beautifully covered with creepers

and woodbine ; the post-office and ye old inn are pictures of rustic loveliness. It was from hence, before I turned into the mountain, that I wired my friend, who was sketching a few miles away, and from whom I had been missing some forty-eight hours, the following, which caused no small amount of curiosity at the rural post-office. The telegram, which has since been kept as a relic by our landlady, ran thus : " Tracking the Langdales searching for glow worms "—singularly true, for on that night, in a certain little vale of which I shall make mention later, I saw the luminous glow of dozens of those shy little creatures. Just a peep into the depths of Great Langdale, with its deep slate quarries and gunpowder manufactory. Much might be written about the beautiful scenery in the lower part of the valley, through which the river Brathay winds. Above, in the recesses of the hills, the grey stone cottages are half hidden by pines and sycamores.* For the present we make a detour through

---

* It was in the Langdale Chapel, some half-century ago, and just after the clergyman had given out his text : " Behold, I come quickly," that the rotten old pulpit collapsed with the parson in it, knocking down an elderly woman in the fall, who, on regaining her feet, remarked, " If I'd been kilt, I'd been reet sarrat, for ye said ye'd come dune quickly."

beautiful wooded bypaths, and reach Little Langdale ; and past the Tarn bearing the latter name the road turns onward to Blea Tarn, beyond which is a magnificent background of hills.   To the left, just before reaching Blea Tarn, a road passes over into the vale of the Duddon, from whence a rough track passes into Eskdale.   Blea Tarn lies on the right of the road near the head of Little Langdale.   In Wordsworth's days its shores were treeless ; it is not so now, for a dark fir wood rises on the mountain sides above the Tarn.

BLEA TARN & LANGDALE PIKES

" Urn-like it was in shape, deep as an urn,
   With rocks encompassed, save that to the south
   Was one small opening where a heath-clad ridge
   Supplied a boundary less abrupt and close
   A quiet, treeless nook, with two green fields,
   A liquid pool that glittered in the sun,
   And one bare dwelling ; one abode, no more."

   Away in the background, west of the Tarn, the Langdale Pikes uprear magnificent and mysterious, like the jagged frontier of some old-world border. Wordsworth, in his " Excursion," says :—

" In genial mood, while at our pastoral banquet thus we sat,
   I could not, ever and anon, forbear
   To glance an upward look on two huge peaks
   That from some other vale peered into this."

" Peered into this " is finely descriptive of the huge Pikes, rising sheer above all into the clouds. Now we bend away north-west into Great Langdale. At the entrance is an old farm, where we took shelter from a sudden storm which swept over the vale

It is a typical old moorland farm, grey and quaint, with curious holes and corners in its thick walls and deep mullions. A few hundred yards beyond is Dungeon Ghyll Hotel, and just to the east of which is Dungeon Ghyll. Ghyll is the dialect of Cumberland and Westmoreland, and means a steep, narrow valley with a stream dashing through it. We follow the stream upward until we reach the solid walls of rock, upwards of fifty feet in height, and some nine or ten feet in width. Into this narrow chasm falls a sheet of water fully sixty feet, the volume varying according to the rainfall. At the top, a rock, at some distant date, has fallen across the ravine, forming a natural bridge.

> " It is a spot which you may see,
> If ever you into Langdale go :
> Into a chasm a mighty block
> Hath fallen and made a bridge of rock :
> The gulf is deep below,
> And in a basin black and small,
> Receives a lofty waterfall."

The Langdales.

Stickle Tarn, the source of Mill Beck, is more to the north, above which tower the Langdale Pikes. Hell Ghyll, Crinkle, and Rossett Ghyll are deep gullies and chasms, well worth exploring, full of romantic and majestic scenery. The solemn and savage grandeur of the scene around the head of Great Langdale is at any time most impressive, but during an overhanging storm is truly appalling. The amphitheatre of dark, sullen crests, Bowfell on one hand and the Pikes on the other, and

Scafell in the background, with Mickledon Ridge, and the dark yawning mouth of glen and chasm, and the faint outline of a path winding upwards over the rocks, by that turbulent stream, falling from the head of the Stake into the Langdale ; the wild and unearthly shriek of the wind, howling and whistling around the peaks, through the passes, disturbing the surface of the tarns, which nature has formed so wisely to act as reservoirs in the crevices of the hills, to-day turbulent like the sea in fury rent. Here and there islands of mist float across the vision like spectral visitants from another world, fit representation of the mysterious reign of chaos and old time, and an entrance into Hades.

Up over the rocks by the zigzag path we climb to the head of Rossett Ghyll, over Esk Hause, past Angle and Sprinkling Tarn, dark and awesome, fit abode for some

Borrowdale, from Rosthwaite.   RODWELL.

unsightly monster. Now under towering peaks, terraced with serrations and needle-like projections, with the snow still deep in the gullies and on the edges of rock which the sun never pierces. Here a mystery of lowering clouds and vapour career around the mountain summits, now hiding crest and precipice, or anon floating down the

valleys, or reeking upwards like sulphurous smoke out of yon deep chasm.* From the summit of the pass magnificent views are to be obtained, if the weather be favourable, in three directions. To the south-east the Langdale and Brathay valleys, and Lake Windermere, with the background of Yorkshire hills ; to the west we look down into

---

* " Many years ago a party of tourists, among whom were two sisters, were on the heights, intending to cross Esk Hause into Borrowdale, and to spend the night at Seathwaite, the first settlement there ; now there is another Seathwaite, on the Duddon, and mistakes frequently arise between them. On Esk Hause one of the ladies lost sight of her party behind some of the rocks scattered among the tarns there, and took a turn to the right instead of the left. A shepherd, of whom she enquired her way to Seathwaite, directed her down the Duddon valley ; and that way she went, till she found herself at Cockley Beck, when the old shepherd farmer who lived there was getting his supper in the dusk of the autumn evening. He used his best endeavour to induce her to stay ill

the deep *cul de sac* formed by the shoulder of Great End and Great Gable. How striking to the mind is the scene! Wasdale, with its solitary lake, is more than a thousand feet below, whilst far up the streams, west, the sea can be descried glittering. To the north, down Borrowdale, the view is remarkable, extending across Derwentwater, begemmed with isles, and Bassenthwaite, to the sunlit slopes of Skiddaw. Here, right up in the heart of the hills, is a lonely tarn ; the solitude is most impressive ; the spot is entirely surrounded by a huge amphitheatre of mountains, whilst the precipice of Scawfell rises nearly two thousand feet overhead ; over sterile peaks (hoary monarchs) are golden gleams and shadows ; down crevice, ravine, and gully, water leaps and swirls, dashing on great boulders, rushing through narrow gorges, breaking and echoing on its madding course, the wild child of the hills shouts loud in her glee. Apart from this sound the silence is almost oppressive. Here, in the most inaccessible peaks, formerly the eagles nested, and the wild boar, wolf, and bustard roamed ; the latter long ago disappeared, but the eagles have been seen here within the memory of many now living. Up in this wild region the Derwent has its numerous feeders, from Sty Head and Sprinkling Tarns the parent stream begins its course, whilst Langsbrath Beck has its rise in the dark waters of Angle Tarn, resting under the left shoulder of Bowfell, and draining the north side of the ridge separating Langsbrath dale and Langdale. This beck joins the main stream just below Rosthwaite in Borrowdale.

Following a rough track we soon reach Seathwaite, the first settlement, a noted sheep-farm ; and further down is Seatoller, where the road from Borrowdale branches off over the famous Honister Pass to Buttermere. Over Rosthwaite Church and the hamlet of Stonethwaite, Dale Head Rock towers like some monster antediluvian ruin, and beyond, the two immense crags guard the gate to Buttermere ; and away up the sweeping curve of Langsbrath dale rise in majesty Eagle Crag, High Raise, Great Gable, and the mighty range of Glaramara, scenes of solitary and striking grandeur. Rosthwaite Church, more to the west, is a quiet, restful spot. One epitaph in the graveyard arrested our attention.

> " Time was I stood, as Thou dost now,
> And viewed the dead as Thou dost me ;
> Ere long 'how'lt lie as low as I,
> And others stand and look on thee.
>
> Weep not for me, I'm dead and gone,
> My husband dear, God's will be done ;
> But on my children pity take,
> And love them for their mother's sake "

---

daylight, but she was bent on going at once, so great would be her sister's terror. As she would not be persuaded the old man went with her, putting his crust into his pocket. It was dark, and the lady was weary, and she was not aware what she was undertaking. After a long struggle she fainted ; the old man was afraid to leave her lest he should not find her again, but he succeeded in reaching the water without losing sight of her white dress ; he dipped his crust, and brought water in his hat to bathe her face. She revived, ate the crust, and strove onwards, persevering on her weary way till between one and two in the morning, when she met her sister and a party coming from Seathwaite in Borrowdale with a dozen lanterns to search for her. She gave her guide " a one pound note " (it was so long ago as that), and afterwards sent him two more."

The situation of Rosthwaite is the perfection of all that is lovely in nature. It is watered by two beautiful streams, and, with the exception of the two hotels, there is a venerable antiquity about the spot, and the immense yew and fir trees add an almost solemn dignity to the valley. Borrowdale is choice in its superfluity of pencil art— a veritable picture gallery—green glades, rock, precipice, mountain, and waving woods, fringed with all the luxuriance of wild vegetation, and the loveliest of rivers winding through. Although nature has dealt so abundantly with her treasures in this valley, report unkindly says that the inhabitants were discontented, for we are told that once on a time they attempted to wall in the cuckoo, and by so doing

Borrowdale.   EDMUND BOGG

retain everlasting spring. The sweet river, like an immortal spirit, flows under the narrow pass, the " jaws of Borrowdale," through exquisite scenery, fringed with birch, alder, pine, and sycamore, the leaves tinged, now with the brown of autumn ; grey, slaty rock strewing the bed of the river, over which the hills and branches cast many a flickering shadow, and seem enchanted by the music of its clear and gushing waters. In the narrowest part of the vale, the stream bends under woods and the deep shadow of the mountain, the waters find a deep, urnlike pool, clear as crystal in a globe ; banks of shingle, feathery branch, and hills, are all reflected, and in its depths the fish can be seen disporting. Music, too, is not wanting, for the water, issuing from the urn into the vale, shimmers and gives forth the most delightful harmony, a trembling strain of sweetness, as if echoing the fasci-

nating memories of the past. A few yards from hence is the famous Bowder stone, and further down the vale is Grange, a little, snug, greystone hamlet. Just before the vale widens to the lake, there is a unique bridge of two spans. Above, towers Castle Crag ; from the summit a glorious view down the vale is obtained. Here the Romans built a fort to hold the wild hill people in check. It was in turn used as a fort by the Saxons and the Normans. With the advent of the latter it passed into the hands of the Derwentwaters, of whom John de Derwentwater, previously mentioned, was the last lineal male descendant. Lower down, and opposite the head of the lake, are the magnificent Falls of Lodore, and near to is Wallow Crag, where the Countess of Derwentwater sought shelter from the fury of the dalespeople. Wild and varied is the scenery from hence. A mighty rock, split into a thousand fragments, lies in huge shapeless masses in the bed of the stream: above, the walls rise perpendicular to a great height. 'Tis at any time a scene that holds the mind with irresistible force; but at flood seasons it is a tumultuous sight, when the beck, in a vast torrent, pours down on rock and precipice. To rest at eventide near the Lodore Hotel, and watch the beauty of the ever-changing surface of the lake in the surpassing glory of declining day—'tis like a golden mirror, and the little islets which here and there rest on its surface appear like priceless gems in a rich setting. When the hills have become clothed in purple, and sunk into slumber, and all sounds are subdued, with the exception of the eternal sound of waters falling down Lodore, a fairer and more tranquil scene the eye can-

Grange.   EDMUND BOGG.

not rest upon, nor the receptive power within us feed on a richer or more luxuriant fare.

A rough path leads to the top of the cliff, just to the east of the falls. The view from this point of vantage, which is several hundred feet sheer above the lake, will amply repay the toil of ascending. The Borrowdale road runs immediately beneath the cliff, and people passing to and fro appear dwarfed to pigmies. The lake, viewed from hence, seems much smaller, resting with such delicacy and repose, a beautiful jewel deeply set in a frame of everlasting hills, which are seen with its emerald isles, rock, and woods, and the gaily painted pleasure-boats floating in its waters. It was an autumn evening when the writer looked on this scene, and the rich variety and harmonious blending of colour was surpassing in loveliness. The vale of the Derwent, with grove, meadow, and scattered hamlet, with the whole surface of Bassenthwaite, and the cloud-capped peaks around it, and Skiddaw, piercing the heavens, gilded with a halo of gold, in the waning sunlight, the perspective vanishing in the purple haze of night.   Added to this scene of enchantment is the continual splash of the waterfall of Lodore, resonant with eternal melody of falling waters—a feast of beauty for the eye, and music for the ear.   A row on the lake amongst its luxuriant isles, in the stillness of evening, by the silver light of the moon, is beautifully described by Southey in the following lines :—

> " The moon arose, she shone upon the lake,
> Which lay one smooth expanse of silver light ;
> She shone upon the hills and rocks, and cast
> Upon their hollows and hidden glens
> A blacker depth of shade."

Watendlath.   EDMUND BOGG.

Some three miles up the glen from Lodore is the rural hamlet of Watendlath, consisting of two or three farms and cottages in a narrow vale or hollow in the mountains, near to a most solitary-looking tarn. The place is a perfect dream of rusticity, primitive bridges, unique cottages, thrown anywise, rustic porches and curious curves and angles, whilst a few gnarled Scotch firs add colour and character to the spot.

THE VALE OF NEWLANDS.

There are some walks which remain as a bright vision of beauty for many years. Such is the writer's memory of the vale of Newlands.   Keswick was alive and gay with visitors, and coaches rattled merrily hither and thither, on that bright spring afternoon, as we passed through the town and over the Greta to Portinscale, and so forward into the beautiful vale of Newlands, the road winding through delightful woods of birch, oak, larch, and pine, with turf-clad slopes adorned richly with wild flowers, rocks, silvery and smooth, and here and there a white cottage peeping through the trees from its surrounding pastures.   Now and again we turn to look at Derwentwater, which lay begemmed, shimmering below like an oval mirror, with its amphitheatre of mountains split into many a gorge and glen. The road winds, the purple hills uprear, the birds give out gladsome song, and glittering beams dance upon the lake. The grey roofs and spires of Keswick, half-shrouded in smoke, with Skiddaw, Blencathra, and Wanthwaite peering down, appears dreamy and restful. Sometimes the sun burst forth in majesty and glory through the mystic veil of cloudscape, fringing the hilltops with a delectable glimmer, dancing amongst the emerald of the larch, and lit with a wondrous hue, rocks and escarpments. To the west Robinson and Castle Crag, Hindscarth and Grassmoor deepen into the purple of night.

At Little Town we pause awhile. The place only consists of three or four poor looking cottages, with "Cat Bells" just to the south. Near to are some disused lead mines; there is a breath of antiquity about the place, and from its appearance its former days have been far more prosperous. The lowly, whitewashed church of Newlands, with its belt of sycamores, is kept locked, and thus secure from the prying eyes of intruders, so we content ourselves with reading the inscriptions of the few tombstones, on some of which are names half English, half Dutch, the reason of which is easy to account for. Some two hundred and fifty years ago the mines of Newland were worked by miners from Augsburg, and at this period produced gold and silver of greater value than the copper from which it was extracted. This was the cause of a dispute between the Lord of the Manor and Queen Elizabeth, and it was then pronounced law that where gold and silver extracted from the lead was of greater value than the copper or lead, the mine was a royal mine, and the property of the crown. This privilege was given up in the reign of William and Mary, on condition that all gold and silver extracted should be disposed of within the Tower of London.

Beyond the Newland Hotel we rise to Keskadale Hawes; the landscape becomes more solitary, Causey Pike and Grassmoor uprearing on the right; to the left is Robinson, deeply fissured and scarred by some convulsion. The scene is wild; the varied aspect hath no limit. Now the road descends from Keskadale to Buttermere. Night has overtaken us, and the scene grows more grand and thrilling; the path runs along the edge of a steep precipice, at the bottom of which a stream pursues its turbulent course, from its rise in Causey Pike, to Crummock Water, adding a weird and wild melody to the scene. A bend in the road, and the mountains around the two lakes uprear ghostly and ominous under the cover of night. Far below, a few lights can be discerned twinkling as we rapidly descend to Buttermere, and bend to the left by the side of the lake, along whose margin a walk of two miles, through sombre avenues to the sound of dark, lapping waters, we reach Gatesgarth, the entrance to Honister, where we rest and shelter for the night.

CHAPTER XIII.

FROM BASSENTHWAITE TO COCKERMOUTH. AND DOWN THE VALE OF LORTON TO LOWESWATER. CRUMMOCK. AND BUTTERMERE.

HE immediate surroundings of Bassenthwaite do not present as much picturesque scenery as many of the other lakes, yet the contour of the hills, as seen from the water, are exceedingly fine, and the margin sloping upward to the hills are variegated with many beautiful phases of nature, and village and hamlet reposing in the vales at the base of the mountains on the west of the water, have a pleasing appearance. On the opposite shore from the Hollin's "High-side" some striking views are obtained. Two or three of the home-steads we visited in this locality are very ancient, one, for instance, in which Jane Davidson has dwelt for upwards of fifty of her eighty-four years, "An it was an owd house," she said, "when ah was a lass. Ye see ahm left bi mysen, an' I want to spend mi days here." The old, yellowy grey, cracked walls are half smothered with creepers and wild rose trees, where the bees hum in and out, and the roof is branched over with the limbs of large apple trees, that spread their pro-tecting arms over the dear and lonely Jane, and the birds carol to her many a lay in the sunshine. The end of the cottage is completely hidden with rich green ivy; here the sparrows rest and chatter, and in the early morning, "they mak' such a fearful din till its fit ta droon yan," said the old lady. On a heap of sticks by the garden wall a lazy kitten basked in the sunshine; an old gate, which must have seen the wear and tear of two or three generations, hangs mouldering by one hinge, and clings, as it were to the wall for support ; nooks and crannies, old railing and walls twist and curve—no straight lines here—even the footpath to the house has a crooked appearance, rises and drops suggesting, with every other object, scenes in touch with memory pictures. She was truly blessed with happy surroundings.

Still along the wooded shores of the lake, with bays, promontories, and overhanging groves, the branches lovingly droop to kiss its waters, and through the park of Armathwaite Hall, with its rich coppices and smooth, velvet, green lawns, we reach the Castle Inn, where the four lanes meet. North-west to Bothal and Aspatria, seven miles ; north-east the road leads to Carlisle, twenty-one miles ; full west, to Cockermouth, six miles ; south, by the shores of the lake, Keswick, seven miles. Bending west, by the Cockermouth road, we cross the Derwent by the Ouse bridge at the head of the lake. Here the surrounding landscape partakes of a soft pastoral charm, more akin to the lowlands. The Derwent wends its course through green, park-like meadows ; a pretty island adorns the centre of the stream, tall reeds and willows overhang its banks. A beautiful river, indeed, is the Derwent, now gliding smoothly along, past farmsteads and cultivated lands, until it joins with the Cocker at Cockermouth, and enters the

Coom Gill. BOWEN.

Solway at Workington. It was at the latter town that Queen Mary landed from a fishing-boat when fleeing from her country and throne. Here she was received by Sir Henry Curwen as became her rank and misfortunes. The apartment where the queen slept was long preserved as she had left it, out of respect to her memory.

" Dear to the loves, and to the Graces vowed,
　The Queen drew back the wimple that she wore ;
And to the throng how touchingly she bowed,
　That hailed her landing on the Cumbrian shore.
　　*　　*　　*　　*　　*　　*
Bright as a star (that from a sombre cloud
Of pine tree foliage poised in air, forth darts,
When a soft summer gale at evening parts

The gloom that did its loveliness enshroud),
She smiled ; but Time, the old Saturnian Seer,
Sighed on the wing as her foot pressed the strand,
With steps prelusive to a long array
Of woes and degradations hand in hand,
Weeping captivity, and shuddering fear,
Stilled by the ensanguined block of Fotheringay."

Before reaching Cockermouth is the village of Embleton, resting at the foot of Wythop and Gale Fells, presents a pleasing feature in the landscape. Cockermouth is a quaint old town, with a population of some five thousand, and is seated where the two rivers, the Derwent and Cocker, unite their waters. Wordsworth says of the first-named :—

"One, the fairest of all rivers, loved   And from his fords and shallows send a voice
    To blend his murmurs with my nurse's song,   That flowed along my dreams."

There is a most beautiful combination of picturesque objects at this spot. The situation of the ruined castle is most striking. It stands in venerable and massive grandeur, high above the river.

"The shadows of those towers, that yet survives
A shattered monument of feudal sway."

Its gateway tower, ornamented with the Arms and Badges of the Umfrevills, Moultons, Lucies, Percies, and Nevills. And the Parish Church, with its Gothic tower

and high pinnacles, and other stately spires tapering above the grey roofs of the old town. The principal street is wide and handsome, and in it stands the house where William Wordsworth was born. It is a house of some pretensions, with a good frontage to the street, its back opens into a garden, which in turn overlooks the Derwent. The poet alludes to it in his poem.

TO A BUTTERFLY.

"Oh ! pleasant, pleasant were the days,
The time, when in our childish plays,
My sister Emmeline and I
Together chased the butterfly !
A very hunter did I rush
Upon the prey :—with leaps and springs
I followed on from brake to bush
But she, God love her ! feared to brush
The dust from off its wings."

A low terrace wall half covered with a closely clipped hedge, intermingled with rose trees, formed a home for the birds who built their nests here. Alluding to the sparrows nests, Wordsworth says :—

"Behold, within the leafy shade   I started—seeming to espy
Those bright blue eggs together laid !   The home and sheltered bed,
On me the chance discovered sight   The sparrow's dwellings, which hard by
Gleamed like a vision of delight.   My Father's house, in wet or dry
                                        My sister Emmeline and I together visited."

Continuing we now follow up the course of the river Cocker, which has its birth in Yew-Crag on the confines of Borrowdale, falls down the Honister Pass, and twines round Gatesgarth Farm, feeds Buttermere and Crummock lakes, and receives fresh inspiration from Loweswater, flows through the beautiful vale of Lorton and enters the Derwent at Cockermouth. A good road leads from the above town to Keswick, which we follow for some distance, and then bend more to the right to the village of Lorton. No place can exceed in soft pastoral charm and sweetness the lovely vale of Lorton, the delicious blending of undulating pasture and cornland, a wimpling stream wandering through the vale gently swelling to the smooth-

rounded summit of the rising hills reminds us of the vale of Yarrow. Looking down the valley mountainwards, it appears as smooth and velvety as a well kept garden,—all is beauty and repose. Midway in the vale stands the village of Lorton, composed of one long narrow street of whitewashed houses with overhanging eaves; there is a primitive and old-world aspect about the place. It was here we met an aged man who had seen ninety-three winters, and had conversed with William Wordsworth before he had reached middle life, and who spoke of the poet familiarly as "William." The old man was fairly erect, and, considering

his ninety-three years, in good health. I met him taking his afternoon walk nearly a mile from his home.

The church stands a fair sized meadow's length from the village. It has a modest tower with tall pinnacles and battlements, and its grey pebbled walls stand out prominent from the green environments and back ground of dark fells; its surrounding features are graphically picturesque. To the south the lake, hills begin to fling out their arms like open jaws as if to scare the intruder, or embrace the village in a firm grasp. The rising fells are dotted with white-walled homesteads and stand out conspicuously from dark green sheltering firwood. The doors of the church were locked, and time being precious, we were unable to search for the keys and so could not gain any knowledge of the interior, with the exception of the modest tower; the exterior walls are in bad taste and uninteresting. We scanned the numerous gravestones but there were no ages equal to our patriarchal friend whom we had just previously met, whose age exceeded the biblical measure of three score and ten, by three and twenty summers. The old Yew tree described by Wordsworth is at High Lorton, but is now only a wreck of its former glory. It stands at a corner of a field fenced off for protection by railings. In its pride and strength the trunk measured twenty-four feet in circumference; one of its main branches was some years ago wrenched off right down to the ground.

> " There is a Yew tree, pride of Lorton vale,
> Which to this day stands single, in the midst
> Of its own darkness, as it stood of yore.
>
> •   •   •   •   •   •
>
> Of vast circumference and gloom profound
> This solitary tree ! a living thing,
> Produced too slowly ever to decay ;
> Of form and aspect too magnificent
> To be destroyed."

At another time the tree was actually sold for fifteen pounds to a cabinet maker at Whitehaven, and two men had begun to stub it up, but fortunately a gentlemen from Cockermouth hearing of its proposed destruction, made overtures to the owner, and thus preserved, though shorn of its ancient dignity, the pride of Lorton vale.

Still progressing up the emerald vale, rich in pasture, cornland, and woods, with mountains now looming in the foreground, majestic and bold, the long ridge of Melbreak, Red Pike, and High Stile being very conspicuous on the right ; Green Gable, Great End, and Great Gable in the distance, and Whiteside and Grassmoor closing in the vision on the left. We cross the river Cocker near the foot of Crummock Water, and from hence the view of mountains is magnificent. A mile west is Loweswater. On our way we turned to look at the rural Post Office, a quaint, antique Cumberland nook known by the name of Gillerthwaite. Loweswater is situated at the entrance of the north-western side of the lake, in a deep, secluded valley. It is only a little over a mile in length from the high ground at the head facing the lake. To the south the scene is wildly grand, whilst a little beyond, looking west, the country recedes more flat and uninteresting to the Solway shore. Some two-and-a-half miles from the edge of the lake is the village of Lamplough, here, on a tributary of the river Maron, which rises on the west side of Blake Fell, there is a very pretty old mill. The church, an old structure judiciously restored, stands on the rising-ground, and has a bell gable containing two bells. The vicarage, and several of the houses, with the village green, are very picturesque. Lamplough Hall was the seat of a very ancient family, several members of which performed deeds of high achievement. A gateway, with the inscription, " John Lamplough, 1575," is all that remains of the old hall.

Here, at the foot of Loweswater, is a good inn—" The Kirkstile," and opposite is the church, a large structure—the largest in western lakeland ; but it possesses no architectural beauty. At the west end of the churchyard, a tombstone records that the mortal body of the Rev. Thomas Cowper rests below. He died January, 1795, aged 74 years, and was minister of this church nigh 50 years. Many years ago, a small reservoir or tarn, on the hill above the lake, burst, and came rolling in one huge wave towards the lake ; a farm stood in its track, and one of the

Post Office, Gillerthwaite.

occupants, a girl, who was outside the house, saw the dark mass of water sweeping downwards. Darting into the house, she informed the inmates (the master and a female), of the occurrence. These two had just reached the outside of the door in their endeavour to escape, when the wave caught them both, swept them into the lake, and their bodies were never discovered, whilst strange to say, the girl, who was first to discover the inundation, was saved by the water forcibly banging the door in her face and holding her prisoner, when she was in the act of following the other persons.

CRUMMOCK WATER.

This Lake is the central of the three occupying the basin of the river Cocker, and is also the largest. On the east are the towering heights of Grassmoor, and the long ridge of Melbreak on the west, whilst the south end is backed by Red Pike and Buttermere Hawes. Three islands give additional charm to this lake; the mountains surrounding have a reddish burnt aspect, which may have been caused at some distant period of time by volcanic eruption. The eastern shore is delightfully diversified with hanging woods, and bays. The surroundings are wildly picturesque, and a magnificent and stern grandeur, approaching the sublime, hangs over the lake, which in turn reflects the deep shadow of the overhanging mountains. In the hollow of the hills between Melbreak and Red Pike, a stream issues from Scale Force — a waterfall of near 200 feet, and the highest in the lake country. The water falls down a narrow chasm at the north end of Red Pike, and in flood-times the scene is awe-inspiring and solemn. Huge rocks hang beetling over the narrow chasm; sombre mist-clouds of spray arise, and the reverberating sounds of falling water is heard. The sides are covered with moss, lichen, fern, mountain ash, and oak, nourished by the constant spray falling over them; and if you visit the spot when the sunlight falls on the spray and foliage, and behold the prismatic hues of innumerable vapoury gems garnished by sunlight, hang on and droop over the foliated encrustments that adorn this fairy gorge, it will long remain a living picture on the tablets of memory. From the neck of land between Crummock and Buttermere, looking south, is a grand scene; the river Cocker, winding 'neath the darkly scowling side of Red Pike, and Buttermere Lake receding under the huge barrier formed by High Stile and the perpendicular mountain wall of Honister. Crossing the Cocker, we pass over the small level area of meadows to Buttermere village, ensconced deeply in the hills, nearly midway between the two lakes. The place only consists of a few houses and two inns, and a small church seated on a knoll overlooking the village.

> " I know a little church, 'mid Cumbrian hills,
> A lower one, methinks, did never claim
> The solemn sanction of that honoured name;
> No symphony, save that of mountain rills,
> The praise in the psalm's rude chorus fills;
> Yet all our ritual asks is there, I ween —
> Font, pulpit, altar, and enclosure green.
>
> Where sleep the dead in loneliness that chills
> The inmost heart. But who can doubt, if there
> The bread of life, unmixed with earthly leaven,
> Be wisely dealt, if those who do repair
> To that rude altar seek to be forgiven
> Through Christ alone — that lovely place will prove
> The house of prayer, of God, the gate of heaven "

There are few people who have not heard of Mary Robinson, the "Beauty of Buttermere." She was born at this place in 1777 or 1778, her father being the innkeeper. A writer, visiting Buttermere in 1792, thus writes of Mary:—" Her hair was thick and long, of a dark brown, and though unadorned with ringlets, did not seem to want them; her face was a fine oval, with full eyes, and lips as sweet as vermilion ; her cheeks had more of the lily than the rose, and, although she had never been out of the village (and, I hope, will have no ambition to wish it), she had a manner about her which seemed better calculated to set off dress, than dress *her.* She was a very Lavinia. When we saw her at her distaff, after she had got the better of her fears, she looked an angel ; and I doubt not but she is the reigning lily of the valley. Ye travellers of the lakes, if you visit this obscure place, such you will find the fair Sally of Buttermere."

Her beauty became the theme of conversation by all who travelled into this district. It happened that a gentleman, styling himself the " Hon. Col. Hope,"

Buttermere.   O. BOWEN.

came to this secluded spot, and, struck with her beauty, he paid his addresses to her, and she became his wife. Sad to relate, this man was a vile impostor, who had fled to the mountains for safety after committing several forgeries. He did not, however, long survive his villainies. He was hanged at Carlisle for his crimes, September 3rd, 1803. After a short period of widowhood, she became the wife of a farmer in the district, and the mother of a family. Thus from the highly romantic phases of life she descended to the austere prosaic.

The road from Buttermere to Gatesgarth passes along the margin of the lake, which is pleasantly shaded by woods, the west side is overhung by frowning mountains, which lend a savage aspect to the scene, and by shutting out the rays of the sun, give a dark and sombre character to the water at the head of the lake.

Sour Milk Ghyll comes fretting and fuming down from a cup-shaped hollow in the steep side of the mountain. Its source is Burtness Tarn, between Red Pike and High Stile ; here, in a circular chain of rocks, the eagles formerly built their eyries, and John Vicars, of Borrowdale, twice robbed the eagles of their young, and at length shot both the parent birds at the head of Buttermere Water. This took place about the beginning of the present century ; since that period eagles have rarely nested in this district.

At the foot of Honister Crag, and a few hundred yards from Buttermere Lake, is a large farmhouse called Gatesgarth, occupied by a well-known dales-family named Nelson. On two occasions, when benighted, we have found excellent provision and comfortable apartments, with most reasonable charges, at this farm ; whilst the wild and magnificent scenery of the immediate surroundings amply repays a short stay here; and if the effusive lines in the visitors' book is any guide, others are of the same opinion. We quote one or two of the many :—

> " Many prize cards within these rooms I see,
> The rooms themselves have been a prize to me ;
> ' Highly commended ' is on every wall,
> Highly commended is this house by all,
> 'Tis well, indeed, to win a prize with sheep,
> But better still to give a weary traveller sleep."

Another tourist, after giving thanks to Mrs. Nelson for her homely kindness, says :—" We ascended Coniston Old Man ; then rowed across the lake, and spent a very pleasant half-hour with Mr. Ruskin, who is always happy to receive tourists at his charming residence." [Query.]

The walls of our sitting-room were covered from floor to ceiling with prize cards ; I counted fifteen hundred, but Mrs. Nelson said the number was far higher. ' Highly Commended,' and ' First,' or ' Second Prize,' is always staring at you from the walls. My artistic friend became nervous and declared that all the sheep reared on the mountain sides, for a thousand years, were staring at him ; but when Mrs. Nelson brought in the finely flavoured ham and eggs, I noticed his appetite was all right."

Edward Nelson, of Gatesgarth, commonly called " Haud Ned," was famed for his breeding of fine mountain sheep, which usually, as the walls testify, gained a prize at the shows near and far. Nelson was a man who often drank deeply of the cup which fires the brain, and was generally the last to leave the market, and many a lonely journey through the hills in storm and darkness must have fallen to his lot.

HONISTER PASS.

It was a boisterous morning on our visit ; lowering clouds, with alternate showers of rain and sunshine, the wind whisked us about as intruders in their wrath. Honister—huge giant of nature, grim and savage, uprears its barrier wall 1,600 feet above ; immense boulders are strewn in the valley around which the road and stream winds, hurled down by storm-fiends, who hold their revelry 'midst floating mists. Where mountains frown, deeply canopied by clouds, and mighty tempests shake the rocky heights that crouch in awe when the wild stream carves its

furrowed course through fear-inspiring ravine ; shriek follows shriek, while sporting
with ponderous mass, driving them forward in madding pace. The colour of the
screes, on either hand, vary from an inky blue to every tint of green and grey.
To-day the wind fairly howls down the pass, and the beck roars in its fury to escape
from the hills.—Such grandeur makes human efforts vain. In the old Border days,
this pass being, as it is to-day, the "gate" into the other dales, was often the scene

of fierce fighting. The
Graemes, formerly the most
notorious freebooters on the
Border, planned and cleverly
executed an expedition into
the lake country, coming in
small parties by intricate and
devious paths, and joining
together at a certain pre-
arranged spot, captured and
drove away all the cattle and
sheep by the Borrowdale
and Honister route. The
war-horn was sounded ! the
alarm of war spread rapidly,
and the Dalesmen were
quickly in hot pursuit. An-
ticipating this, the raiders
separated, one party pushing
forward with the captured
booty, whilst the other laid
in ambush in the rocks of
Yew Crag and Honister, and
sprang forth to the wild
yells of the clan, just as the
English party reached the

Honister Pass.

neck of the pass. Volleys of musketry rang from the crags, and arrows flew through
the air, and many a steed fled in terror, riderless, through the glen, amongst which
was the white steed of the English leader, who was shot by the elder Graeme.

Furious at their loss, the Dalesmen scaled the ambuscade of their foes, and in the
wild hand-to-hand *melee* which took place, many of the Border clan bit the dust,
amongst whom was the younger Graeme. The English, who in point of numbers

were overmatched, now dashed down the pass, gathering in force, as their war shout rang loudly and echoed among the mountains, hoping to recover their cattle or retaliate on the Scottish Border. Who can picture the feelings of that old chieftain, over whose form 70 winters had passed, and who had never trembled nor fled from the mighty in war? Now, with emotion of wild grief, tears streamed down his furrowed and weather-beaten cheeks, as he stretched his trembling hands over the corpse of his son, the pride of his clan ; the warriors, leaning on their shields, watched in silence the wild tumults of sorrow convulse the frame of their aged chief. Then the body was tenderly deposited in a recess on the heights of Honister, and every clansman helped to raise a cairn over the corpse of the brave ; on the summit they affixed his bonnet, shield, and claymore, that neither friend nor foe should thereafter pass it with irreverence. No one can point us to the burial place of the chieftain, but you can still hear, if your imagination is sufficiently acute, the shriek of spirits, or see dim ghosts careering o'er the mountains when the storm-fiend is abroad, and the torrent, swollen by rains, sweeps with resistless fury roaring down.

> " Red came the river down, and loud and oft
> The angry spirit of the water shrieked."

On the extreme end of Honister overlooking Gatesgarth, a small wooden cross arrests the attention of the traveller. It is erected to the memory of F. M., a young lady, aged 18, who accidentally fell from the rocks and was killed, Sept. 8th, 1887. The following lines are inscribed on the cross :—

> " PEACE, PERFECT PEACE,
> DEATH SHADOWING US AND OURS."

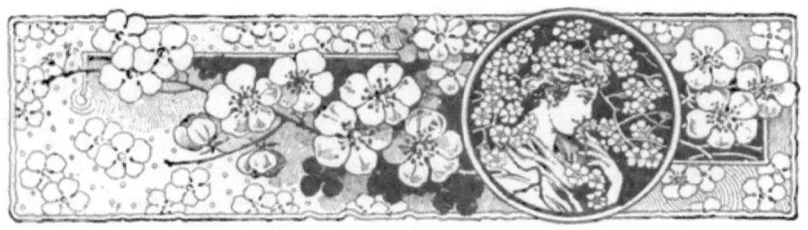

CHAPTER XIV.

OVER SCARF GAP AND BLACK SAIL TO WASDALE.·

EAVING Gatesgarth and Honister, we proceed by way of Scarf Gap and Black Sail to Wasdale. It is a stiffish pull over the mountain passes, yet only what a "rambler" would term child's play. 'Tis morning, but I well remember passing over Scarf Gap with a friend in the twilight, when the *cul de sac*, south of Buttermere Lake, yawned ominously, a grim barrier, which some mighty glacier had scooped, while the shadowy outline of mountains, piled mass above mass, brooded in solemn majesty over Honister Crag, like the entrance gate to a strange unknown world, inhabited by mighty Titans. This morning, we have a good view of the two lakes from our vantage ground, over which the cloud shadows are passing, adding greatly to the beauty of the whole. Mist gilded by sunshine creeps round the crests of distant hills, dimly visible through their vapoury shroud. A sunbeam like a rare gem flashes on a huge monolith of nature, and as suddenly disappears, leaving dark grim shadows in its place. So brilliant was the light, we turn in wonder, and just over the verge of the mountains, snow-like clouds are parting asunder, and gliding like aerial spirits, a richly tinted cobalt sky shows through the rift, and the firwood in the vale becomes suffused in splendour. 'Tis a phantasmagoria, every moment changing. Yonder above the shores of Crummock, clouds and shadows before the chariot of zephyr climb to the highest ridges, domes, and pinnacles of nature's temples, carrying the mind upwards to the regions of the

sublime and the infinite.   Now forward across the mammoth skeleton of an old
world over whose backbone the wind wails a requiem.   Yet here in the mountain
fastnesses and solitude, a spray of stag-horn moss and Alpine ladies mantle greets
us amongst the lichen covered rocks, pencilled by nature's hand assumes every conceivable device, shape, and hue that mock the highest effort of human skill.   Sometimes like a stronghold, where human beings cannot enter the inmost recesses, or
fathom the secret of its construction.   From the summit of Scarf Gap, which lies
between Haystack and High Crag, the scene is indescribably bold and majestic.

Storm on Great Gable.   BOWEN.

A remarkable feature near the
head of Ennerdale is the great
number of round hillocks, no
doubt formed by *débris* washed
from the mountain side.   They
have the appearance of tumuli,
and fancy pictures the burial place
of some Celtic tribe of which the
bards have been silent, and
nothing speaks of their deeds
except Liza's wild stream.   They
are of varying size, clothed with
grass, and are striking objects to
the traveller.   Looking across the
stream, the scene is one of wild
magnificence, the pillar rising a
jagged awful mass of solid rock,
the most imposing and wonderful
in England.   Farther west Ennerdale Water can be descried, the
head of the lake is by far the most
savage and picturesque.

From the summit of Black Sail
two remarkable scenes unfold ; on
one hand lies the vale of the Liza, the mountains in the foreground are deep in
shadow ; across the middle distance a gleam of sunshine lights up the patches of
grass and moss, beautiful in colour as cloth of gold ; the peaks and ridges of the
background of hills were also suffused with light.   Clouds fold and unfold, opening
to the soul of man magnificent vistas, in nature's solemn temple, jagged peaks and
mountains towering abrupt and precipitous, or sweeping in more graceful outline

like the waves rolling on a tempestuous sea, the ear is ravished with the eternal melody of water, whilst the glory of earth, cloud, and sky are around us. At the gate, near the summit of Black Sail, leading down to Wasdale, another mystic scene unfolds. As we scrambled down the rough track into the jaws of Mosedale, the mountains on either side appearing like giant buttresses to nature's cathedral, for the upper vale is entirely roofed with a dark mist cloud, hiding the crests of Kirk Fell, Yewbarrow, and Great Gable, furrowed and seamed by scar and rent, the water leaping and dashing over the rocks, blend into a confused melody, and the wind howling through the pass adds its wild unearthly dirge, as we drop down the mountain path and reach the solitary hamlet of Wasdale Head.

WASDALE HEAD.*

This little green glade in the mountains appears to the traveller almost like an oasis in the desert. The extent of the level area is only about 400 acres, which, if planted with trees, would have a far greater charm. Instead, the eye is everywhere arrested by a perfect labyrinth of bluish grey stone walls, which run from the centre of the little basin, far up the sides of the mountains, like a vast array of mathematical figures, and tell of the ancient lines of demarkation and allotments, where every yard of land was precious to the people (probably refugees or outlaws), British or Saxon, hiding from the strong hand of the conqueror. The primitive milking sheds for goats and small herds, invariably open to the south, and, with other indications, are very significant of the past. The place is almost completely shut in by lake and mountain; the only perceptible outlet, excepting to the west, are two wild mountain paths up Mosedale and over Black Sail, or the Sty Head pass. There is a church—one of the humblest in the land—yet a perfect study for the antiquary. It is a very low building, with three windows, and contains eight pews, which hold forty-eight people. The population in 1887 was only forty-six, so if all the inhabitants attended service, there is still room for two strangers. Although the dedication of the church is unknown, it

* Green says, in 1819, "Wastdale Head is a narrow, but fruitful vale, and, if riddled of its stone walls, and more profusely planted, would truly be a pastoral paradise'. All its inhabitants are shepherds, and live at the feet of the most stupendous mountains ; these are Yewbarrow and Kirk Fell, Great Gable and Lingmell—the latter is the ground work of the Pikes. Through the half circle formed by the intersections of Yewbarrow and Kirk Fell is presented the Pillar. There are at Wastdale Head six families, three of them are landowners. The vestiges of many ruined cottages show that this village was once more considerable. There is no mill, public house, shop, or tradesman in the valley, notwithstanding it is a considerable distance from any market town, being upwards of fifteen miles from either Egremont or Keswick. An inn at Wastdale Head would be a great accommodation to strangers, but by the courteous yeomanry who occasionally receive them, this want is, to a considerable degree, supplied."

is no doubt a branch of the mother church, " St. Bee's," 8th century. Part of the ancient walls are still in existence, and, instead of lime, burnt seaweed and shells have been used in the construction. The timbers were black bog oak, which, in the first instance, had done duty in ships, and which had probably been wrecked on the coast nine miles distant. But previous to this there is supposed to have been a wooden church, or cell, built by the ancient Britons, who fled thither for safety during the times of the Diocletian persecution, and is said to have become famous as the head—" Wattle Cell ;" for we have every reason to believe that at this period Christianity had already taken deep root in Britain. There are traces of a very ancient college, such as the West Britons had for the training of their clergy and choir, besides other indications which point unmistakably to this place having been in touch with men of culture at a very remote period. Ancient usages, and the donations of bread and wine, point to the Culdee, Cult, and Scottish ritual in the vale, at a very early date. There was a most ancient and unique cup, probably dating from the 14th century, whilst the small font of red sandstone, under two feet in height, is a mystery to the antiquary. There was formerly a Runic cross, but this has now disappeared, and no burial takes place now in the little churchyard, although it is supposed there did formerly, yet not the slightest sign of any grave mound is seen, Netherwasdale, at the west end of the lake, doing duty for both. The lowly church, with flagged roof and walls, thickly coated with whitewash, and quaint bell gable with single bell, affords a striking contrast to its screen of green yew trees. To the south, Ling Mell, glaring in the afternoon sunlight, rises unshapely like the back of a huge mastodon.

William Ritson, or Old Will, as he was better known, who died a few years ago at a patriarchal age, was one of the best known characters in the dale. By some he was styled "Master," or "Gaffer," but he was generally dubbed the "King o' Wasdale." He was a most powerful wrestler in his young days. He once had a famous encounter with Christopher North, whom he threw twice out of the three rounds ; yet he often remarked that " Maister Wilson was a veira bad un te lick," and many a story could he recount of Wilson's mad pranks in this region. He had also been conversant and acted as guide to most of the lake worthies of the old school. His house long afforded shelter to tourists, but has now grown to large dimensions, and is generally the head-quarters of numbers of visitors, chiefly men who test their powers of endurance and skill by climbing into the most inaccessible rocks of Scafell.

John of Wasdale, the name of a renowned knight who dwelt here and owned this valley as far back as the Plantagenet kings, and these monarchs were, on two or three occasions, his guests when hunting the huge deer, wild ox and boar, which still haunted this forest at that period. Elizabeth Wasdale, the last of this family, died at a great age some two or three years ago. She dwelt on the north side of the lake adjoining the romantic glen there.

There are no knights in the valley in these prosaic days, at least not attired in chain or clanking mail. But the last time the writer passed that way he observed within the entrance porch of the inn a vast array of shoes, heavily nailed and plated with iron. There would at least be thirty pairs, and from appearance in size, they shod thirty giants. Hovering around for some time to understand the meaning of such a sight, there presently emerged a number of stalwart fellows, armed, or I should say provided with pike and hatchet, and coils of rope. I felt rather nervous and abashed as they passed, long limbed, sinewy men, attired in thick, heavy tweed. One of them cast a contemptuous glance at my poor thin boots, and I thought I heard him remark to a companion, "Look, 'Mist of the Mountain,' at that poor fellow on tramp in his Sunday boots." There is a certain amount of danger in rock climbing, and three men at least have lost their lives on the Scafell range of late years.

Will Ritson.

Just one or two items from the visitors' book, which dates from 1858. One lady, from a busy industrial centre of Yorkshire, writes : "This is an alpine corner of our England that ought to be more known and visited. The air is pure as crystal, strong as wine, and after the hard work of a long and trying winter, we returned quite rested to our duties." Another tourist declares—

"Nor have these eyes by greener hills
Been soothed in all my wanderings."

On July 12th, 1869, a Miss Knowles wrote—

"Oh Wasdale, where are thy charms,
That poets have found in thy face ;
Better dwell in the midst of alarms,
Than stay in this watery place."

Another person who seems to deplore the exertion he was put to in ascending the Pikes, and who evidently was not meant for a cragsman, writes :—

Of Scawfell Pike I clomt the height ;
   And when I got upon it,
With all my soul, with all my might,
   I wished I hadn't done it.

My blythe companion lay at ease,
   No heights had he to scale !
And smoked the pipe of utter peace,
   Reclining down the vale.

Woe to the man on clambering bent !
   He finds but falls and strains,
And mists, and much bewilderment,
   And divers aches and pains.

But well for him who, in the vale,
   Reclining smokes in peace ;
No strains are his, no heights to scale,
   Body and mind at ease.

I scrambled down ; my limbs, though sound,
   Were most severely shaken ;
Oft when I thought I'd reached smooth ground,
   I found I was mistaken !

Let he who wills go climb the hills,
   My taste with his don't tally ;
Let he who wills go climb the hills,
   But I'll stay in the valley !

Three streams meet beyond the hamlet, and pour their united waters into the lake. The road to Netherwasdale passes under the south base of Yewbarrow and Middle Fell. On the south side of the lake an almost imperceptible path leads over Burnmoor and past the tarn, situated in an amphitheatre of mountain, and forward to Boot, in Eskdale.

From the head of the lake, Scafell, Seafell, Great Gable, and Yewbarrow tower sublimely into the clouds, indented with many a scar and fissure. Wastwater has been termed the "Lake of Solitude," and this name is not inapplicable, for to the casual visitor, who perhaps hurries through this region, the lake appears black and gloomy, even on a summer's day. No village, homestead, garden, nor blossom-flecked hedgerows weaving and lacing sweet meadows and cornfields ripe for the sickle ; nor the umbrageous pomp of many-coloured woodlands, with waving boughs, drinking the subtle hues from the sunlight ; nor the tremulous trilling of joyous birds are here ; but if the brief study of one single autumn day was spent in noticing the almost magical effects of colour, varied as a rainbow, and the light and shade falling on the Screes, different conclusions would be arrived at. Yet the spot is very weird, particularly as night comes, and you listen to the wild moaning sound caused by the wind-current ; then it verily seems haunted with spirits of a lost world. Such was the impression made on the writer.

The sun had sunk below the verge of the horizon ; at our feet lay the lake, walled in by mountains and roofed with night clouds ; the dull grey road winding west along the shores of the lake ; the *débris* composing the Screes deepening to the colour of old gold. Not a sound, not a voice but that of nature—the sound of lapping waves and the moaning of the wind-current. The scene is grand at night, when nature draws her curtain aside, and a virgin moon pours a silvery flood of light around, and the bright evening orb hangs over Wastwater, the far-receding vault bespangled with stars, and the distant Fells fall into shadow, the wild solemnity of a deep peacefulness, which in like solitudes can only be known; this silence imparts splendour to the scene, and even the sighing of the wind seems part of the silence.

Waves of grey mist half shroud the lake. 'Tis the day passing into night, the solemnity of nature blending with the longings of the soul. Hark! list! 'tis the wild shriek of a solitary bird; we scan the darkening surface of the lake, and in a lighter wave of mist we see the outline of a large heron, which seemed to have partaken of the same hue as the water as it flapped slowly, with extended wings, along the bosom of the lake, uttering three or four melancholy wails, and putting the last touch of perfection to this night picture.

The Screes is the name given to a mountain near, 2,000 feet in height, and running for three miles along the south-east shore, taking its name from the *débris*. The upper rocks are soft and crumbling, and between them, at intervals, are deeply dented fissures, worthy the efforts of an experienced climber. From the top to the bottom is a fine angle or slope, which dips sheer down into the lake. As seen from the opposite shore the appearance is almost artificial, like a tip from a huge quarry. These Screes are the most extensive in the lake district, and lend a character peculiarly distinct to this lake.

The sun has passed the meridian. We are on the heath north of the Strands Road. Here is a mountain farm, overlooking a beautiful gorge; the water gurgles round and over the rocks which vainly seek to bar its course, then leaps and dashes past many a lovely nook. In that sweet murmur and restless force is blended the music and pathos of the past with the beauty of the living present. Here in this quiet hour we rest, and drink in the glory of moor, sky, and lake stream. Graceful birches feather and droop o'er its banks, richly-hued mosses blend with golden furze, and blue rocks—worn into curious shapes by the churning of centuries—the deep brown, and in some cases yellow, bed of the stream, or, again, patches of white foam like driven snow. Such are the influences which arrest our attention, with the now almost matchless beauty of the lake as it glitters in the afternoon sun, all strongly appealing to our sympathies and imagination.

Past Wasdale Hall, and near the foot of the lake, are beautiful woodland walks, and a most marvellous view of the whole lake, which seems to float on the bases of huge mountains, from whose inspiration they rise, as it were, in majestic contour, the most striking mass of peaks in England.

The hamlet of Netherwastdale is a little distant from the west end of the lake, and midway between the head of the dale and the sea. The surroundings are finely diversified; it is one of those quiet nooks entirely hidden from the world, well sheltered from the north by the knolls, which are beautified by growths of trees. There is a small, plain church, with a burial-ground attached, where the dalespeople sleep after their life's toil.

Amongst the tombstones is one to the memory of William Ritson, previously mentioned, late of Wasdale Head. The church possesses a very antique pewter tankard and plate, also a rare chalice of beaten silver, on which is the following inscription :—

✠ This + Is + The + Gift + Of + Robart + Gun-
sone + Sone + Of + Antonie + Gonsone + Of
✠ Toshtorne + Free + Mane + Of + Londone
+ This + Is + The + Communion + Cupe
✠ Of + Mastell + Church +
R.
G.

The Gonsons, or Gunsens, of Wasdale, were a very ancient yeoman family, many of whom were interred at Gosforth. There are two good inns at this place. A lane leading west, clustering in the early autumn with fern and wild fruit, brings

Gosforth Cross.

the traveller in about four miles to Gosforth. In the twelfth century it was written Gosford, or Goseford, from a fen or morass, inhabited by vast numbers of wild geese; this is most probable, for there was formerly a marsh two miles in length and half-a-mile in breadth, caused by the overflow before the artificial banking of the river. The village is of considerable size, having about thirteen hundred inhabitants. There is a very tall cross, with slender shaft, covered with intricate carving, typical of the conversion of the inhabitants from paganism to Christianity, and is said to be the tallest, as well as one of the most remarkable, crosses in the kingdom, and is supposed to have been erected early in the seventh century. There are fragments of two other Runic crosses in the church, and many indications which point to the antiquity of this place. On the north side of the church is a site still known as Chapel Croft, where, tradition reports, was formerly a chapel ; fragments of the building were scattered around within memory of many now living. Near to is the site of a spring, called "Holy Wells." A little more than a mile west is Seascale, a quiet, modern seaside resort, and, on our visit, as far as the eye could reach, only one solitary sail specked the glittering Solway.

Now down the charming old lanes and byways, and up the rough path which crosses the fells yonder, we drop down to Boot, at the head of Eskdale. Near to, in the wood, is an ancient sawmill, its motive power gained from an antique water-wheel; the structure is charmingly hidden in trees, and grown over with lichen and grey and golden moss, the sunlight playing hide-and-seek on the old roof and wheel, forms a charming picture. Near to is a picturesque bridge of one span, roughly built together, and almost choked with creeper and ivy. Boot is a small rural dale-village, primitive enough to please the most fastidious. In the walls of some of the cottages large boulders of natural rock have been utilized in the construction of the homestead. On our visit the sports were being held, which comprised racing, wrestling, throwing the hammer, the fell race, the high leap, the long leap, putting the stone, hitch and kick, the old Hellenic game of quoits, in fact all the old Scottish athletic games, except tossing the kaber, a six or more yards pole, or young tree; the base resting on the palm of the athlete's hand, supported against his shoulder, he runs in semi-bent form, to make it fall on the ground on its base—that is the feat of tossing the kaber.

The scenery of Eskdale is finely diversified, a grand foreground of mountains, from whence the river winds through a wildly-romantic valley to the sea, near Ravenglass. Rock, hill, knoll, river, stream and cascade—fell-sides clothed richly with

A Mountain Stream, Eskdale.   RODWELL.

gorse; large patches of unreclaimed moorland, where the heather blooms and wild fruit ripens; huge crags on which the broad leaves of ferns wave and festoon gracefully; glades of firwood, oak, birch,. and hazel skirt the hillsides, and silvery glimpses of rivers winding to the Solway, at full tide the waters swelling to a great width. Most of the homesteads are of primitive construction, chiefly of unhewn stone, and roofed with thick slate; generally, these old houses have an ample porch, and the walls, if not newly whitewashed, partake of a grey, sober aspect, and harmonise and blend with the surrounding landscape. Many genteel residences have sprung into existence of late years, and such are generally too obtrusive, and tend to destroy the

P

romance and poetic charm of Eskdale. The little miniature railroad, however, seems almost to add to, instead of destroy, the dignity and beauty of the district; its entire length is under eight miles. It is an independent railway, and has six stations between Boot and Ravenglass; the gauge of the line is only 3 feet. The stations are curious-looking places, something like a platelayers' shanty, and are opened and closed as the train arrives and departs. One of them is composed of an old boat turned partly over (see illustration). The guard performs several duties besides his own, being station-master, ticket distributor, collector, and porter. He is most obliging, and should a likely passenger be descried anywhere within, say a quarter of a mile, he will draw up the train, whose speed generally averages eight miles an hour, to ascertain whether or not he is going up. This is not fiction, for we have been so obliged.

The writer on one occasion was passing from Wasdale to Eskdale, just when the sun was setting behind the darkening hills, expecting to arrive at Boot in time to

Station—Eskdale Line.

catch the last train for Ravenglass, but after hurrying and several times mistaking the path in the gathering gloom, arrived only to find the last train had gone, the station in darkness, and not a sound or a vestige of humanity around. I was obliged to be at Ravenglass that night, and not being acquainted with the road, walked the entire distance, 8 miles, in the dark, up the line.

It was a murky, damp, yet warm night, and the host of glow-worms which lighted their innocuous fires on that memorable tramp I shall never forget. The shy little creatures shone with a phosphorescent brilliance most bright and dazzling, which now and again startled me, not being familiar with the soft and luminous glow of almost unearthly light, lustrous as the gems of Golconda. On and on I tramped, under beetling rock and over moor, here and there to the sound of a stream rushing under the line, until I arrived at Ravenglass, none the worse for my adventure; it was an experience I shall not soon forget. When the anxiety subsided, and reflecting on the gain I possessed, I was more than compensated for the toil and discomfort of that walk up the Eskdale line.

Muncaster Hall, originally spelt Mulcastre, stands on a rising green plateau, charmingly surrounded and completely hidden, even at a few yards distance, by the forest. Its walls, partly covered with ivy, with battlemented roof, presents a commanding and pleasing picture. The place received its name from a Roman camp, which stood a few hundred yards nearer the sea. Near to this camp are the remains of a Roman villa ; the walls still standing measure some twelve feet in height, being the highest fragment of Roman work in Great Britain. After the departure of the Romans, it is supposed to have been the residence of a British prince, for Camden states that a certain king (Evelin) had his palace here, of whom abundant stories are told. The situation is fine, close to the Solway shore, with the tidal estuaries of the Esk and the Mite to the north and south.

Muncaster Church is delightfully situated in a setting of nature's handiwork. The churchyard contains a short Saxon or runic cross. There are numerous monuments and memorials to the Pennington family ; several of the brasses are very ancient. These commemorate Sir William Penyton, 1301 ; William Penyton, 1390 ; Syr William Penyngton, Knight, 1533 ; William Penyngton, Armr, 1543. One inscription is still in its original place, on a freestone slab in the floor of the chancel. It covers the remains of " Syr John Penyngton, sone of John Penyngtone, grandchild of ye Syr

Ancient Cross, Muncaster Churchyard.   EDMUND GOOD.

John who resseved Holye Kinge Harrye at Molcastre.   .   .   .   .   He was a brave captain.   .   .   .   .   he stoutlie headed his souldiers at Floddon Field. Died MDXVIII."

Ravenglass stands by the coast, about a mile away. It is a poorly-built place, and, when the tide is low, with long stretches of sand and mud banks. Yet the varying hue of the water towards eventide is most exquisite. A century ago the village was the resort of smugglers, who ran their contraband cargoes under cover of night amongst the sandhills or numerous creeks adjoining.

Waberthwaite is a secluded little hamlet situated on the south side of the Esk, near to where it falls into the sea. The original settlement was made by an ancestor of the Wayberghs, now Whyberghs ; hence we have Wayberghthwaite. During the restoration of the church, several fragments of an earlier structure, probably Saxon, were found. One of these is the shaft of an ancient cross, upon which is the figure of an animal struggling in bonds. There are also other fragments, all of which suggest a tenth century date. The font is of very primitive workmanship ; the old pulpit, still in use, was the gift of Abraham Chambers, 1670. The church is prettily adorned by trees, and a few gaunt Scotch firs lend character and contrast. When the Esk is at full tide, the water washes up to the churchyard. A more peaceful and secluded place would be difficult to find. The living is in the hands of the Penningtons of Muncaster, and until 1844, the parson at this place fulfilled the duties of both parishes. Up to the above date, the service was held in the morning at Waberthwaite, "of a suitable time and length " to allow the rector to cross the river Esk by the stepping-stones " free of tide," so as to be able to perform his duties in the afternoon at Muncaster.

Eskdale is full of beautiful and interesting places, on which time will not allow us to dwell longer. We must hurry over Birker and Ulpha Moor, by way of Crosbythwaite, to the vale of the Duddon This is a long and rather uninteresting tramp across a wide moorland waste, until we drop through the wood and hazel-fringed lanes, and the beautiful valley of the Duddon, with the stream winding under the trees to the sea, spreads before us.

CHAPTER XV.

THE VALE OF THE DUDDON, CONISTON, AND WINDERMERE.

ULPHA KIRK is a small hamlet, where the inhabitants still retain their primitive manners. The inn is in a charming situation, and that crude dwelling with yellow-washed walls, where evergreens and rose trees climb, is the rural post-office. Ulpha church has been recently restored, yet the old yellow-washed walls are still the same, with ancient window and lych-gate. Some sixty years ago, a blind priest officiated here. One Sunday morning, the kirk bell rang before all the people were ready for service; one stout, heavy-footed farmer came in last of all, "thunnerin down the aisle." "Wha's comin' noo?" inquired the blind preacher. On being told by the clerk that it was John T——, he asked, "A-foot or a-horseback?"

The churchyard stands high above the river. Wordsworth says :—

> " The Kirk of Ulpha to the pilgrim's eye
> Is welcome as a star that doth present
> Its shining forehead through the peaceful rent
> Of a dark cloud, diffused through half the sky."

The view of the homesteads from the east side of the picturesque bridge, which here crosses the stream, is indeed very charming. Here, in the bed of the Duddon, we noticed the curious perforations and pot-holes in the rocks, caused by the action of the swirling waters. Right upon the Fells we came on an elderly man mowing bracken, but were almost startled to hear he had reached the great age of 88 years. It was then six in the evening, and he told us that, with the exception of a rest for dinner, he had been engaged on the moor since eight in the morning. His name was Robert Dawson. To a remark of ours, he replied : "Ah, but things hev changed since ah wor a lad." We took a photograph, and then went on our way rejoicing, almost feeling as if a span had been added to our life by the appearance of this hale octogenarian.

The valley between Ulpha and Broughton Bridge is delightfully wooded, and, seen from the high fell-sides, forms many exquisite and charming pictures, but we must now return and follow the Duddon to its source. Above Ulpha the valley narrows, and you pass cool green glades ; the river, in its frantic rush, leaps onward resonant with melody, filling the entire vale with its song. Soon we reach Seathwaite, three miles up from Ulpha. Its little church, embowered in trees, and its miniature belfry, appear modest and rural through the clustering foliage. Here it was that the wonderful clergyman, Robert Walker, spent 66 years of his life. When he first entered upon his duties, the living was only five pounds per annum, and never, during his lifetime, more than £50. He married young, and brought up a large family, all of whom were well educated, one of them becoming a clergyman. He died in

Ulpha Moors, and Robert Dawson.   OWEN BOWEN.

1802, aged 93 years, leaving a fortune of £2,000. Yet withal he was kind and generous to the needy, and a faithful pastor to his little flock. A secret to this accumulation may be better understood when we are told there was no public-house in Seathwaite in those days, and the reverend gentleman, besides the duties of parson, appears to have been the local brewer, and sold the ale to the people at a small profit. He also spun the wool needed for the family clothing, acted as schoolmaster to the children of his parishioners, assisted as a labourer for hire during the hay harvest and sheep shearing, and as clerk and surveyor on the same terms. He had also two acres of land, a few sheep, and a couple of cows. He was the most unique factotum on record for a parson. A plain blue slab, under the old yew tree, records his death and that of his wife, both dying at the ripe old age of 93, within a few months of each other.

Now over the beautiful white stepping-stones of Wordsworth's, past the "fairy chasm," where the rocks have been scooped and carved into the most fantastic shapes by the churning of ages. Still upwards we climb to Cockley Bridge; here a path crosses the moors, west, into Eskdale, from whence the vision stretches far away to the glittering Solway; and, a little distance from the bridge, on the rising ground, the grand contour of the Pikes are outlined majestically against the sky—southward, the Duddon, like a silver thread, can be descried winding onward to the bay at Broughton. There is a cottage and a few trees near the bridge, but not the sheltering pine trees of Wordsworth's time—

" 'Mid sheltering pines, this cottage rural and grey."

Glen Ulpha and Birker Fell.   G. H. ROOMELL.

Past the cottage we climb up the rough mountain track, drear and melancholy, with scarcely an easy place for the foot to rest, and thus reach the source of the Duddon (in Wrynose), near the three-shire stone, the meeting point of Cumberland, Westmoreland, and Lancashire. Proceeding, we drop down to Fell Foot, Little Langdale, and into the delightful vale of Tilberthwaite. This path leading to Coniston is most charming, fairy little dells, babbling brooks, patches of moorland covered with gorse, moss-covered rocks, long waving lines of grey stone walls running up hill and down dale, enriched in colour by climbing lichen, patches of sweet wild thyme and masses of brown-tinged bracken; sombre woodlands, where the hazel and other trees overhang their branches and lave the stream, impregnated with the silvery music of innumerable waterfalls; rustic homesteads with antique porch, towering heights with dark, pine-covered slopes, lovely vistas and hues of richest colour, lead us under the shadow of Wetherlam, 2,592 feet, and that storm-riven mountain of rock, "Old Man," 2,632 feet high, to Coniston Lake, which is a little over six miles in length, three-quarters of a mile in width, and is in position north and south. It is beautifully wooded down to the edge of the water, particularly at the north end.

The village is a long straggling place, with many interesting bits of old architecture. John Ruskin, the great art critic, resides at Brantwood—above the east side of the lake. Coniston, rich in possessing Ruskin, and honoured by his choice of dwelling in her midst, whose eye hath penetrated deeper into nature's mysteries, or gifted with so subtle a receptiveness, combined with high and noble sympathies, encircled with a halo of pure sincerity—the greatest prose writer of his generation : his other compeers are gone. As John Morley says : " There was, first of all, Carlyle ; there was Macaulay, and there is Mr. Ruskin. Those are all giants, and they have the rights of giants." Dow Crag, a little to the south of " Old Man " mountain, rises perpendicularly to a thousand feet, split from base to top by yawning gullies of terrible aspect, is the climber's happy hunting ground. The neighbourhood of Coniston abounds in beautiful and interesting places ; the mountains in the vicinity are bold and imposing. It would be difficult to find any place more delightfully

Dame Tyson's Cottage.

romantic than the scenery of Yewdale, Glen Mary, or Ravens Crag. Here it was that Wordsworth and his fellow-students used to harry the ravens which nested in the vicinity, and scoured the woods in search of wild fruit. Hawkshead lies about midway between Coniston and Windermere. It is a most antique little town, and Wordsworth is indelibly associated with this place ; here he spent his happy schoolboy days, and many of the pictures which he so truthfully describes still remain, notably the cottage of Dame Tyson, with whom he resided, and whose kindness to him could only have been equalled by a mother.

> " Ye lowly cottage wherein we dwelt,
> A ministration of your own was yours ;
> Can I forget you, being as you were.
> So beautiful among the pleasant fields
> In which ye stood ?"

And again he pictures the spot from his bedroom :—

> " That lowly bed, whence I had heard the wind
> Roar, and the rain beat hard ; where I so oft
> Had lain awake on summer nights to watch
> The moon in splendour couched among the leaves
> Of a tall ash, that near our cottage stood ;
> Had watched her with fixed eyes, while to and fro,
> In the dark summit of the waving tree,
> She rocked with every impulse of the breeze."

Flag Street, or we ought to say Alley, is perhaps the most antique and picturesque. It is very narrow, and paved with flags, from whence it received its name :
overhanging eaves and roofs twist in the most inconceivably irregular manner,
with quaint nooks and angles, overhanging beam and rafter. Down the centre a
small brook babbles, now and again partly covered. This is the brook mentioned by
the poet : " Unruly child of mountain
birth," but which

> " Soon as he was boxed
> Within our garden, found himself at once,
> As if by trick insidious and unkind,
> Stripped of his voice, and left to dimple down
> (Without an effort and without a will),
> A channel framed by man's officious care."

Flag Street, Hawkshead.

The old Grammar School is still
standing, with wide, low, and antique
window and doorway, over which is a
sundial. The interior is whitewashed,
and the old desks, on which many of
the schoolboys carved their names,
still remain. Wordsworth's name is
still there, covered by glass to preserve
it from injury. The venerable Parish
Church stands on an eminence near
by—

> " The snow-white church upon the hill."

A flavour of antiquity surrounds it ;
there is a plain yet severe originality
about the interior.

No spot in the Lakes presents more rustic glimpses of the simplicity of the past ;
or memory which recall visions of the gentle muse. For was it not the scenery
around Coniston, the glorious pageantry of the sky, and the gilding of the hilltops,
that suggested to the inborn genius his first impulse of spontaneous poetry ? Pro-

ceeding, we pass along the east side of Esthwaite Water. It was here that, as the young poet rowed across its starlit waters, and the huge peak of Wetherlam following him (as it seemed), was suggested to him the dim conception "Unknown modes of being." In "The Prelude," he speaks of Esthwaite Lake :—

" One summer evening (led by her), I found
A little boat tied to a willow tree
Within a rocky cove, its usual home ;
Straight I unloosed her chain, and stepping in,
Pushed from the shore . . . . lustily.
I dipped my oars into the silent lake,
And, as I rose upon the stroke, my boat
Went tearing through the water like a swan ;
When, from behind that craggy steep, till then

The horizon's bound, a huge peak, black and huge,
As if by voluntary power instinct,
Upreared its head ; I struck and struck again,
And growing still in stature and grim shape,
Towered up between me and the stars, and still,
For so it seemed, with purpose of its own,
And measured motion like a living thing,
Strode after me."

Again, in "The Prelude," he speaks of Esthwaite Lake :—

" Well do I call to mind the very week
When I was first entrusted to the care
Of that sweet valley ; when its paths, its shores
And brooks, were like a dream of novelty
To my half-infant thoughts."

This lake is a little over two miles in length, with undulating margins of sweet pastoral beauty.

Past Sawrey there is a lane called Scotch Gate (Way). During the rebellion of 1745, the Highlanders were said to be coming this way, so the inhabitants, carrying all their valuables with them, took refuge in a solitary building named "Cook's Braw Bog-house." Here we are at Windermere Ferry, and here is the Ferry Hotel, a large building sumptuously furnished. From hence are some of the finest views, both up and down the lake. "Formerly," says Harriet Martineau, "it was impossible to get over by the ferry after dusk, and if you should arrive at the Nab too late, you may call all night, but the boat will not come." On which hangs a tale, known as the "Crier of the Claife," the name of a ghost or spirit, who, tradition says, long haunted this district.

About the 15th century, one stormy night, a party of travellers were making merry at the ferry-house, then a humble tavern, when a call for the boat was heard from the Nab. A quiet, sober boatman obeyed the call, though the night was wild and fearful. When he ought to be returning, the tavern guests stepped out upon the shore, to see whom he would bring. He returned alone, ghastly and dumb with horror. Next morning he was in a high fever, and in a few days he died, without having been prevailed upon to say what he had seen. For weeks after there were shouts, yells, and howlings at the Nab on every stormy night, and no boatman would attend to any call after dark. Things came to such a pass that a monk from

Furness, who dwelt on one of the islands of the lake, was applied to, to exorcise the Nab. On Christmas Day, he assembled all the inhabitants of Chapel Island, and performed, in their presence, services which would forever confine the ghost to the quarry in the wood behind the ferry, now called "the Crier of Claife." Some say that the priest conducted the people to the quarry, and laid the ghost then and there. (Laid though it be, nobody goes there at night.) It is still told how the foxhounds, in eager chase, would come to a full stop at that place ; and how within the last generation, a schoolmaster, from Colthouse, who left home to pass the Crier, was never seen more. The Crier Quarry, and Crier Wood, are spots well known, near to High Wray, in a delightfully wooded district, above the shores of Lake Windermere.

Looking up the lake from the ferry, the view is inexpressibly charming, the high sloping banks beautifully clothed in woods down to the water's edge, the innumerable tints of foliage, and the sweet verdure of the Emerald Isles ; the boats gliding hither and thither, and the varied colours of the ladies' costumes, all presenting a charming contrast and variety. Sail up the lake ; the richest foliage rounds off towards the sky, and glimpses of mansions, embowered in the luxurious splendour of velvety lawns and many-tinted woods. 'Tis like a dream, when bathed in the rose-coloured radiance of a fairy, transfusing sunset. But to drink in all the tranquil beauty

HILDESHEIMER & Co.   Waterhead.   F. W. HAYES.

and commanding views must be seen, for language is feeble, and words cannot paint such delightful charm. Professor Wilson has remarked : " From one view of the lake there was nothing to compare in the Hanging Gardens of Babylon." "There is," he adds, " the widest breadth of water, the richest foregrounds of woods, the most magnificent background of mountains, not only in Westmoreland, but, believe me, in the world." There is scarcely to be found one bit of uninteresting scenery from Waterhead, at the north end of the lake, to the estuary of the Leven, which drains the lake into the sea at Leven Sands, Morecambe Bay (see picture of the Cockle Gatherers on Leven Sands). It is positively delightful to watch the waves glimmer and sparkle, the ever-changing hue of the woods in the sunlight, with here and there a patch of purple, and cloud-shadow sweeping the hoary mountain crests—domes of nature's magnificent architecture, the most imposing background in Great Britain.

From Orrest Head is a most splendid prospect ; below lies the whole surface of Windermere, and beyond, to the north and west, all the famous lake mountains, whilst away to the south, the waves can be seen shimmering at Morecambe Bay. Elleray, on the slope of Orrest Head, was the residence of Wilson, one of the noblest figures and most generous natures of all the lake worthies.   He it was who so gallantly defended Wordsworth against the carping criticism of Jefferies ;[*] " and," says one, " Wilson never showed to so much advantage as when he walked by the side of his great master, whose greatness he was one of the first to detect."   " Who that was present," says Dr. Russell,[†] when describing the burial of James Hogg, the shepherd poet, in Ettrick kirkyard, " can forget the noble form of Wilson, a model for a sculptor, as he

The Cockle Gatherers on Leven Sands.   DRAWN BY GILBERT FOST- P.

stood at the top of the grave, with his cloak wrapped round him, his head uncovered, his long auburn hair streaming in the wind, while tears flowed down his manly countenance."

Just beyond, where the lanes meet, and situated in fine pasture land, is old Calgarth Hall, and, with Belle Isle, was formerly the property of the Philipsons, whose

---

[*] The Edinburgh reviewers were too severe on the early writings of Wordsworth, Byron, etc., etc., but such an array of master minds, connected with a magazine, has never appeared—Jeffery, Brougham, Macaulay, Smith, Scott, Wilson, etc., etc. Three of the above were created Lords, and one a Baronet. As a matter of fact, they revolutionized the entire literature of Europe.

[†] Dr. Russell's father was minister of Ettrick (who was succeeded by the Rev. Charles Paton. He died in 1818).

arms are still to be seen carved, amidst a profusion of arabesque devices, over the kitchen fireplace.* The hall has the reputation of being haunted, besides which there is a skull legend. The skulls, for there were two, occupied a cupboard in the interior, and all attempts to get rid of them failed ; they were buried, burnt, and ground to powder, and dispersed to the winds, sunk in the well, and thrown into the lake ; but all this was of no avail, for they were always found again in one particular position. Now and again the two ghastly objects were said to attend banquets at Armboth Hall, on the shores of Thirlmere, and join in the midnight revels there. This is the way it was done, as related by the late Dr. Gibson :—

" To Calgarth Hall, in the midnight cold,
Two headless skeletons crossed the fold,
Undid the bars, unlatched the door,
And over the step passed down the floor,
Where the jolly round porter sat sleeping.

With a patter their feet on the pavement fall,
And they traversed the stairs to that win-
    dow'd wall,
Where, out of a niche, at the witch-hour dark,
Each lifts a skull, all grinning and stark,
And fits it on with a creaking.

Then forth they go with a ghostly march,
And bending low at the portal arch,
Through Calgarth woods, o'er Rydal braes,
And over the pass by Dunmaile Raise,
The two their course are keeping."

HILDESHEIMER & CO.   Belle Isle.   F. W. HAYES.

Here, with other spectral visitants, they held high revel till the first streaks of dawn warned them that it was time to recross Dunmaile, and return to Calgarth Hall.

" The skeletons, too, rush through the yard ;
They push the door they left unbarred,
Laid by their skulls in the niched wall.
And flew like wind from Calgarth Hall.
Where the round porter was sleeping.

As out they rattled, the wind rushed in,
And slammed the doors with a terrible din ;
The grey cock crew, the dogs were raised,
And the old porter rubbed his eyes, amazed,
At the dawn so coldly breaking. '

* During the Civil War the estates were owned by two brothers, who espoused the Royal cause. The youngest, from his desperate exploits, acquired the appellation of " Robin the Devil." Briggs, an officer in Cromwell's army, and who resided in Kendall, hearing that Major Philipson was secreted in Belle Isle, went thither, thinking to take him prisoner. The Major, however, withstood a siege, until his brother came to his relief, and the attack was repulsed. Soon after this affair, the Major, with a small troop of horse, rode off one Sunday morning in search of his enemy. On reaching Kendall, he was told that Colonel Briggs was at prayers. Riding up to the church, and posting his men at the entrance, he dismounted and rushed into the church in full armour. Fortunately, Colonel Briggs was not present. The congregation, on seeing the threatening attitude of Philipson, became alarmed, and attempted to take him prisoner. He managed to gain the door and leap upon his horse. The girths of the saddle, however, had already been cut, and he was nearly taken prisoner. The man who attempted to detain him fell by his hand, and the town was soon in arms ; but he rode off without saddle, and reached Belle Isle in safety."

Mr. Conway, in *Harper's Magazine*, thus accounts for the cause of the appearance of these two skulls at Calgarth Hall:—"Calgarth was first owned by a farmer named Cook, and his wife Dorothy. But their little estate was coveted by a wealthy Justice of the Peace, Myles Philipson, who, unable to persuade them to sell it, brought a false charge of theft against them. The offence was then capital, and, as Philipson was the judge, Cook and his wife were condemned to death. Before her death, however, Dorothy pronounced her seven curses on Calgarth, and prophesied that while its walls stood they would haunt it night and day. From that day forth the Philipsons had two skulls as their guests, which never left them, in spite of their efforts to destroy them, till the family sank into poverty, and at length disappeared." *

Leaving Bowness, with its antique church so delightfully sheltered in trees by

the lake, and past Windermere, with charming villa residences surrounded by the most luxuriant of leafy foliage, and just a peep at the magnificent hotels, with every appointment of modern luxury and comfort, we follow the high road to Kendal, which crosses the higher reaches of Gilpin Beck, and past the

Sunset, Windermere.   NICHOLSON.

quaint hamlet of Crook, with its row of white cottages, facing south. The view all along the route is romantic; sweet little pastoral valleys, the land broken by numerous watercourses; in the middle distance are dwarf hills covered with gorse, whose green and prickly branches are crowned with golden flowers, and the green fronds of the

---

* There is a farmstead called Threlkeld Place, which was formerly haunted in this manner. The skull was found there by a new tenant in a dark room which had been unused by his predecessor. It was promptly buried, but, on going to the room soon after, it was found again in the same niche in the wall. The farmer in his alarm carried it to St. Bees Head and cast it into the sea only to find that it was at home to receive him on his return. Other means were employed to get rid of it, but without effect. There is no difference in the legend of the skull that used to take up an ominous position at the foot of the staircase at Hayfell in Westmoreland; no efforts were successful in displacing it altogether. As often as it was removed, so often did it reappear. At Kickersgill, not

bracken are full of life and freshness, the brushwood and bramble with trails of many tints upon the leaves, the rooks are calling across the pastures from the wood-ways, and the rhapsody of ringing song comes pealing from beyond the cloudlets that spread the azure sky; and beyond, Whitbarrow, Underbarrow Scar, uprise most commanding.

The little river Gilpin has its source in Borwick Fold, and, after a few miles' run, empties near the estuary of the Kent, Morecambe Bay. The stream has its renown, and is supposed to have received its name, so tradition says, from a Richard de Gylpin, who slew the savage wild boar which had so long, to the mortal fear of the inhabitants of Kendal, infested the district. Several names hereabout, no doubt, attest to the truth of this story; such, for instance, as Gylpin's Stile, Gylpin's Bridge, near Crook, and barrow, or burrow (Underbarrow), the den or sty of the wild boar.

The De Gulespins, or De Gylpins, took their name from a place in Normandy, and are supposed to have emigrated to this part about the time of the Conquest. They were two brothers, Walchelin and Joscelin. According to tradition, near the close of the twelfth century, a ferocious boar, more savage and terrible than the "felon sow of Rokeby," infested this district, its den being in Scout Scar, Underbarrow, at that period situ-

A Bit of Windermere.   F. W. HAYES.

ated in the depths of a dark forest which stretched west and south across Whitbarrow, to the shores of Windermere and the mouth of the Kent and the Leven. Here, in the dense solitude of luxuriant nature, the wild beasts roamed at pleasure; here might have been seen massive, antique oaks, coeval with Druidic times, and the gloom of their foliage was so dense and impenetrable, that pilgrims or travellers passing to and from Kendal (then a small place rising into importance, under the protection of a baron's stronghold), to Our Lady's Chapel, Lady's Holm, Windermere, shuddered with fear, for tales of the boar's malignant aspect and unwonted ferocity were

far from Ravenstonedale, the visible phenomenon took the shape of crockery, which refused to "shift" with its owners to a new farmstead, returning as often as it was removed. The skull at Brougham Hall was a much more formidable and disagreeable visitant; unless it was kept in the house the inmates were never allowed to rest by reason of diabolical disturbances and unearthly noises throughout the night. Whatever was done with it, buried or drowned, it had to be restored, or the ghosts of the former owners of the hall could not rest in peace. To prevent awkward contingencies, it was built into the wall, and has given no trouble ever since.

circulated far and wide. Things came to such a state that few dared pass the neighbourhood of Underbarrow after nightfall. A champion at length stepped forth in the person of Richard de Gylpin, who tracked the infernal beast to its lair in the intricate and dense gloom of the forest; a terrific fight ensued, in which, though severely wounded, De Gylpin came off the victor, for the grisly beast was slain, and henceforth pilgrims and wayfarers were free to pass to and from Kendal to worship at Furness or Lady's Holm. The knight, after this exploit, took for his Arms: "In a Field Or,.

a sanglier or, Boar-sable, armed and tusked Gules," which his posterity have borne ever since.

> " De Gylpin having kill'd the boar,
> A pine branch o'er his helmet wields;
> A sanglier in a field of Or,
> Arm'd and tusk'd gules, adorn'd his
>   shields."

The picture of the fight, I believe, may still be seen at Scaleby Castle, which was built by the Gylpins. The hound is represented dying, and the boar, desperately wounded, brought to bay. For this great enterprise, Gylpin was presented by Sir William de Fleming, Lord of Lancaster and Baron of Kendal, with the manor of Kentmere, in the reign of King John.

Now we have reached the old town of Kendal, standing by the banks of the river Kent. This river takes its rise in High Street; some four miles from its source is Kentmere Here formerly was a large mere or lake, which has now been drained; the place is pent in by mountains. Kentmere Hall, a ruined peel tower, now a farmhouse, in olden times belonged to De Gylpin, of wild boar fame. Bernard Gylpin, the apostle of the north, was born at this place in 1517; his courage was not a whit less remarkable than that of his redoubtable ancestor; he did earnest work, ofttimes in peril, always endeavouring to raise the minds of the people to a loftier ideal. He died at the age of sixty-six, a noble champion, faithful and fearless in the cause of his fellow-beings. There is a story anent the building of the present Kentmere Hall. Ten men had long been trying to lift the very heavy chimney beam of the kitchen into position, but failed to do so. During the attempt, Hugh Hird, the Troutbeck giant, came past, and took the beam and placed it into position, six feet from the ground, where it still remains, and is 30 feet long and 13 inches by 12 inches thick. A pastime of this man was that of tearing up trees bodily by their roots, an herculean task, which ultimately killed him. This took place in the days of bluff King Hal, and Lord Dacre wanting a quick messenger to carry news of a Scotch freebooting expedition to the king, then at London, sent Hugh Hird on foot thither.

A rough and long journey in those days. When he arrived, the King received him graciously, and, on being asked what he would have for dinner, he said, "The sunny side of a wether." This puzzled the King and his attendants most sadly. At last they found out that a wether was a sheep, but it was a long time before they could tell which was the sunny side. At length the King bethought himself that the sun shone on all sides of a sheep, and he therefore ordered the whole sheep to be cooked, which Hugh Hird devoured for his dinner. When he had done, he stroked down his waistcoat, and told the King he had not had such a good dinner since he left Troutbeck. A few such men, says one, would soon cause a famine in the country.[*]

Further down the vale is Kendal, by far the largest and most prosperous town in Westmoreland, standing chiefly on the west bank of the river. It was anciently known as Kirby Kendal, or the church town, in the vale of the Kent. The main thoroughfare is nearly a mile in length, very irregular and quaint ; but the town has been greatly improved of late years. The remains of Kendal Castle occupy the summit of a lofty eminence, which commands a fine view of the town and the vale of the Kent, that clear and rapid stream which, night and day, sings an unwearied song. The ground on which the ruins stand is a long, narrow oval, surrounded by a deep, dry moat, which is probably of much earlier construction than that of the Norman fortress now in ruins, which it surrounds, dating from the early years of the 12th century. The moat is no doubt the work of Saxon or Dane, and protected a rude fortress, erected in pre-Conquest days. The castle is not associated with any of the remarkable episodes of war in this country ; it is chiefly interesting by reason of its being the birthplace of Catherine Parr, the eighth spouse of King Henry. We do not suppose that the men of Kendal were not trusty and brave, but the town lay wide of the troublous parts of the county, and the almost inaccessible hills of the lake country for an army to traverse, was between them and the marauding Scot ; they thus escaped

---

[*] ROBERT HALL.—Rab Ha', of Glasgow, in the last generation, a powerful half-witted town worthy whom everybody knew, eat for a wager a calf at one meal. He at length killed himself by over-eating, and was found dead in the street.

many of the calamities attendant on war.   Still the archers of Kendal were renowned far and wide, and the old chronicler of Flodden says :

> " These are the bows of Kent-dale bold,
> Who fierce will fight, and never flee."

It was here, as we have already observed, and during the troublous times which ended in the Scottish defeat at Flodden, that Catherine Parr, the last queen of King Henry the Eighth, was born, a lady who, as Pennant says, " had the good fortune to descend to the grave with her head, merely by outliving her tyrant."

Mrs. Sigourney, writing of this ruin, says :

> " Next we sought
> Yon lonely castle, with its ruined towers,
> Around whose base the tangled foliage, mix'd
> With shapeless stones, proclaims no frequent foot
> Intrudes among its desolate domain ;
>
> Yet here, the legend saith, thine infant eye
> First saw the light, Catherine, the latest spouse
> Of the eighth Tudor's bluff and burly king ;
> Here did thy childhood share the joyous sports
> That well it loves."

The manufacture of a coarse cloth, for which Kendal was so long famous, was commenced by Flemish weavers, under the guidance of John Kemp, who settled here under letters of protection from Edward the Third, and for four centuries the Kendal cloth was the common clothing of the poor of the country.   As a proof of the vast importance of the Kendal trade, during the early part of the 18th century, it is on record that 354 pack-horses, carrying goods passed to and from the town every week.

Ruins of Kendal Castle.

The Parish Church of Kendal, with its square tower and interior of great width, is an object of much interest.   It is of perpendicular Gothic architecture, but the oldest part dates from about 1200.   The interior is remarkable, containing nave, clerestory, four aisles, chancel, and three chapels belonging to the Parrs, Bellinghams, and Stricklands.

> " There was an ancient church,
> Dark browed and Saxon arched, and ivy clad ;
> And there amidst its hallow'd aisles we trod,
> Reading the mural tablets of the dead,
> Or poring o'er the dimly-sculptured names
> Upon its sunken pavement."

The Parr chapel contains a large black marble tombstone, which bears no inscription; suspended above the Bellingham chapel is an ancient helmet, which, story says, belonged to Philipson, *alias* "Robin the Devil," who, as we have already written, swore to be revenged on Colonel Briggs, and led a troop of horse into Kendal during divine service, stationed his soldiers outside, whilst he rode up and down the nave and aisle in search of his enemy. Sir Walter Scott, in his notes to "Rokeby," says that he actually discharged a pistol at the head of his enemy. Be this as it may, the congregation becoming alarmed, and the townsmen coming to the rescue, he

Robin the Devil in Kendal Church.

retreated towards the entrance, but, unfortunately, his charger slipped and fell on the pavement; yet he was able to raise it with whip and spur, and rode safely out of the church. As he passed under the portal arch, his helmet was struck off, and he galloped out of the town bareheaded, and, one chronicler says, without saddle. Scott, in "Rokeby," has used this incident for the character of "Bertram of Risingham":—

    " The utmost crowd have heard a sound
       Like horse's hoof on a hardened ground;
       Nearer it came, and yet more near,—
       The very death's-men paused to hear.

'Tis in the churchyard now—the tread
Hath waked the dwelling of the dead;
Fresh sod, and old sepulchral stone,
Return the tramp in varied tone;

All eyes upon the gateway hung,
When through the Gothic arch there sprung
A horseman armed, at headlong speed—
Sable his cloak, his plume, his steed,
Fire from the flinty floor was spurned,
The vaults unwonted clang returned !—
One instant's glance around he threw,
From saddle-bow his pistol drew,
Grimly determined was his look !
His charger with the spurs he strook,
All scattered backward as he came.

*   *   *   *   *   *   *

Full levelled at the Baron's head,
Rung the report, the bullet's sped.

*   *   *   *   *   *   *

While yet the smoke the deed conceals,
Bertram his ready charger wheels,
But floundered on the pavement floor
The steed, and down the rider bore,
And bursting in the headlong sway,
The faithless saddle-girths gave way."

It was a daring and sacrilegious deed, and well illustrates the bitterness and animosity which existed between the rival parties during the Civil War.

The country lying between Kendal and Kirkby Lonsdale is delightfully interesting. To the south the view extends to the gleaming sands of Morecambe. To the north, hill rises behind hill, swelling upwards until the vision is arrested by the giant peaks of the Lake country, but we cannot linger by the way. Few places can lay claim to more picturesque surroundings than Kirkby Lonsdale; seen from the Sedbergh road, it has a most charming and romantic appearance. The situation is fine and imposing, standing high above the river, the smoke ascending spirally from the grey stone dwellings subdued into a low tone of silver grey by the evening sunlight. The river Lune, flowing from lofty fells down delightful slopes, a living jewel with all the characteristic surroundings and conditions of a thing beautiful ; here a delightful bend or limpid pool, here flashing and leaping over rock and cascade, then hurrying onward makes a bold sweeping curve past the church and town standing high above, and through glade, wood, and meadow ; 'tis a perfect Eldorado of delight, echoing and reverberating in its frantic haste, filling the valley with a gladsome melody. Kirkby Lonsdale (The-Kirk-by-Lune-dale) still retains many quaint features of the past ; this, added to its cleanliness and fine situation, makes it a most desirable spot to spend a holiday. Its most characteristic features, architecturally, are the old parish church and the bridge, both designed, we should imagine, during the early Norman era by the same architect ; for the interior of the church still contains most of the features of the original Norman Gothic ; that stability and massiveness of cylindrical column and arch, almost immovable in vast strength, typical, we might say, of the strong Norman character. The first Norman building erected in this country was by a Saxon, Edward the Confessor, whose youth had been spent in Normandy. He founded the Abbey of Westminster, and the church was consecrated for divine service in 1065, only a few days before his death (a year before the Norman Conquest). It seemed like a preparation of what was to follow, for William the Norman and Matilda were soon after crowned in the abbey by a Saxon prelate. This first Norman church was rude and clumsy, yet it was auspicious—the capitals left plain for painting or carving afterwards. Undoubtedly both Saxon and Norman founded upon Roman work, and though prompted by the Constantinal model, they were not exact either in proportion or detail, but let their fancy have full scope, which at length produced that beautiful style of architecture known as Norman Gothic, which continued to improve until the reign of the 2nd Henry, when the Crusades produced the sublime elegance of the transition period, fine examples of which can be seen in Canterbury and other of our English Cathedrals.

Several immense hostelries, dating even from pre-coaching days, prove the importance of this town in olden times, The view from the grave-yard up the valley of the Lune is exceptionally grand and inspiring.

The Devil's Bridge, a remarkable structure, com-posed of three beautifully fluted arches, and so named from having, it is said, been built by his Satanic majesty ; if so it is certainly inconsistent and in direct contradiction to his general character, and the good that has come out of evil in this instance is most remarkable. Res-pecting the building, the legend which nearly all Kirkby people will tell you, is as follows :—A cow

The Devil's Bridge.   SIMPSON

belonging to a poor woman had strayed across the river at some convenient wading place, and not having returned with the town herd at milking time, the woman went forth to seek her. In the meantime the water had risen considerably, and, not being able to cross the river, the woman was in a dilemma, for her good man, a labourer, and her cow, were on the opposite side. At this juncture the

Devil, in human form, appeared on the other bank, no doubt assuming the soft guile of the tempter, promised to build a bridge, on condition that the first living thing which passed over should become his lawful prize; to this the woman gladly assented. Darkness deepened rapidly—necessary for diabolical thought and deed, which in this instance was frustrated by the forethought of the woman, whose husband or herself had been singled out for the victim which was to propitiate the building of the bridge. At the appointed hour she returned, bringing with her a dog, and a delicious morsel wherewith to tempt it. The bridge was complete, and there stood his sable majesty, anxiously awaiting his victim. Suddenly, across the bridge, she threw the tempting morsel, and after it sprang the dog. The Devil, seeing how cleverly he had been outwitted, gave forth a terrific howl, which aroused all the inhabitants in the old town, who at once rushed down to the river to ascertain the cause, thinking there had been an earthquake, instead of which they were agreeably astonished to find a sub-stantial bridge, across which the woman, accompanied by her husband and dog, were driving the cow. And there still stands the remarkable structure to witness or attest the truth, as story says, if I lie, and as a further proof, below the bridge is still to be seen the Devil's Neck Collar—a rock with a large perforation, which he lost from his neck in that wild unearthly plunge from the bridge, on finding his hellish scheme thwarted.

All the way down Lunedale, from Kirkby to Hornby, and on to Lancaster, the valley is rich in antiquarian and historical associations, and delightful in secluded pastoral charm. A few hundred yards up the stream from Devil's Bridge is the village of Casterton, sequestered in trees, a most charming place, situated near the river, on the banks of a little ravine; and Underley Hall, just beyond, surrounded by magnificent timber and rich green lawn, forms, with other objects, a landscape of rare beauty.

CHAPTER XVI.

HIGH RIBBLESDALE

WHITAKER, in his great book " The Antiquities of Craven," says :—

"The beauties of Ribblesdale may be said to expire at Horton ; for in tracing the course of the Ribble upwards, the woods gradually dwindle, the verdure of the fields diminishes, and the stream becomes a mountain torrent, hurrying along a shallow and desolate valley, which conducts the persevering inquirer to a spring in the ridge of Cam, the origin of Belisama."

This is in part true, but when Whitaker wrote the admiration of natural scenery as a cult was almost unknown. The wild solitude and desolate beauty of moor and mountain appealed uncomfortably to the travellers of those days, and they generally failed to see either the grand or the beautiful. To-day the average walker will find the interest of the valley become absorbing among the hills and pot holes, and its beauty culminate in the gills and on the summits of High Ribblesdale.

Horton and Ribblehead are the best centres from which to explore High Ribblesdale. Horton is an ancient village mentioned in Domesday Book, and straggles for a mile or more along either side of the Settle and Hawes road. The church, a long, low building, with a flat leaded roof, and a sturdy square tower, is the monument of nearly all that is historical in Horton, and dates from the 12th century.

The great and dominant natural feature of the village is Pen-y-ghent, 2,273 feet, perhaps the most beautiful mountain in Yorkshire. There is a capital bathing place for those who know where to find it. About half-a-mile below Horton Bridge, on the river's right bank, are a number of thorn trees on the water's edge, some 300 yards above the private foot-bridge. Here a long pool at the tail of a rapid forms a perfect natural bath. At its head a great rock, covered with short soft grass, juts into the stream, and the swimmer may safely dive into either the pool below, or the bubbling waters of the rapid. The lower part of the pool is shallow.

The ascent of Pen-y-ghent is the most obvious expedition, and it can be made to combine several other interesting features by taking the best route. The way should not

Hull Pot.   S. W. CUTTRISS.

be difficult to find in clear weather, with the help of an ordnance map. Starting from the church, Horton Beck should be followed, past the kennels of the Pen-y-ghent Beagles, and the trout hatchery to Dow Gill, a sort of miniature Malham Cove. Here the water from Hull Pot reappears, and flows over a natural staircase of rock into the stream bed beneath. The passage from which the water issues, may, in dry weather, be traversed for some distance The white limestone is overgrown with fern and flower, thorn and tree. The rowan thrusts its red berries through the beech leaves, and the firs rear their dark heads against the sky. It is a pleasant place to do nothing in, and the lazy are sometimes rewarded by the sight of an odd cock pheasant, whose brilliant plumage lightens the dusky fir trees. Above Dow Gill, the way is along the bottom of a little valley. This valley has at one time been the bed of Horton Beck, and contains another smaller cove, and some fantastic bits of rock scenery. It ends on the open moor, close to Hull Pot. This pot is oval in shape, about 200 feet long, 50 feet wide, and 60 feet deep, and is seen to the greatest advantage after heavy rain. It may be descended in the south-east corner, by a fissure in the rock. This fissure was blocked for some years by an accumulation of stones, but these were removed three years ago, and it is not difficult to climb down into the Pot. In wet weather, a considerable quantity of water accumulates in the bottom. Opposite, Hull Pot Beck pours its water into the hole in a fine fall, some 50 feet in height. The fall gives a great charm to the place. If the morning sun be shining, its brown and cream waters throw out thousands of sparkling liquid diamonds, which, rising again in spray, encircle the foot of the fall with a tiny glittering rainbow. The water disappears in the north-west corner, behind some huge boulders. In dry weather, a small passage to the right of the descent can be explored for some 12 or 15 feet. It also contains a waterfall, which can be dimly seen falling into darkness by candle light.

Hunt Pot is close by, a little to the south-east. It is a deep, narrow rift in the limestone, an uncanny place, to be avoided in foggy weather. This hole has been recently descended. From Hull Pot the ascent of Pen-y-ghent can be easily made by the Saddle, and thence along the ridge to the cairn. The path to the Saddle is a pony track, and it is far more interesting to traverse the western face, and climb the rocks of the nose or southern end of the mountain. By this route Pen-y-ghent is best appreciated. More imposing perhaps from a distance, for a close view there is no place from whence the mountain is so well seen. Above the first slope its side is striped grey and green with grass and scree. Higher the limestone surrounds the mountain like a ruined wall. Buttress and tower stand up in shattered strength, and through the breaches King Frost shoots many a great stone split from the rocks above.

Sombre and dark beyond the limestone are the millstone grits of the summit. Split and broken, seamed and wrinkled in their struggle with the great destroyers, heat and cold, wind and rain, they give to the southern end of Pen-y-ghent a nobility of outline often lacking in our Yorkshire Hills. The way is nowhere difficult. The slopes are steeper and rougher than by the path, but there are as compensations curious fossils, and rare flowers and mosses among the stones. Short climbs, easy or difficult, can be found among the higher rocks. From the cairn, if it be clear, may be seen a glorious panorama of mountains. But the weather may be bad, the clouds low, the distance hidden, yet there is charm—the charm of grey solitude. The pale watery sun struggles to disperse the gathering gloom with ill success. A great white wreath of steam hangs round the flanks of Whernside long after the train has vanished into the depths of Blea Moor. Quietly and quickly Pen-y-ghent disappears in clinging vapour, but there still remains the strange, weird beauty of the mist as it sweeps by a twisting, trailing mass of phantoms in the wake of the wind. Perhaps it is best of all to stand on Pen-y-ghent's green brow on a fine autumnal afternoon. Then the sinking sun bewitches the scene with his golden rays. Great shafts of light, the spokes of his chariot wheels, irradiate the heavens. Ribblesdale is for the nonce an enchanted valley. Below, the houses of Horton make a dull setting to the dim shimmer of the church's leaden roof. The river, a golden chain, winds through its green margins of meadow. Each little tree-topped knoll wears a crown of leaves turned into red gold by the first frost. Patches of white, the premature snows of October, linger in the deeper hollows of the highlands, and skirt the northern bases of the rough stone walls. In the distance the smoke of Settle masks the entrance of High Ribblesdale, and mingling with the golden haze becomes a veil through whose mysterious beauty are darkly seen the hills of Lancashire. The air is magnificent with its glorious smell of sea and heather. Surely nature is most lavish to those who seek her in high places, and from her hill altars gives joy and health to those who, dwelling in the grimy shadows of our great towns, want new thoughts in their minds, new pictures in their memories, and the vigour of new blood in their veins.

If Pen-y-ghent is so obvious, some of the other sights round Horton are not so easily found. Still time and patience, a good map and a civil and inquiring tongue will reveal most of them. Jackdaw Hole is another pit in the limestone about two miles north of the New Inn, on the edge of the moor. It is some 40 feet deep, and the climb down is rather difficult and dirty, the walls being covered with soil and vegetation. There is no apparent exit, although at its northern end is a small chamber. The principal feature of the place is the enormous nettles growing in the bottom. One mile further up the valley, in a pretty little glen, is High Birkwith Cave. This cave has been explored a distance of 600 feet. The first few yards are very unpleasant travelling, the method of procedure being a wriggle over rough limestone, in whose many little hollows are pools of water. Further in a rift in the rock gives standing room, and a waterfall is seen on the left. In dry weather this fall may be climbed and the passage followed for 550 feet, when it ends in a pool on whose further side the roof and the water meet. Formerly, the farmstead of High Birkwith was an inn of some importance, where men and horses were wont to halt and rest on their journeys 'twixt Hawes and Settle. A short distance from High Birkwith, in a field near the next farmhouse, Old Ing, is another cave. Its entrance is curious and somewhat difficult to find, as it slopes down gradually like a mining level in the more or less even ground of the pasture. A stream enters at the side, and its exploration means wading. The first 200 yards are easy going, care being taken to step on the thin rock ledges that divide the deeper pools. Then a small waterfall and a deep pool are encountered. There is choice of two ways over these obstacles. One down the fall and through the pool, which may be passed on the right by cautious feeling for foothold, without getting wet above the middle. The other, drier but more difficult, is a traverse along the rock wall, covered with calcareous deposit, on the left. Beyond the passage gradually narrows, and ends in a deep pool of still water some 400 yards from the entrance.

On the right-hand side of the road up the valley, five minutes' walk from Old Ing farm, is Calf Hole. It is 56 feet deep, and is crossed in the middle by a natural limestone bridge. This bridge, at first sight, makes it appear to be a kind of Siamese twins pot hole. The water which falls into Calf Hole emerges at Brow Gill Head, and is crossed further down by another natural arch known as God's Bridge. Though it might be possible to climb down this hole, it is more safely descended by ropes from the highest part of the bank near the road. From this point a landing can be made on a large rock, and the water at the bottom avoided. The stream flows into a passage to the left and can be followed for some 200 yards, when it disappears under a small heap of boulders. The water varies very considerably in depth, and, reflecting the dark rock, has a black, sullen, and gener-

ally uninviting appearance. The deeper pools can be avoided by careful traverses of the rock walls, though the holds are not of the best, and it has been proved possible to slip off into the water. After the stream disappears the passage becomes dry and gradually lower, until moving along, stretched at full length on its floor thickly covered with loose stones, whose only uniformity is their nonconformity, is, to put it mildly, disagreeable. It also trends upward, and, after some 200 feet, was abandoned, as it did not appear likely to lead into Brow Gill Cave. This cave can be found by continuing up the road to a barn on its left, about 300 yards

Brow Gill Head.   E. W. CUTTRISS.

from Calf Hole, and then following the path through the fields to the stream below. Brow Gill Cave is perhaps the most pleasant in the district, and can be easily explored. The entrance is a rude arch in the limestone scar, about 15 feet high. The first 200 feet are easy along the rocks to the right. The limestone is worn into a variety of curious shapes, with sharp knife edges. Then a few yards of wriggling leads into a long lateral fissure 50 to 60 feet high. To the right this fissure can be passed without difficulty by climbing over the huge blocks of stone that fill the bottom. Beyond is a fine chamber, in which is a waterfall flanked by a yellow stalactic pillar. Apparently, the only way to make further progress is to climb the fall, a wet and nasty business, but the discovery of a jagged curtain of rock on the left wall of the fissure provided a means of turning it. Behind this curtain is an easy rock climb, or staircase, of 40 feet, and, by following the passages in the roof, it is possible to stand on the lip of the fall, in the rushing water, and peer into the weird dimness of the chamber below, with its chaotic pile of big boulders.   Above the waterfall the passages become lower and lower, until further progress involves lying down in the stream itself.

From Horton some good expeditions can be made on the western side of the valley.   The limestone scars and terraces of Moughton and Crummack Dale, and the ice-borne boulders of Norber, will delight equally the scientific and the mere lover of the curious and picturesque.   Ingleboro', with its great pot hole, Gaping Ghyll, is within easy distance.

For years Gaping Ghyll Hole has exercised upon the minds of many travellers, from Clapham to the summit of Ingleboro', the fascination of the unknown, as they turned aside from the path to gaze into its dark depth.   Forty years ago, an attempt to descend it was made, but failed.   It remained for a Frenchman, M. Martel, one of the greatest living speleologists, to secure the honour of making the first descent.   On Thursday, August 1st, 1895, he descended, by means of rope ladders, to the bottom of the pot hole, a distance of 360 feet.   What this means is perhaps most apparent to a man when he makes his first attempt to climb a rope ladder.   To the writer, who has since had the good fortune to see the great Frenchman's climb from the bottom, it appears to have been a splendid feat of pluck and endurance.   An interesting article on his experiences appeared in the *Bradford Observer*, of August 3rd, and he contributed a most graphic account of his adventures to the *Alpine Club Journal*, May, 1896.

The second descent was made on May 11th, by Mr. Edward Calvert.   On the following day it was again descended by him, and five other members of his party. Mr. Calvert had been making preparations to descend the pot hole as far back as the Easter of the previous year, and had already made an unsuccessful attempt in September, 1895.   This second descent varied in its most important details entirely from that of M. Martel, which was made over the brink of the great hole itself, by means of rope ladders.   This was made by way of a lateral fissure, to the north of the main hole and by means of ropes and a windlass.   To the use of this fissure, in a great measure, was due the success of the later expeditions.   The ledge, 190 feet below the edge of the great hole, which gave M. Martel a welcome rest on his ascent, was a serious difficulty to overcome in lowering a man to the bottom.   From the end of the fissure to the cavern floor the drop is absolutely sheer.   Falling water, a grave hindrance, in any but the driest weather, to the passage of the main hole, is, by this route, almost entirely avoided.   With Fell Beck at its normal summer level, it is only an incidental inconvenience of no serious moment.   The two methods have their disciples.   A strong argument in favour of Mr. Calvert's is, the average time occupied in descending and ascending, and the absence of exhaustion.   The average descent by rope and windlass occupied four minutes, the average ascent five minutes. M. Martel was 23 minutes descending, and 28 minutes climbing his rope ladder. The rope ladder is the more sporting, the rope and windlass the more convenient.

The entrance to the lateral fissure is masked by some large blocks of stone, under which it is necessary to crawl. The short passage then entered is narrow and dangerous, and should not be visited without lights. The necessary tackle having been fixed, and the members of the party* allotted their various duties, on the evening of May 11th, Mr. Calvert made the second descent of Gaping Ghyll, and returned safely to the surface, after an absence of 15 minutes. The following day six members† of the party were lowered to the bottom, and a partial exploration of the great cavern was made. Passages

Gaping Ghyll Cavern.

leading out of it in several directions were discovered and followed for some

---

* Messrs. Ed. Calvert, T. Gray, T. S. Booth, J. A. Green, S. W. Cuttriss, Lewis Moore, F. Ellet, J. Lister, A. Kirk, R. Emsley, and B. Mason.—*Bradford Observer*, May 14th, 1896.

† Messrs. Calvert, Gray, Booth, Green, Cuttriss and Moore.

distance. The party received considerable assistance from some of the many visitors in the arduous work attending such an expedition.

On this and the second expedition a telephone was put down the main hole, and was of the greatest service to the explorers.

A fortnight later, at Whitsuntide, another and larger party, largely composed of members of the Yorkshire Ramblers' Club, assembled at Gaping Ghyll, under the leader-ship of Mr. Calvert. On this occasion a considerable number of descents were made, and the tackle, carefully managed, did its work admirably, to the great credit of its engineers. The brief account of an ordinary descent may be interesting. The man about to descend first puts on a suit of oilskins. This is necessary, because the line of descent traverses a small waterfall for some distance. He then buckles a stout leather belt round his body above the waist and enters the fissure. Here the life line, a rope worked by hand independently of the windlass, is tied round him, and he is ready to find his way into the boatswain's chair. This chair, a plank attached to the main or windlass rope, is steadied by a light line tied beneath it reaching to the bottom of the hole. The two ropes are worked from the bank outside, and pass under wooden pulleys to the jib, a stout beam projecting over the hole, with an iron pulley at its extreme end for the main rope, and another on its side for the life line to pass through. The narrow-ness of the passage, still further contracted by the timbers which stay and support the jib, makes it necessary for the intending passenger to climb out over the hole to enter his seat. Face outward, with left arm round the jib, he feels with his feet for the seat hanging below him. His legs once over the seat, he slides easily into it, and releases his hold of the jib. The leather belt is attached to the main line by a hook to support his body. He is then given a long bamboo pole, which he holds with both hands. Upon his use of this pole much of his comfort and pleasure on the trip will depend. By touch-ing, when possible, the walls on either side with it, he will be able to check a decided tendency to twist. This twisting never attained a high degree of velocity, but it is not always agreeable in ascending to find the life line has taken a certain number of turns round the main rope, and that so many turns must be made in an opposite direction, in mid-air, to free it and allow the main rope to pass over the jib pulley. The man is now ready, and the command "Lower slowly!" is passed out to the men on the windlass. For the first 30 feet the shaft is narrow, and dimly lighted by an oil lamp on the jib end. He will find it necessary to use his feet to keep clear of the rock ledges on the near side. Gradually it gets wider and lighter, and as he becomes more accustomed to his seat and the use of his pole, he begins to appreciate the magnificent weirdness of the scene through which he is passing. Some 60 feet down, a small waterfall spurts out of the rock wall, and falls in a long trail of mist and spray to the bottom. A hanging curtain of glistening limestone shuts off, with jagged edge, his view of the main chasm. Below this curtain the two holes unite, and he is able to look up the waterworn sides of Gaping Ghyll, with their myriad drops of glittering water, to the green lip of its funnel-shaped mouth, and catch a distant glimpse of the heavens above. The light, a filtered sunshine without warmth or colour, illumines the place with natural fitness, and he drops down through the great Hall, with its huge walls of rock, in a mist of falling water, awed by a scene which is most strangely grand. When he has gained his feet amongst the pools and boulders of the bottom, his first impulse will be to get clear of the seat, and his next to get out of the falling water.

M. Martel thus describes his impressions of this great cavern :—

" I despair of giving my readers any idea of the view on which I gazed as I stood at the foot of my ladder, and at a respectful distance from the waterfall. There were no stalactites or sparkling diamonds of carbonate of lime to be seen (the cave is too frequently filled with water for that), but an immense cathedral un-supported by a single pillar. There was one vast hall, 500 feet long, 80 to 100 feet high, 66-116 feet broad. Thus, it is one of the five or six largest caves known at present to exist in the whole world, and the scene ranks among the most impres-sive that I ever expected to come across in my underground wander-ings, particularly by reason of the

Gaping Ghyll—Stalactites.   R. W. GUTTRIES.

fantastic dropping of water, and the darting of the daylight through the funnel in the gigantic vault."[*]

Great walls of rock, rent with deep vertical fissures, carry the dome-like roof, and the sand and silt of the floor are banked and seamed by the action of flowing water. The only living thing discovered was a small plant (unfortunately lost) growing in the sand on the edge of the daylight. At either end are heaps of boulders, piled in steep confusion to the very roof, and over these lies the way into the passages which lead out of the cavern. Some of these passages have been explored, especially those in the

---

[*] *Alpine Club Journal,* May, 1896.

direction of Clapham Cave. They were found to contain many beautiful stalactites and stalagmites of dazzling whiteness and strange eccentricity of form.

* One hundred and sixty-two yards from the top of the boulders at this, the south-east, end of the great cavern, another cave of immense size was found. The descent into this was a matter of some considerable difficulty. A huge bank of slippery clay, at a steep angle, with a sheer drop of 30 feet at the bottom, required great care and the use of a rope ladder to descend it. The aneroid barometer showed the vertical distance from the entrance to the floor of this second chamber

Gaping Ghyll—Stalactites.   S. W. CUTTRISS.

to be 150 feet. Its length was estimated to be considerably greater than its height, and the width of the widest part was fully half the length. To again reach the passage beyond, another heap of loose stones had to be climbed. This passage was followed to its terminus, a distance of some 400 yards. The story of Gaping Ghyll, at present, goes no further. If an outlet, passable by man, into Clapham Cave exists, it has yet to be found. Determined attempts to force it have been made from the Cave itself, but they have not yet reached the desired goal. It remains an interesting problem, a north-west passage at our own doors, and it contains all the exciting elements of romantic exploration.

Several days may be well spent round Ribblehead. The station and viaduct are not picturesque, but must be accepted as inevitable. Chapel-le-Dale, though outside the scope of this chapter, should not go unmentioned. Lying between two of the highest mountains in Yorkshire, Whernside and Ingleboro', it contains, in its short

---

* The party who conducted the exploration at Whitsuntide were Messrs. E. Calvert, F. Ellet, T. S. Booth, S. W. Cuttriss, J. A. Green, and J. Firth. Whilst these gentlemen had the excitement, a great deal of very uninteresting work—absolutely necessary, however, to the success of the undertaking—was patiently carried out by Messrs. A. Barran, G. T. Lowe, Lewis Moore, Leonard Moore, Ralph Smith, W. Ramsden, J. Firth, C. Scriven, F. Holtzmann, and Ben Mason. Several of the latter gentlemen (Messrs. Barran, Lowe, Leonard Moore, Ramsden, Scriven, and Holtzmann) also descended during the work.—*Bradford Observer,* May 30th, 1896.

length of six miles, perhaps, more that is curious than any other similar valley in England. Flanked by scar and mountain, its caves and pot holes, glens and waterfalls, are equalled in interest by the relics and traditions of its human occupation through the centuries. The ascent of Whernside from Ribblehead requires no description. The mountain is a very plain one, and can be climbed more or less easily anywhere. With a little discretion in the choice of the way of getting there, it is best to go straight for the cairn. The views to the north and west are very fine, and to the south Ingleboro' is seen on its most picturesque side. The great feature of the valley of the Ribble below is the succession of Drumlins, low rounded hills, formed by the glaciers which filled the valley in the Ice Age.

In Kingsdale, the valley between Whernside and Greygareth, are several noted caves and pot holes. Rowten Pot, the deepest yet explored, was descended for the first time on July 4th, 1897, by four members of the Yorkshire Ramblers' Club, Messrs. T. Booth, S. W. Cuttriss, W. Parsons, and J. W. Swithenbank. Four previous attempts had been made by members of the Club at various times. This pot hole is about five miles from Ingleton, at an elevation of 1,200 feet above the sea, nearly opposite the farmhouse of Braida Garth. Rowten Pot, or Rowan Tree Hole, is a great surface rent in the limestone, about 80 feet by 40 feet, with a total vertical depth of 365 feet. Unlike Gaping Ghyll, Rowten Pot is more picturesque near the surface. It descends in a succession of pitches, and the ledge from which the actual work of the descent commences is 100 feet below the surface. This ledge, with its natural bridge of limestone crossing the yawning gulf, has considerable beauty of a weird kind. The descent was made by rope ladders, and was rendered unpleasant by the waterfalls. The bottom is disappointing, and, although interesting on account of its curious limestone formations, cannot be compared with the great cavern of Gaping Ghyll for grandeur.

Alum Pot, another of our greater pot holes, is an hour's walk from Ribblehead by way of Selside, or it may be reached more directly by skirting the base of Parks Fell. It is a huge hole in the limestone in a small plantation, surrounded by a stone wall. It has been descended several times, and was explored in 1870 by Prof. Dawkins and party. The actual descent involves a considerable amount of preparation, but Long Churn, which enters Alum Pot some 40 or 50 feet below the surface, can be traversed in dry weather without difficulty. This passage commences 150 yards above the Pot hole, and is good if wet going. There are three small waterfalls in it, and caution is necessary if swimming is to be avoided. Some of the pools are ten or twelve feet deep. The rock is light in colour, and its reflection gives a beautiful bright transparency to the water. The third waterfall, with a drop of ten feet, should be climbed down with care as the ledge below it is somewhat narrow, and shelves downward into a deep pool.

R

There is plenty of head room, and as the passage approaches Alum Pot it opens out into a chamber of considerable size. Stalactites are plentiful in this chamber, but they are covered with a soft calcareous deposit, and lack beauty of form and brilliancy. By standing on the lip of the waterfall, which here falls into the Pot, it is possible to see some distance into the shadowy depths of the awful chasm below. At this point the real difficulties of the descent commence.

The most charming excursion from Ribblehead is to Ling Gill, an hour's easy walking through the fields, by way of Nether Lodge. The Gill is a beautiful ravine in the limestone. Romantic rather than savage, it is decked with ferns and flowers. Its bold limestone scars, for the most part masked by foliage, are best admired from below. They are generally rotten, and the vegetation upon them is loosely rooted. Along

Thornes Gill   S. W. CUTTRISS

the bottom the bright waters of Cam Beck run swiftly in and out, and round about the great boulders, with two waterfalls, and a constant succession of cascades and little rapids. By following a path along the right bank, the first, and largest, waterfall may be turned, and a descent made to the bed of the stream above it. From this point it is a very pleasant scramble up the Gill. To the photographer and the botanist it is a quiet paradise. The rocks are, it is true, slippery and some of the pools deep, but the possibility of a wetting gives an additional zest to the pleasure of overcoming their difficulties. The greatest charms of Ling Gill are the details that make the whole, and the visitor must not rest content with casual glances from the path above. The varied beauties of lichen-patched boulders and mossy nooks, the graces of leaf and flower, the silent golden pools with their lurking trout can only be really seen, and the silvery voices of the chattering rapids truly heard by the scrambler. At the head of the Gill the stream is crossed by an ancient stone bridge which carries the old pack horse road from Horton to Hawes. In the parapet is a stone, bearing the following inscription : " This bridge was repaired at the charge of the whole West Riding, Anno. 1765."

Below the inn at Gearstones is another ravine in the limestone, Thornes Gill. This does not possess the charm and beauty of Ling Gill, but it is interesting for its many curious pools and the remains of its old bridge. The eccentricities of water acting upon limestone are here seen to great advantage. There is also a cave in the

Gill, Katnot, or Kap Nut Hole. This can be explored for a quarter of a mile, but it is wet and dirty, and without special interest. The stream flowing through Thornes Gill may be rightly considered the head waters of the Ribble. It is known as Gale Beck, and not until its junction with Cam Beck does it become the River Ribble.

In this place, probably, no apology is needed for a sport which has grown considerably during the last two or three years. This sport has been called mountaineering reversed, cave hunting, pot-holing, and, by the Philistines, mouldy warping. Its pursuers have dignified it with the more scientific name, speleology. Its pleasures are more real than apparent, and, when seeking them, it is wise to remember the rules of the game. The greater pot holes should not, and probably will not, be attempted without an adequate supply of the necessary tackle, and the assistance of a strong party. It is the less obvious dangers of the smaller ones which call for a few words of caution. A nasty fall, a sprained ankle, a deep pool, an insufficient supply of light, wet matches, are some of the unpleasant contingencies. Small things they may be in themselves, but they contain possibilities of serious peril to a solitary explorer or a weak party. Some of our caverns and water sinks are dangerous when heavy showers are hanging about. They flood quickly, and for a dry river bed to become a boiling torrent is sometimes only a matter of minutes. There is, perhaps, no ideal number for a party, but it should consist of not fewer than three men, of whom at least one should have some experience. Each member of it should possess a waterproof match-box, well filled, and a supply of spare candles. Mining candles are the best. A climbing-rope is easily carried, and is always useful, often indispensable. For the rest, common sense, care, and an eye to the weather, will enable the explorers to safely visit the majority of our Yorkshire caves and pot holes. Many of these have still left the charm of novelty. Much of the published information, about even the better known ones, is in need of correction. Strangeness and beauty are often closely allied below, as above ground, and, to those who find them, they contain attractions only less powerful than those which, sooner or later, draw men, who walk lovingly, from the dust and ruts of our highways to the wider freedom of hill and mountain, moor and fell.

LEWIS MOORE.

CHAPTER XVII.

FROM PENYGHENT TO PENDLE HILL.

IN the concluding chapter of this work we follow the windings of the Ribble from Penyghent to Pendle Hill. An old couplet says—

"Pendle Hill, and Penyghent, and little Ingleborough,
You'll not find three such hills, and search all England through."

A wild and wonderful tract of hill country is that lying between Penyghent, Cam Fell, Whernside, Greygareth, and Ingleborough, measuring, roughly, some ten square miles.

The Golden Lion, in the primitive village of Horton, is a capital centre for the tourist to fix his head-quarters, when ascending the mountains, or following the various streams to their source, or descending into the wondrous caverns and pot holes abounding in this district. It was a dark, boisterous October night that found us tramping towards the village of Horton ; the wind howled, and the clouds swished rapidly past overhead ; rain descended in torrents ; the wild mountain country became enshrouded in mystery and silence : a light here and there gleamed from a grey stone dwelling ; further

The Hayfield.   t. BOGG.

up the village one solitary lamp, over the entrance of the Golden Lion, tried in vain to pierce the gloom. A ray of light, however, fell on the venerable lych gate, just across the roadway, and dimly, like a shadow thrown from bygone ages, the grand old tower of Horton Church loomed out of the darkness, typical of a religious light burning through the dark ages of a far past. There was a motley gathering at the Golden Lion on that night, quarrymen from the limestone quarries, and the dalesmen of the district, thirsty souls, we should imagine, by the amount of beer we saw consumed. Three farmers, who had been to Clapham Fair on that day, were benighted here on our visit ; their homes lay some eight or ten miles over the moors, and it would have been sheer foolhardiness to have attempted the journey in the dense darkness of that night. One, an elderly man, who had spent upwards of half-a-century in crossing and re-crossing the moors, attempted the

Horton Church

journey ; he missed his way, and his horse floundered in a bog, and he was glad to grope his way back to the inn. We joined them in company later on, and jolly fellows we found them, yet withal shrewd, stark, and strikingly original.

Horton Church is a venerable structure ; it has been judiciously restored, but still retains most of its primitive Norman features. The body of the church dates, we should imagine, from the latter part of the eleventh or beginning of the twelfth century ; the tower from the fourteenth. One writer says it has no architectural beauty, and is rude and uncouth. With this opinion we beg leave to differ, it stands there in solitary meekness and humility, amidst the mountains, as it has done for upwards of 700 years, and though built in a semi-barbarous age by rough workmen, and out of rough materials, it is a symbol of architecture the most impressive and sublime in Upper Ribblesdale. Work of that period was severe, that which could only be done by an axe, adze, and primitive chisel, for all churches were timber roofed, stout and short columns with plain caps (not even the chevron nail head or cushion enrichments), square abacus, its lower half chamfered to the cap carrying the round arch, all in keeping with the simple tastes of those who dwelt there in the early Norman days. The venerable building, toned by near 800 winters, is in perfect harmony, and partakes of the general characteristics of the surroundings. A lych gate, both on the east and west, gives access to the churchyard. Thirty generations of people sleep around these walls, and thirty generations of children have been carried through the lych gate and under the Norman portal arch to be baptized in the antique font, and afterwards have worshipped and knelt beside the altar in prayer.

A stream which rises in the wilds between Penyghent and Cosh Knot, and in its run to the Ribble ofttimes plays at hide and seek, disappearing into the earth and again reappearing, flows past the east end of the church, and empties into the infant Ribble just below. We cross the bridge and follow the stream upwards. The charm of colour on this autumn day is most delightful ; we notice the picturesque craven homesteads along the banks, with quaint porch and mullions, and listen to the music of the deep brown sienne water, and note the golden colour of the trees, the rich green of the moss, the whiteness of the old hipping stones, the flickering shadows and sombre shade of the gorge, the white and silvery grey of the pack clouds scudding onward overhead, and the shadow chasing the light across the hill tops. Up Douk Gill we wander past the trout hatchery ; until the beautiful gorge ends in a half-circling amphitheatre of beetling rock, a veritable Malham Cove, only on a smaller scale. Two or three fir trees stand defiantly on the very brink of the precipice, as if defying the elements to hurl them down. The cove occupies the south-eastern spur of Penyghent, and the limestone ridge rises from hence to the summit. There is a cave-like entrance at the foot of the cove, but the cavity soon closes abruptly. The whole of the half-circle of rock is honeycombed by water, and the continual roar at flood time is simply deafening. Douk is Anglo-Saxon—a douking shower—very heavy rain. The entrance to the glen is charmingly embowered by foliage, under which in the noonday sunlight, the waters flash like a myriad gems.

Just to the south of Penyghent may be seen the giant's graves ; unfortunately, a practical farmer in this district has removed the large stone grave covers to make gate posts ! still the depressions which mark the spot can be found by those who seek and enquire. The largest grave measured 27 by 25 feet, and another, supposed to be the grave of some mighty chief of pre-historic ages, is 27 by 8. In those far-off days the lines of demarcation between the contending tribes would no doubt be

Penyghent, the hill which separates Ribblesdale and Wharfedale, and many a fierce fight would take place for supremacy at the neck of the pass.

From the summit of Penyghent, 2,273 feet, the scene around us is wildly grand, wave after wave of mountain ridges, in this ocean of hills, spread interminably as far as the eye can perceive, as if they were an army of giants coming through the portals of the sky, no patch of corn or sign of cultivated lands whatever; the hills have a bare monotonous aspect— yet far down into the deep valley there is rich pasturage—the whole face of nature seems to have been torn and convulsed by some mighty conflict or upheaval, the plough of the Great Creator, glacier, storm, and flood having scooped out vale and gorge, and thrown aside vast accumulations of earth; ridge and peak peer down into the deeply furrowed vales; here and there are depressions, as if formed for the purpose of entrance gates into the other vales. Huge, dark, cumulus clouds hang their beetling form over the scene, and tints of cobalt sky peep from the vault of heaven, with now and again a gleam of sunshine piercing the clouds, lighting up the heather with a wondrous halo, like unto a cloth of gold, which gives strange contrast against the dark shadow of Ingleborough, almost awe-inspiring in its density of gloom. Within a few yards of our position the ravens nest in the overhanging crag, and we can hear the dismal croak of these birds of ill omen, which gives to the spot a touch of weird and wild romance.

The Litton River, or Skirfare, which joins the Wharfe below Kettlewell, is here repre- sented by a moor-born stream; twining in many a semicircle in its onward march, from yonder hill flows Cosh Beck; above is Horses Head, Raisgill Hag, and Langstrothdale, whilst farther afield, in the gap to the north, is Widdale and Wild Boar's Fell. Eastward, the outlines of hills rise and fall like waves on a stormy sea. North-westward is Ling Gill and Ribblehead, Whernside and Greygareth. West, the limestone rocks of Maughton Fell and the whole of the Ingleborough range, through Lunedale to Morecambe. The river can be descried winding onward from the place of its birth through the valley to Settle, which seems to snugly repose a few miles below us to the south, still further Pendle Hill uprises in the background. Ugh! how the wind whistles, the mountain grass shivers, the heather and nature assume a sombre hue. Ingleborough appears grim and cold in shadowy outline, as the sun departed, fringing with delectable glimmer the machiolated outlines of cloud-forms, whilst above are long streaks of pale chrome across a cold, pearly sky, other snowy cloud-forms are rising, whose very appearance make us shiver with cold. No one can understand perfectly the surrounding country without ascending one of these mountains.

Penyghent has been seared and scarred by many furious storms, but the most disastrous, during the memory of man, was in July, 1881, when the mountain seemed deluged with water, and waves rolled down the slopes and inundated the valley, leaving the mountain seared and storm-riven, as it still remains; but we must now hurry down to the valley, the sun has set and darkness is growing apace. On the slope between here and Douk Gill are numerous pot holes, which are very dangerous in the dark, as there is no protecting fence, in fact the whole base of this mountain is honeycombed by hidden passages and water-worn channels ; Hull and Hunt Pots are perhaps the grandest. Hunt Pot is really a pot in the floor of a pot : a beck falls into the black abyss 170 feet below, and then flows, so we are told, under the bed of the stream which flows from Hull Pot. As we have said, there is no fence round the holes, and many poor sheep, during a winter's storm, have lost their lives in these death-traps.

Stud Fold is a small hamlet a mile or so below Horton ; the indentions made by the huge limestone quarries on the opposite side of the valley appear like a huge blot on the bold face of nature. Midway between Horton and Settle is Sherwood House, a typical Craven homestead ; here the vale of the Ribble narrows, and the river passes through the deep gorge and over a bed or serrated rock, and the roar and hum of falling water makes wild melody. Further down is Stainforth ; a beautiful wooded precipice shelters the village from the south-east ; to the north-east two ravines unite, in one of which is Cattrick Force, a remarkable cascade or waterfall well worthy of a visit ; from hence the beck winds through a bower of foliage to the entrance of the village ; here the old hipping stones cross the rivulet, everything is charming, houses, beck, and fells all form pleasing pictures.

Now we are in the district of the celebrated Craven Fault composed of gritstone which runs across the Limestone range from Ingleton to Threshfield. A geological fault—a disturbance or displacement of strata thrown by the convulsions of nature ; one portion of a locality may subside and another be forced upwards—upheaval and subsidial. A fault may be the result of very violent or gradual movement, then a second displacement may, and has taken place of lower strata thrusting itself upwards through the ponderous weight that lays upon it. The Craven Fault is a similar phenomenon.

Stackhouse is delightfully situated amongst trees on the south side of the river, and from hence to Settle the land is rich in green pastures, and the windings of the Ribble now partake more of the character of a Lowland river. Langcliffe is a large village about a mile from Settle, and is a place with marked characteristics. The spot is ancient, and is mentioned in Domesday survey ; Cross Green, or the Middle Row, has an antique appearance, and an individuality peculiar to the village. The church, resting under the Fells, is modern ; on the green is a fountain and old elm tree with seats around, where the village politicians discuss local and national subjects. Old Langcliffe appears to have been completely destroyed during the forays of the Randolphs and Douglases, and the town is said to have stood some distance from the present site. An ancient inn, now demolished, was known by the sign of the "Naked Woman." The original stone figure of a naked person, of crude workmanship, which reminds us of a child's first attempt at drawing, is built in the walls of a house, on which site formerly stood the inn. Langcliffe has been the cradle of many original and eccentric characters, of which space forbids mention.

Settle, the capital of Upper Ribblesdale, lies deeply embosomed, as it were, in a hollow or cavity ; nestling calm and peaceful, surrounded on three sides by rock and wild moorland, shelving upwards to Malham and Arncliffe Moors on the one hand, and Penyghent and Ingleborough on the other. Seen from the train, in the hazy tone of evening light, half veiled by shadow and smoke, ascending through the trees which fringe the fells so delectably, and the scarred head of Castleberg rock, rising imme-

diately above to the height of 300 feet : the hazy outlines of the distant hill tops lit by the fading rays of the setting sun ; the charm and pensive haze of beauty that then hangs over the old town, reminds us of some fairy-haunted nook in Rhineland. Settle is an

View from the Meadows, Settle Penyghent in background. MORREN.

ancient market town, and was flourishing when some of our emporiums in the West Riding were barely in existence. The name "Setl" or "Setel" is old Saxon, meaning a station, or place of rest. The same meaning applies to the Settle. Langsettle,* which is still a necessary appendage in most of the Craven homesteads.

There is still to-day, even when many genteel residences have sprung into existence, a 17th Century aspect about the place ; not that the little town is any way behind the times in matters of Art, Science, Literature, or general Education, but quite the reverse is the fact. For a place of its size there is certainly a forward movement in

*A long, high-backed wooden seat on which several persons can sit at one time.

those matters, and it possessed quite a large Subscription Library at a time when those institutions were very rare even in the large towns.   The main thoroughfare is wide and clean ; the most characteristic features, apart from three or four ancient inns, are the old Shambles, in the centre of the Market Square, which Pennant describes, on his visit " as a shabby French town, with a place in the middle" ; and the Poet Gray, who visited Settle in 1767, is anything but flattering, for he says " it was the neatness and civility of his landlady which caused him to stay over two nights " ; whilst of the town, he describes " as only possessing about a dozen good-looking houses ; the rest, he says, are old and low, with little wooden porticos in front."   Yet the Shambles, or "place in the middle," gives a dignity, character, and old-world charm, which, if demolished, would for ever destroy that venerable antiquity which it adds to the place.   The Folly is another antiquated building, whose builder has, perhaps,

thought to raise a memorial to his name ; if so, the Folly, the name given to the house, tells its own story.   It is an imposing Stuart mansion, with a goodly array of windows, whose deep mullions lend an antique character to the house.   Victoria Cave, discovered in 1837, and the Ebbing and Flowing Well, each within a mile and a half from Settle, are interesting objects of curiosity.

Giggleswick, on the west side of the Ribble, is less than a mile from Settle.   The centre of the bridge divides the two parishes.   The path leading by the bank of the Ribble through the meadows to Giggleswick are sweet in pastoral richness, and allied to the gurgling melody of river, and the picturesque range of limestone scars, commencing with the towering canopy of Castleberg, and rising from hence, tier above tier, until the vision is terminated by the lofty brow of Penyghent, towering above all like a huge wart on the face of nature, completing the picture.

Giggleswick possesses charms both for the artist, antiquary, historian and geologist of perhaps more surpassing interest than any other spot in Upper Ribblesdale. The church is a large spacious edifice, most judiciously restored ; apparently of 14th Century date, and is supposed to be the third structure which has stood on this site, it has a wide nave, two aisles, and large chancel.   In the south aisle is a finely carved Alms Box, with date 1684, on which is inscribed " Remember the Pore."   The pulpit and reading-desk, most elaborately carved, are of the same date.   During the restoration of the church in 1891, a full length effigy of a knight in plate mail was discovered, supposed to represent Sir Richard Tempest, also portions of other effigies sadly mutilated.

There is no dissenting chapel in the village ; it is pre-eminently a church town. There is a story of a dissenter preaching at the village cross, when Mr. Chapman, the vicar, and Rowland Ingram passed by, the latter remarked that a stop ought to be put to that sort of thing, but the kind old vicar replied, " For 50 years I have been trying to do the people of this village good, but they are too much for me ; let this fellow try his hand." The preacher tried, but, 'tis said, he also failed ; let us hope otherwise.

The Black Bull Hostel adjoining, and built partly into the churchyard, is very quaint and curious. A low, ancient porch and doorway, studded with iron bolts, give access from the house into the churchyard. So if a worshipper needs any refresh

Church and Cross. Giggleswick.

ment, he can obtain it without leaving the churchyard, very convenient to those who come from distant places to church.

The schools, for which Giggleswick is famous, are indissolubly associated with the church, she being the parent. The first grammar school was founded in 1507, by James Carr, and stood in the "church garth"; it was a plain-looking structure without any architectural adornment. The third, which now stands just without the precincts of the churchyard, is a goodly building, but is now only used as a lumber room or a joiners' shop, where the boys are taught joinery. The handsome new schools stand on a commanding elevation above the road leading to Clapham, and is a most flourishing institution.

Regarding the nomenclature of Giggleswick, we cannot say. Several learned gentlemen have pronounced it to be the "Wick of Gikel," the name of a Saxon. Others are of different opinion, and say the name is derived from guggle, the gugglian or gurgling of waters, neither of which, we should imagine, is right. The beauty of the place is apparent to anyone who has eyes to see and a soul to drink in the beauty and charms of this spot. Apart from its beauty and old customs, there is a spell of antiquity tinged with romance pervading the spot. The old-time stone cross and remains of the stocks, the lych gate, and the characteristic church seen under the branches of stately elms, the babbling brook, with its clear, limpid waters telling the same tale and singing its dulcet strain in the same measure as it did to those who trod its banks long, long ago ; and the rows of antique cottages, with old-world interiors and deep mullions, and whitewash, and creamy walls, over which the richly-hued Virginia creepers droop and festoon so gracefully, charm of colour, beauty of line, here nature and art combine to form interesting pictures.

From Settle the river winds onwards through the low-lying meadows or "ings" (here so called)—Rathmell on one side and Long Preston on the other. Dobson says of the former place that it is known throughout this district as Rathmell in England, concerning which we subjoin the following droll story.

The story goes that once upon a time, when the hay was being gathered from the " ings," a haymaker, having partaken somewhat freely of " 'lowance," fell asleep on a haycock, and was left in the hayfield by his companions. Heavy rain came on, the Ribble overflowed its banks, and the haycock, or "hub," as the inhabitants of Craven would call it, along with its sleeping occupant, was floated a mile or two down the river. The following morning he was roused by a farmer from his perilous position, and was asked his name ; "Tommy Jooanson" [Thomas Johnson] was the reply. "What, Tommy Jooanson a' Ramill?" [of Rathmell]. "Aye, Ramell i' England," replied Tommy, who, surveying the country, and seeing a broad lake occupying the valley, instead of the familiar features of his Craven homestead, appeared to think he had been floated to some foreign land, an event in those days, when the French and English were deemed natural enemies, not considered very desirable for an Englishman. Ever since the village has been styled, from Tommy's description of it, " Rathmell in England."

Long Preston, four miles from Settle, is situated at the foot of the Fells ; here the most interesting items, pictorial and legendary, are, first, the peculiar character and length of this town (the lang-priest town), with its two draw-wells ; secondly, the antiquarian charm still lingering around the walls of the venerable kirk ; thirdly, the legendary romance woven around the story of Langpreston Peggy.

" Long Preston Peg to Proud Preston went,
　To see the Scotch rebels it was her intent.
　A noble Scotch lord, as he passed by,
　On this Yorkshire damsel did soon cast an eye.

He called to his servants, which on him did wait—
　' Go down to yon girl who stands in the gate,
　That sings with a voice so soft and so sweet,
　And in my name do her lovingly greet.' " *

A bracing moorland walk from Settle to Long Preston is by way of the now almost disused coach road, which passes at a great altitude over the Settle and Preston moors, from whence the low-lying country to the south can be finely descried with the Ribble winding onward to the sea.

From Long Preston, a walk of less than two miles, brings us to Hellifield Peel, a fortified residence surrounded by a deep moat, and called into requisition during the unsettled period which followed the fruitless attempt of the first and second Edwards to subjugate the unconquerable Scot. It was for centuries the home of the Hamerton family, whose burying place was at Long Preston. Opposite to the Park, the river curves gracefully to the south-west through rich green pastures and woods of varied growth and hue, until we arrive at Gisburn, a charming spot just above the confluence of the Ribble and Stockbeck (the latter a beautiful stream winding through picturesque scenery) stands Gisburn

Long Preston Church.

Hall, the ancestral home of the Listers—Lords of Ribblesdale. From an architectural point of view the mansion is not at all striking, but the natural beauty of the scenery, and richness of the timber, is perhaps unequalled in Lower Ribbles-

---

* " It is well known at Long Preston, near Settle, in Yorkshire, that in the year 1745, a buxom, handsome young woman of that place, anxious to see the Pretender and his army, went to Preston, in Lancashire, for that purpose, a distance of thirty-eight miles, and, after gratifying her curiosity, and staying for some time in or near the rebel camp, returned to her native village. This became so much the subject of general conversation that it was the occasion of producing a ballad which obtained as much notoriety in Ribblesdale as the famous historical ballad of Chevy Chase. The gentleman who has furnished this anecdote says that he has frequently heard her sing the very song of which she herself was the subject, twenty-five years after the occurrence, and she had then, though advanced in life, the remains of a handsome face and fine person, which had doubtless been impaired by time, and a strong propensity to indulge in spirituous liquors. The strain of
　" Long Preston Peggy to Proud Preston went,
　To see the bold rebels it was her intent.'
was seldom carolled from her lips till she had been treated with a half-a-dozen or more glasses of spirits."

dale.   The river flows in graceful curves, reflecting the beautiful imagery in its clear sienna water.   The old bridge and mill are perhaps the most romantic, for here are intermingled the charms of woodland, the delight of a beautiful river, and the interest surrounding antiquated buildings, pleasing alike to all who delight in ruminating over themes of bygone centuries.   In the walls of the mill are sculptured devices of the Percy family, the lion rampant of Brabant and the arms of the Lucies—to some, probably, these memorials of noble houses built in the walls of the old mill may appear inglorious—to the writer, although relics brought from a noble abbey now mouldering in ruins, and placed in the walls during repairs and at random, no richer setting can be found, appealing to our inmost soul with almost double force.   Amongst the legends of Robin Hood is one relating how Guy, a stout yeoman of Gisburn, had an encounter with the outlaw in the Barnesdale forest, after each had astonished the other by their skill in shooting arrows at a wand stuck in the ground.   Guy demanded of Robin his name and occupation—

> "Now tell me thy name, good fellow," say'd he,
>   Under the leaves of lyne.
> "Nay by my faith," quoth bold Robin,
>   "Till thou hast told me thine."

> "I dwell by dale and downe," quoth he,
>   "And Robin to take I'm sworne ;
> And when I am called by my right name
>   I am Guy, of good Gisborne."

> "My dwelling is in the wood," says Robin,
>   "By thee I set right noughte ;
> I am Robin Hood of Barnesdale,
>   Whom thou so long hast sought."

A combat with swords was the result.   Guy was slain, and Robin, attired in some of the dead man's garments, and with the aid of Guy's bugle-horn, artfully deceived the Sheriff of Nottingham, and liberated all his merry men.

A herd of wild cattle, descendants of those which formerly ranged the forests of England, was formerly kept in the park at Gisburn, but are now extinct.

The town of Gisburn stands about half a mile from the bridge immediately on the outskirts of the park, and, with its church, contains much that will interest the stranger.   Further down the river is Bolton Hall and Park.   The hall is said by Whitaker to be one of the oldest houses in Craven.   This was the ancestral home of the Pudseys, and the place where Henry the Sixth found shelter after the disastrous battle of Hexham, so fatal to his cause, and it was here that he was betrayed, and carried prisoner to London.   Here, also, towards the end of the sixteenth century dwelt William Pudsey, a godson of Queen Elizabeth's.   This young squire brought himself under the penalty of the law by working the mines on his property, which, containing both gold and silver, can only be worked under a grant from the Crown. But what was even a more serious crime, and punishable by death, he not only worked the mines, but coined the silver into shillings.

"Oh, then he made, and thought no ill,
    The Pudsay shillings, his debts to pay,—
Still, at the Mint by Bolton Mill,
    The dross of his works is seen to-day."

He soon became a marked man, and justice was on his track; he was obliged to hide in the woods and secret places in the district. During his hiding he chanced to espy two local elves, Lob and Michil :—

"For once by Aithera hoile I hear,
Betwixt the gloaming and the day,
  He lighted on those Goblins queer.
They gave him there a magical bit—
  The strangest thing you ever could see—
And charged him aye to remember it

If ever he chanced to be forced to flee;
For it would nourish a drooping horse
  From evening red to morning gray,
And help him by its magical force
  To gallop away for the livelong day."

And once, the legend says, that had it not been for this magical bit he would have been captured, for the soldiers were already about to seize him, when he ran to the stable, placed the bit in the mouth of his wanton grey, and leapt into the saddle.

"Out of the gates himself he flung,
  Rainsber Scaur before him lay ;—
'Now for a leap, or I shall be hung ;
  Now for a leap,' quoth brave Pudsay

Into his steed he drove the spur,—
  Fearfully he did snort and neigh—
Yet, though at first he was hard to stir,
  Over the Scaur sprang Wanton Gray.

Ninety feet or more he fell.
  Still he had cleared each bush and tree,
And dipped in the Ribble's raging swell,
  And never came on to his bended knee.

Slowly he gained the other bank ;
  A scalding tear rose to his ee
As, with his garments dripping and dank,
  A long adieu to his home bade he."

He rode till he found Queen Elizabeth, who was on board a ship in the Thames, when he alighted, sought her presence, and craved her pardon.

Whalley Abbey.

"Queen Bess she laughed, Queen Bess she smiled,
  She thought on many a bygone day ;
And then she pardoned her own godchild,
  Who on the deck before her lay.

She gave him then her hand to kiss ;
  So, while the tears stood in his ee,
His heart was brought from bale to bliss :—
  'But no more Pudsay shillings !' said she."

Onward the river winds past the Abbey of Salley, beautifully situated, and forward to the interesting old town of Clithero, and further still, the Ribble divides Great Mitton on the one hand, and Mitton Hall on the other.

All about us, says William Howitt, during his visit, as we ascended to Mitton, were green whispering trees, and peeps into meadows rich with cattle ; and the sound of two rivers—the Hodder and the Ribble, which unite just below—came up to us delightfully. The church is a plain, unpretending structure, with low square tower ; but it delights you as you approach with the green sequestered beauty of its churchyard, and on your entrance, with such a group of effigied tombs as few village churches can show.

A little to the west is Stonyhurst College, the chief of Roman Catholic schools in England. Some three miles east from Mitton, on the banks of the Calder,

is Whalley Abbey, founded in 1294. Near to the Abbey is Whalley Church, said to have been founded A.D. 596. Three Saxon crosses of the above period are now to be seen in the churchyard. In many a semicircle the river now flows past Ribchester, an ancient spot, and though now of

Church of St. Cuthbert, Lytham.

small importance, it was, as its remains have amply proved, a flourishing Roman city nigh 1800 years ago. Old Leland says : " Ribchester is now a poore thing, it hath been an ancient towne, great squaried stones, vaults, and antique coynes be found there." Now past the ancient town of Walton-le-Dale, and along the charming riverside path, and, through a park-like landscape, Preston, with its bridges and hotels, tapering spires, towers, and tall chimneys, comes in view, and the Ribble emerges into the arm of the sea at Lytham.

The curtain is falling, shadows deepen, the light is dim, the distant landscape seems preparing for rest, the whispering streams speak of repose ; we will not break this dream of peace, but kiss the hand, and breathe a kind farewell.

EDMUND BOGG.

FINIS.